A CANTICLE FOR BREAD & STONES
(A NOVEL)

by

Emilio De Grazia

A CANTICLE FOR BREAD & STONES
BY
EMILIO DE GRAZIA

Published
by
Lone Oak Press, Ltd.
304 11th Avenue Southeast
Rochester, Minnesota 55904

Symbol of faith, the cathedral was also a symbol of love.   All men labored there. The peasants offered their all, the work of their strong arms. They pulled carts, and carried stones on their shoulders.... The burgess gave his silver, the baron his land, and the artist his genius.... The dead too were associated with the living, for the church was paved with tombstones, and past generations with joined hands continued to pray in the old church where past and present are united in one and the same feeling of love. The cathedral was the city's consciousness.

Emile Mâle

"Adam: Wheresoever she was, there *was Eden."*

Mark Twain

This work is dedicated to

Carole Stoa Senn,

The enduring human spirit,
star-crossed.

1. *...it's damned hard to find words – make sense of what women have to do with my little impulse to save the world.*

Guido, waiting with patience at death's door, believed above all in his tomatoes.

"There were two or three real nice ones for sure," he told me, his eyes dancing as he tapped the floor with his walking stick. He'd been a grocer all his life, with an attachment to the old store stronger than his grip on life.

"He's ninety-three," my mother, who has terrible dreams every night, complained, "so he's got funny ideas in his head. He really believes he *owns* the old store."

"I don't want to live that old," my father said. "When you get that old what's the use? You just get in the way."

"Like Heino Slutzke, the Jew shoemaker," Mamma said. "For all those years he couldn't remember, not even his name."

But our names are impossible to forget. For centuries we've named ourselves after great people, grand ideas, and saints. My great grandfather's name was Raphael. His son, my Nonno, is Guido, and his son's son, my father, is Paul, who says my mother, Gloria, gave all the kids their names. My sister, a college freshman barely eighteen and somehow blond, is Beatrice, and my younger brother, who plays piano in barrooms for twenty bucks a night, is Bruno, a name that doesn't wash clean the way the others do.

That leaves my grandmother Rosina, my wife Sandra, and just me, Sal. Salvatore.

Savior. Think of that. When I was a kid I had a hard time living a name like that down. Now I'm stuck with living up to it.

It's also my fate to be an Amato. Though the females in the family don't show up in the word, Amato in the singular means Loved. Among ourselves we use the name as a last resort, but when outsiders get nasty with us it's like a barbed wire fence to keep them away.

There's a magnet too: The big cathedral, St. Paul's, that stands on the hill within view of our neighborhood. Over the years we family members have put more and more distance between ourselves, a space measurable in city blocks. But no one in the family has moved beyond walking distance of anyone else, and nobody owns a car except Papa, a big 1962 Buick he keeps locked in the garage. He says it takes money to run cars, but that's just his way of having it both ways: He wants his big American car, but he doesn't want it going anywhere because he figures we'll use it to get away from St. Paul's, that dome and facade always in our sky, those grey stones invisibly weighing on us like gravity.

We have a family connection to St. Paul's: Though somebody fired him before he finished the job, my great-grandfather Raphael came all the way from San Giovanni, a town south of Naples, to help supervise the building of the thing. Pierre Vente, the French architect who was like a brother to Raphael, kept their destination a secret until the very end. Guido said his father couldn't believe how far he had to go after he stepped off the boat in New York – hundreds of miles past towns and hills and fields full of corn and grass until finally he came to a city with a wide river running through. "Where are we?" Raphael asked when he stepped from the steamboat and looked around. The French architect laughed. "America."

So where is our city? And where am I? I look around and what do I see: Guido's grocery store with no groceries in it, the store he never really owned; and St. Paul's on The Hill, the big old cathedral that somehow went wrong for Raphael. I can't be proud of these facts. So when people ask where I live I tell them what the Frenchman said: "America."

One time I asked Mamma about Raphael's beliefs: "He must have been a man of great faith to leave everything behind and come all the way here."

"Oh yes," she replied with a roll of her eyes. "I knew him too, before your father married me in St. Paul's. And you

2

wouldn't believe all the stories we heard about him from your Nonna Serafina, God bless her, my own mother, before she went back to Italy. Every day Raphael got up in the dark – and he went to Mass before going to work."

"After he lost his job working on St. Paul's?"

"You don't have to go to Mass every day to be a Catholic," she snapped. "It broke his heart. They brought in somebody else to finish St. Paul's, but it didn't make him a heathen atheist."

"Did he ever go back to St. Paul's...I mean after they fired him?"

"They didn't *fire* him, Sal. They just got somebody else to finish the job."

"Why?"

"Because, that's why. He was stubborn – like you. Like a stubborn brat. He had to have everything his way, just his way and nobody else. Everything just right or he'd blow his top. When everybody went home after work he'd go see what they did to it. And he always came back shaking his head, talking to himself. Some of the things he said – you wouldn't believe."

"Like what?"

"He called them all crooks."

"Who?"

"The ones who kicked him out."

"What did he do, Mamma – I mean at St. Paul's?"

"What do you mean, Sal? He worked, that's what. We all work."

"I mean what part did he work on? What was his job?"

"The stones. He was in charge of the stones. He built the walls."

"Tell me one thing for sure. Who fired him? Who took his job away?"

She threw her hands up. "How should I know? I just wish I'd see you in Mass someday, Sal. Sometimes I think you don't know how hard I work to save a few pennies for a rainy day."

She works hard and worries more than any of us. "And there's something else I want to say: Someday we're going to find your Nonno dead in the back of that old store."

"Then what are we going to do with Rosina?" Papa wonders. "You expect her to live in that apartment all by herself with that Virgin Mary of hers?"

3

I don't know, we all say to ourselves, I don't know. But for sure we would want Rosina to die in a few days. It would be terrible and sad but easiest if she died right away.

"And what are we going to do with you, Sal?" Mamma complains. "When are you going to make something of your life?"

I don't know how to keep her off my back. I'm a little too short but not bad looking for my twenty-eight years, five of them spent in college (BA in history, City University) infatuated with a few of the theoretical facts of life. Bruno and I lucked out of doing time in Vietnam, but I've done six years worth of minimum wage hours pumping gas, delivering laundry, and doing other similarly significant work on my way to being freshly unemployed. With a wife waitressing to make some dough and a mother making me fresh bread, I have too much time to make anything small of myself, anything less than a little savior of the world. But I'm not a character in some book. I'm choosy and stubborn and generally confused, especially when I see a pretty woman walking by.

"I don't think I'll do anything right now," I tell Mamma. "I think I'll just take a walk."

"Go ahead, go ahead, take your walk," my father says as he dismisses me with a wave of his hand. "My boy the bum. Pretty soon everyone will be calling you The Bum."

I end up sitting in some joint full of empty coffee cups, a bunch of newspapers under my elbow and a book propped in front of my nose. Now and then I go through the want ads, but when a beautiful woman approaches I have no choice: I follow with my eyes until she comes close; then as she walks away I send forth a shadow that lengthens until it covers her and we both disappear.

No savior, I know, should be moved by lust. But who are they, all these women everywhere? I can't call them tomatoes the way my Nonno Guido does. At ninety-three a man can get away with saying almost anything. All I know is that it's damned hard to find words – make sense of what women have to do with my little impulse to save the world.

2. *"...and then they broke his heart like it was just another stone."*

"It's your Mommy," Sandy said as she handed me the phone. After six years of marriage she no longer smiled when she heard Mamma's voice on the other end.

"Sal?" she started in with that voice of hers. "I had a dream last night. A terrible dream. Your father had an accident at work – one of the big machines cut off his leg. They want me to bring him home and I'm pushing him out on a stretcher when they call me back. They tell me I forgot the leg. They're all laughing at me, Sal. And your father, Sal, he's lying on the stretcher screaming and suffering, and right on top of him I put the leg. And it's so heavy and I need help, but I look around and God only knows where you are."

"Jeez, Mamma, Papa's retired now."

"Where were you Sal? I've been trying to reach you for the last two hours. Where have you been?"

I lied right to Sandy's face. "I was out, Mamma, looking for a job."

"Did you find something, Sal? You're a smart boy. I don't see why they don't give you a job."

"Nothing yet, Mamma. That was a terrible dream you had."

"And Bruno just called. He wants you to get your Nonno out of the old store. Bruno has to play piano at eight all the way on the east side tonight, and your Nonno won't budge. Here it's October and he sits all alone back there, Sal. He's going to catch a cold and die. You just wait and see what I just said."

"I'll go over soon as I can."

"And then you call me back right away. Okay Sal? You have to call."

Unless the snow and winter winds locked him in like everyone else, Guido found his way back to the old store every morning before dawn. After stoking up the wood stove and putting the coffee on, he stared out the window for the first signs of traffic in the street. It took only a hint of light to thaw his blood. As soon as the sun rose above rooftops and trees Guido made his way to the store's back yard, a space no larger than the front lawn of a small suburban house, his garden and little park. In the old days, when all the shelves were stocked and straight, the floors free of any speck, and the business slow, Guido would steal toward the back of the store. With his white apron on he would hoe here and there around the vegetables, looking under leaves for weeds hiding in the dark and trimming sprigs yellowed by too much watering.

The far end of the yard was marked by a fence made of wrinkled boards. Years ago Guido had built a small shack just inside, its one window facing the side of a three-car garage just next door. In this shed Guido kept his tools, jelly jars full of seeds, and any used lumber he could find. What he could not fit inside – a roll of chicken wire, old water pipes, old planks – he threw on top, never forgetting where he put a thing. One year he started raising a few chickens in the shed, but somebody – he always suspected the owner of the poultry market a mile away – complained, and he got an official letter requiring him to be rid of the chickens within two days. "Why should you stick your nose in my business?" he said to the letter in his hand. "What do you know about chickens in America – those bags of skin and bone you buy in the stores that ain't got no taste at all? Besides, I don't own this place, so who says these chickens are mine?"

He had never owned the store. When Guido came from the Old Country as a twelve year-old, Uncle Marco, then renting the space, put him to work for the eleven years it took Guido to go back to San Giovanni for a wife. When he returned to America with Rosina as his bride, Uncle Marco handed him the lease and keys. "You can have it," he said. "I want to go back where I belong." Two days later the newlyweds carried a steel bed, a dresser, a card table and two chairs into the

6

apartment upstairs from the store, and when the store went out of business fifty-three years later Guido and Rosina were still sleeping in the same bed. "I come to this country in 1895," Guido said to anyone who would listen to his stories, "and they tell me I have to work if I want to get ahead. I tell them if I have anything left in my head I'm going to go back to the Old Country where I belong. But they tell me to work, so I work. Sixty-five years I'm in Marco's store, and God only knows how many bushel baskets full of rent I pay. And how many years ago was it the lawyer says I finally bought the place, and then he turns his other cheek and says I lost it all because I miss two payments in a row? What do you mean I lost it all? It's the law, the lawyer says. So what should I do? He says if I want to get ahead in America, I have to work."

The grocery store finally closed its doors in the autumn of 1959. Guido tried to sell every last apple, cabbage, and pear, but when the fruit began to rot on the shelves he scooped it into pails and added it to the compost in back. He and Rosina stayed in the apartment upstairs, even after big trucks kept appearing with their cargo carefully stacked box-by-box to the ceiling in the old store below. "I ask the driver what's in the boxes, anything good to eat? And what do you think? Nuts, bolts, screws, rivets – all kinds of sizes in those boxes down there. I say look Rosina, we got a good foundation under us now."

The old store was a warehouse for fifteen years before trucks suddenly appeared and began carting everything out. During all these warehouse years the sign in the window still said "MARCO'S," though everyone called it Guido's store. Then one day the sign was taken down and Guido heard footsteps below. A vacuum cleaner repairman moved in, but he was gone before he got his own sign up. A long-haired boy came next, claiming he'd make a go of it showing old-time movies three times a week. After the movies he and his friends crashed on the three sofas he'd dragged in from the Salvation Army store, the music beating on into the wee hours until the night the police knocked the door in and arrested everyone for smoking dope.

"After that," Guido explained, "we didn't know what to do. Here we are upstairs all the time, and it's like a coffin down there. In the winter you like to sit by a window and look, but you gotta have something going on inside. I say to Rosina let's go back to Italy, but she says no, I don't want to go nowhere no more."

Then a little man in a plaid sportcoat moved in, bringing with him birdcages and tropical fish. For a month he hammered and sawed, trying to give the place the look of an old wooden ship. He hauled in cages full of gerbils, hamsters, even snakes, and let two pugs run loose inside. On the morning of his grand opening, he finished carving his sign and hung it over the door. Swinging back and forth in the wind, the sign said "THE ARK." Everything went well for almost a year, but in January he found all but one of his birds dead. "Some sort of chill," he said with tears in his eyes. "God only knows what." He began moving his animals out on the day I got my second job pumping gas, so I wasn't even around to help. By the next morning the old store was empty again downstairs, The Ark looking as if it had been hit by a hurricane.

"What a terrible, terrible thing," Guido said. "The animals stunk up the place when the doors were closed, but the birdshit was something else. My tomatoes in back couldn't get enough. And here I had all I wanted free. Now where you gonna get stuff like that these days?"

"Who's renting it now?" I asked Guido after our Noah moved out.

"A Jew," Guido said. "I can tell he's a Jew."

The Jew turned out to be Seymour Markels, Professor of History at City University.

"Professor? He looks like a bum to me," Guido said when I told him about Markels. "What's he doing with all that hair on his face?"

"What's he doing in the store? That's what I want to know. This guy is smart. I had him for a class."

"Those Jews are all smart," Guido said, touching a finger to his head. "But I don't want him talking sweet to Rosina when I got my back turned on her."

I was there the morning the cab pulled up loaded down with boxes full of old books. Yes, of course Markels remembered me – second row seat near the windows. But whatever happened to that pretty girl I brought to class one rainy day? He lifted an eyebrow when I told him I married her,

8

and I didn't have the courage to ask why he was suddenly ex-Professor Markels.

We unloaded books all day from the cab that came and went, and the next morning he taped a sign, crayoned on cardboard, in the window: "USED BOOKS." Then a pickup truck delivered an old stuffed chair that Markels placed in the midst of books stacked on the floor. At night I could see into the place, the bare bulb hanging from a ceiling line, Markels slumped in his chair asleep, a book open on his lap and a half-dozen beer bottles at his feet. I stayed away, uncomfortable with the fact my honored professor had come to this.

He lasted two months. On a rainy day, right after noon, a black man came into the store and pointed a gun at him, took eighteen dollars, and complained as he threw the wallet on the floor. "This ain't shit. You ain't nothin', man."

Markels' face seemed more drawn after that, and his hands began to shake. He stayed on a few more days, slumped in the fat chair every night until he fell asleep, the empty bottles on the floor until the next day.

Then Guido called in the middle of the night. The front window had a big hole in it. I came right over and nailed two pieces of plywood in place, but the next morning Markels began loading his books into a cab that came and went. Before leaving he scrawled his new address on a scrap of paper for me. "Man overboard," he said. "Come see me. I need somebody to talk smart with me."

Within a week my father decided it was time to find a new apartment for Guido and Rosina. Guido locked himself in and swore we would have to carry him out dead, but when I told Rosina the apartment was just five blocks from the store Guido finally looked through a crack in the door. "And Nonno, listen to this," I said. "Bruno's moving in. You'll be able to come and go as you please." We all came right after Easter to move them out, my father leading first Rosina and then Guido down the stairs by the hand.

On June 1, 1975, Bruno moved in. "To get some peace and quiet," he said, "and a little new work done."

And he still pays the rent. He took his bed out of my old room in the Third Street house and put it in the same place where Guido and Rosina slept all those years. Rosina's kitchen is the same, even the pine cupboard left behind when my father

9

led her and Guido down the stairs. But it's a rare night when a light is visible in the bedroom window upstairs. Bruno said right to Mamma's face that he sleeps up there, but I know he lied. If he sleeps in the store, it's downstairs in the old green chair with nothing but a blanket covering him.

Without the animals the store has a different smell. It's all full of piano now, the old upright Bruno bought from Danko, the junk dealer on the corner just down the street. I helped him roll it down the sidewalk to the store, and watched as Danko rubbed a special oil in the wood. "Damn lovely old thing," Danko said, "if you bring out what's in the wood. Probably make it sing all the better for you." Bruno ran his fingers up and down the keys, and the very next day a short grey-haired man with a German accent tuned it by ear. Bruno never got the piano too far past the front door. You can see it when you're walking by, and if you hear him playing you'll want to stop.

But Bruno opens the door only on the hottest days. He's mainly got one thing on his mind – the music he scribbles down in notebooks piled next to his chair. But then maybe he's also afraid. Whenever I stand on the street and face the row of broken-down shops, a few of them beginning to lean like old drunks, or when I see the losers, alone or in twos or threes, wandering, pausing to look in windows in which there is next to nothing for sale, sitting on curbs because there's nowhere to go – then I know it's time to be afraid.

And I don't know what to make of the building directly across from Guido's old store, its window boarded up after a rock shattered the glass, its agenda carelessly splashed like warpaint on the plywood boards: "SOCIALIST WORKERS HDQ. WORKERS UNITE."

Before somebody's rock broke that window too I saw Bruno, lost in some crazy blue tune, reflected there. The reflection put him inside the Headquarters instead of in Guido's old place. In fact he does spend a good part of his time across the street, the time he claims to be sleeping where he belongs.

It was chilly when I walked over to take Guido home. A woman lugging a shopping bag stopped to stare as I stood at the door of the old store, its new window blank in the glare of the low autumn sun. Some of the books Markels had left behind were stacked against a side wall, a few in neat piles on the floor, but there was little else in the room. Bruno had pushed aside a few things – a pair of boots, wastebasket, old display case – to get his piano toward the front, just to the left of a flap of canvas sail from the store's Ark days hanging like a curtain just inside the door. On opposite sides of the piano bench he had situated his chair and a weak-legged table with a lamp on it. Toward the back stood the pot-bellied stove, relic from a farm, and next to his woodpile a big pushbroom leaned like a teenager with nothing to do.

Hunched in his chair he stared past me at the traffic outside, motionless until I put a quarter on the table next to him. "Could you spare a cup of coffee for a dime?"

He nodded a curt thank you my way.

"Keep the change," I said, "for a song."

The word required him to look at me. "Plenty of songs later. I work tonight at eight."

"I came to get Nonno. Is he in back?"

"Watching his tomatoes rot."

The old man was sitting on a wooden crate next to the old shed, a shadow across his face. As I approached he looked up as if interrupted from a conversation with himself. "The sonofabitches are no good this year," he mumbled. "First no rain, then too much rain." He lifted a finger to accuse the sky.

I brought another wooden box in close and sat down. "How's Nonna?" I asked.

Guido shook his head. "She's home with that Holy Mother of hers, like usual. She's no good any more. I ask her to do it every chance I get, but she's never talks back at night. You call that my fault? What can I do?"

I waited for him to tap his stick on the ground, but he remained still, his eyes distant and sad. "She asks about you every day."

"Yes, it's been too long. I'll go tomorrow." I had no excuse. She was lonely, abandoned. It was my fault. Someday she would die and that too would be my fault.

But I felt at ease with the old man. Every time we sat alone I wanted the two of us to start having some sort of final say.

"Tell me, Nonno. What do you think of that crazy brother of mine?"

11

"A good boy. All that music in his head. If everybody leaves him alone."

"You mean if his woman Kate leaves him alone?"

"Who? I mean your mother...and that father of yours."

I wanted to rush in to say yes but nodded instead. "I think Mamma's happy with him now...since he moved here."

"No, no, no," the old man shook his head. "She still comes here. Tells him to clean the place up, brings him soup, tells him to get a job. Then she comes when he's gone, cleans the place up and goes away mad."

"He should get a job."

"You should get a job." Guido tried to pull his words from the fire. "One of my Papa's men said you gotta eat if you want to work. 'You think I'm crazy,' my Papa said to him, 'eating so I can work? Don't make me sick.' There in the Old Country we worked so we could eat. And we had sun when I was a boy, and walked to the sea almost every night. Here we go outside and it's a freezer half the year, so you might as well eat so you can work and die."

"And have nothing to show for it."

"That's the sonofabitch of it." The old man squinted out of one red eye and tapped his stick on the ground. "That's the goddamned sonofabitch of it. The rich get richer here. That's all. The rest of us can't even go back to the Old Country to die."

He fell into a silent stare, bitter and sharp. As I looked at him I saw myself sitting on the wooden box, my body not bowed yet like his but my own eyes and lines – my eyebrows and the downward turn of my mouth – visible in the old man's face, the two of us waiting together for the silences between words to pass, waiting, hands limp, with nothing to do.

He broke the silence. "You look for a job today?"

"Not yet."

"So what did you do all day?"

"I was thinking of going to St. Paul's."

"Bah!" With his stick he stabbed the sky in the direction of the cathedral dome. "Why waste your time there?"

"Just to look around." Because St. Paul's went wrong. That's what Guido kept saying, shaking his head as if he knew something he couldn't explain, some history lurking in the stories his father had told him. Guido had told me about his

12

father's coming to the neighborhood when it was no more than wooden shacks heaped at the base of the bare hill on which the cathedral was destined to stand, the mansions built on the wooded ridge called The Hill nothing more than dreams as foggy as the mist that rose off the river carrying barges and steamboats to the scene on summer nights. And Guido told me that Raphael and Pierre Vente, his friend the French architect, stepped off a steamboat at a place called Old River Park.

I heard myself asking the same question again. "You never told me the whole story, Nonno – why St. Paul's went wrong." He had told me that Vente asked Raphael to supervise the cutting and placement of the stone, had picked him out from all the men of Italy, persuaded him finally to leave his village for America and call his family afterward, that together they set sail for New York in the summer of 1888. And Guido told me how Vente and Raphael wandered the decks every day dreaming of the most beautiful church in the world.

"Tell me more, Nonno."

Guido's hand curled into a fist on his walking stick. "They were betrayed. Vente and my papa were betrayed. The men who brought him here broke his heart. I was five when he left us in Italy, then he called us here to be with him when I was twelve, and then they broke his heart like it was just another stone."

3. *"The crazy one, the witch."*

"When he was sixteen years old," Guido began, "my papa packed a bag and set out on foot from San Giovanni to see what there was in the world." Guido remembered his father's hands – how big and rough they were from stones, from mixing cement for ceilings and walls, from scratching the earth with a *zappa* so that a little corn would grow here, a tomato there. Already Raphael knew what his profession was, a destiny inherited through a long line of fathers who passed on their mastery of stone to sons who added their initials to obscure corners of the houses, terraces, churches and monuments they built, all these men doomed to carving their own names on the tombs in the *camposanto* that one day would hold their remains. "'See,' Papa would say as he led me by hand through the streets of the town, 'this is the house your great-grandfather Settimio built, and there is the porch your Nonno added on. And there across the way is Massimo's house – look at the window arches on that house, how the stones are all perfectly in place. Ancient they are, those arches. God only knows whose father built Massimo's house. Maybe God himself had a hand in it.'"

Guido said Raphael kept looking back at San Giovanni as he walked away, but not to console the mother waving her hanky at him from the balcony of her house. His eyes were always searching for the girls, especially the prettiest one, Aurora, who had followed him to the edge of town. "'Don't you worry about me,' he said to Aurora before he started down the road, 'and don't think I'll forget. San Giovanni is my home. I'll carry you always with me, and one day I will return.'"

15

He pointed to his heart and blew Aurora a kiss as the road curved downward toward the sea. Then he disappeared from view.

Raphael's father was the only one who could console and explain. Let him go, let the boy go, he said, for he needed to go. What future was there in San Giovanni for him, a town with fewer than five hundred leftover souls? What could he do here? Work in the marshes with his *zappa* until the malaria caught him too? Pile stones on some terraced mountainside so some landlord could grow a half-dozen more tomato plants? Or maybe see himself marched away into what they called the army in those days, all for the greater glory of an Italy existing in the minds of politicians in the north? Let him go, his papa said. Who knows what the boy will see. Besides, he would never starve – he had mastered his trade. "My papa cut stone," Guido said, "like he sliced bread with a knife."

On the second night of his travels the boy knocked on the door of a house not far from the road, and a woman, widowed for years, let him in. What did he see when he entered her house? Right in the middle of the floor an unmade bed and a jungle all around. Imagine if you can – vines covering the walls, a fig tree growing right into the window, basil in pots, oregano, hot peppers hanging down like horns, ferns and mushrooms coming right out between the planks on the floor. God only knows what she offered him that night – a crust of bread, a piece of cheese, the milk of one of the goats tethered to trees surrounding her house. And God alone knows what she gave him to drink with that crust of bread, for as soon as the moon rose over the mountaintops a drowsiness came over him and he fell helpless into her bed, feverish and delirious.

Guido tapped the ground with his stick. "Eh, what could he do? They say that widow made love potions out of menstrual blood."

"Did he get sick, Nonno?"

"Sick? Why sick? He was bewitched. And in his seven weeks with her she taught him many useful things."

The widow, old beyond years, put cold towels over his forehead and eyes, but the fever raged on through the night. To slake his thirst she fed him her potions one spoonful at a time, and all night she stood over him, fanning his face with the feathers of a goose. "'Where am I?' he mumbled in his delirium. 'What is happening to me?'

"Papa told me he slept all that first day, if you can call it sleep. For what is it when a man walks a dizzy line between here and there, between day and night, between this world and the next? 'I died that night,' Papa told me, 'and where would I be if I had not opened my eyes again? Neither here nor there or God knows where. But I kept coming back from the dead, and now here I am still. And God only knows what I saw when my eyes were open or shut, whose face it was looking down at me.'"

I had to ask Guido a question now and then. "They say, Nonno, that just before you die you see a tunnel, a brilliant light. Is that what your papa saw?"

Guido's eyes opened wide. "He told me what he saw – and there was no light. Scorpions dancing over a bed of coals, and everywhere the odor of manure, sweat and fish, and when he tried to swallow always a lump in his throat. So how could he say one word? He was like a drunk – drowning and flying at once, turning this way and that, his legs paralyzed and running while he tried to catch up."

Guido paused and looked away.

"Then what, Nonno?"

Guido kept gazing away. "Give me time," he said. "I'm old. When you got all those years and then death to look at every single day, then everything happens at once. That's why it's better just to shut up, what the hell. So imagine if you can: My father only sixteen, and what did he know? Here he was, in a strange house, his head spinning from drinking too much wine mixed with the milk of goats, and a widow in black looking down at him with maybe the Evil Eye, fanning his face with the feathers of a goose. What did he know? What did he see?"

"What was the widow's name, Nonno?"

"Widow? He sees Aurora, the girl in the white dress, alone on the edge of San Giovanni, waving goodbye to him. The widow sat him at a table and taught him everything, and within three months he's with Pierre Vente in France, looking at churches there. He wrote letters to us. 'I saw another Maria today – she was beautiful, delicate, all very nice. And she's more than six hundred years old. When I entered her I could

17

not help myself – my soul flew to heaven as I fell on my knees.' It was there, in France, he found his wife, my own Mamma, God bless her soul, a woman whose story is lost, someone so beautiful men could not lay eyes on her without having a little attack of the heart. But what do you think – she refused to live in San Giovanni as his wife, and one night took off with an opera singer who ran away with her to France. We never saw her again. So what could Papa say when he found himself in that unmade bed with the jungle all around him in the room, he away from home for the very first night, all sick and tired, opening his eyes to that widow looking down at him? Only one word came out: 'Mamma.'"

"Mamma?"

"Yep, the woman in widow's black, feeding him the bitter soup one spoonful at a time, holding him prisoner in her house for God only knows how long until he finally learned how to read."

"Read?"

"Nobody went to school in those days. She made him sit still seven weeks until he learned to read and write."

"But how did he get all the way to America?"

"The same way he got to Rome and France,' Guido said as he stood and began taking small steps toward the back fence. "Little by little. He had that lump in his pants right between his legs. Everywhere he went that thing led him by the nose."

I knew a few things about Guido's history – how he came within two years of owning the old store before the Depression suddenly fell on us, how he took out another loan, lost more money, and almost paid his new mortgage off the year Rosina fell ill. For months she tried to die so he would not have to pay her bills, but Guido was forced to sell, renting from the man he sold to for way too much, a man named Waldman who eventually built one of the big houses on The Hill. When he pronounced the name Guido always twisted his lips as if he were uttering a curse. Waldman, young at the time, always coming on the last day of the month to collect, the two of them always making haste to get the business done. How one day a notice came instructing Guido to pay by check. Guido walking into a bank, demanding that the president himself explain how a check could pay the rent, after an hour throwing his hands up in a fit and opening a checking account. And Waldman promising to sell the store back, then retreating to the other side of the invisible fence separating the palaces on The Hill from the apartments and shops below. Guido never saw him again, never wanted to.

"Now," I said as I cornered Guido again, "tell me more about your father and St. Paul's."

Guido scratched in the dirt as he spoke. "Somebody gives a piece of land to the church right on The Hill and a bishop writes to Pierre Vente. He wants an architect, the best in France. The high ground is a good place for a cathedral – all the big houses behind it going up like churches anyway. Then they rope it off, hire a bunch of Irishmen and every Italian they can find, and they start bringing stone in from the west. It takes years. When I first came I used to watch – the stone all piled up, the scaffold looking like it's going to fall down, and the women coming just before dark with the babies in their arms. We wait on the grass outside the ropes for the sun to go down. Then we walk home to the old store. I'm not even thirteen then – can't talk English except a word here or there. In those days it was nothing to leave the family behind in the Old Country, make a little money in America and send for them. Can you believe I came in 1895, where all the time goes these days? To me my father was a god. I wanted to tell the Irish kids that, but how many words did I have then? Yes, thank you, please."

"What did he do after they fired him from the cathedral job?"

"He went back to Italy, back and forth every couple years."

"What did he do?"

"He couldn't make my mother happy no way, and Aurora was married to a *carabinieri* chief. So Papa came back here again, worked in the old store with me and cut stones for the rich men building their houses behind St. Paul's. For him that stonework was like nothing. His heart was not in his work. When the Depression came he went back to Italy again, but by then my mother was long gone with her opera singer to Paris."

"Wasn't there a church to build in Italy?"

Guido's eyes, glazed with a confusion of years, narrowed as he spoke. "We had a brown stone house halfway up the mountainside. On clear days we looked at the ocean from the

19

balcony, and Mamma had to carry water in a big pot on her head from the fountain in the piazza. We threw grain out so the pigeons would come, so we always had plenty to eat. Papa sat half the day in the piazza and argued with everyone about politics and God. When there was a church to be built, they called him and he went away. The rest of his time he spent in the garden with his *zappa*."

"Nonno," I asked, "was the plan for St. Paul's your father's – I mean the original plan?"

"Both of them – the Frenchman and Papa had the plan."

"Then when the walls went up – when the walls finally got built – they were your father's walls?"

"The walls? What do you mean *walls*?"

"I mean the walls your father came to build."

"My boy, my boy," the old man said shaking his head, "in the best cathedral you have supports, not walls. So you have to form every stone just right, or else everything comes down. That's what the Frenchman and my father said right to the bishop's face."

"What bishop?"

"Bishop Oliver. I was a boy and no one ever saw the bishop then. All these years and never did I see him once."

"When did the bishop die?"

"Die? He ain't dead, the sonofabitch. Whenever I go to bed and feel a chill in my bones, I know he ain't dead. Men like him don't die. They go to heaven where they belong."

The old man stabbed the air with his walking stick.

I let a silence fall. "Nonno, Bruno has to work tonight."

He didn't lift his head. "You come here to take me away."

"Mamma called. I came to walk home with you."

He drew a small circle in the dirt with his stick and poked a dot in the center. He then looked up at me, his head nodding with the tremulousness of age. "I am not afraid to die, so when I die I will die here."

He took a folded envelope from his shirt pocket and held it in front of me. "All these years and what do we have? Seventy years, and now they raise the rent again. That Waldman sonofabitch. He wants fifty bucks more out of Bruno every month again. Can you believe?"

"And you'll pay, without Bruno knowing it."

The old man said nothing, looked away. Poking his way forward with his stick, he made his way to a bare spot of ground near the shed. Here his fig tree once stood, rising in its glory days to more than twenty feet, its branches heavy every August with fruit.

"What you gonna do?" the old man said, shaking his head.

He had watched the tree come and go, losing it to long dry winters that froze the ground two feet deep. But soon enough a new sprig, carefully wrapped in a parcel, crossed the sea by boat, and within three years the sprig had branched into a little tree.

"I tried everything, so what you gonna do?"

He cut it back and wrapped it in burlap bags, watching it from his back window on the coldest January days. Then he built a wooden shack to its height, stuffing the tower full of leaves and grass. As the tree grew the tower grew with it, coming down only when Guido lost the tree a third time.

Still the tree had to be. He faithfully watered a new sprig every day until it was as high as the fence. Then he pruned it back to its barest bones, tied a rope to its top branch, and bowed it over as close to the ground as it would go. It tried to spring up in the middle of a November storm, and that's when he went out in the dark, dug a trench alongside, tied it down to a stake driven into the ground, and covered it with dirt, leaves and cow manure some farmer brought in the trunk of his car.

The next August I was seven years old. "Here, eat," he said as he opened the fig with his thumbs. "Yuk," I said. "It looks like somebody's insides."

"I don't know what to do any more," Guido said, poking at the bare spot with his stick. "All these years, and now I gotta do without. I write to that Old Country over there. I'm Raphael's son, I say. And nobody writes back. What a shame. The figs there they grow like weeds."

He poked the bare ground one last time before walking on, pausing before a half-dozen withered tomato plants still tied up on poles. Then he returned to his crate, sat, and stared at the ground.

Words from behind the wooden fence. A shuffling, the sound of an old pail turned upside down. Then over the top of the fence a face. "Guido, you seen Sam?"

21

Santo, seventy years old, lived across the alley in a two-room flat. Pulled far back on his balding head was a ragged New York Yankee baseball cap. "You seen Sam?" he asked again, his face resting on arms folded on top of the fence. From the crack between the boards I could see he was standing on the upside-down pail.

"I ain't seen nobody yet," said Guido, waving him away. "You got some deal with him?"

"Maybe," Santo said as his face dropped below the top of the fence. "Donna Anna wants him too."

Guido hushed his words. "He wants my ashes. I know what he wants." Guido put his finger to his head and winked.

"Ashes?"

"The ones from the stove inside."

"Bruno's wood stove?"

"Sure, what else?"

"Ashes?"

Guido's eyes grew big. "He's got the seeds this year – and everybody knows. Last year you saw – my tomatoes brown all around, and this year you can just look around and see for yourself." He gestured obscenely at the sky. "Too much rain and what you got? A mess. It's the seed. That's what it is – the seed."

"I don't know about these things, Nonno."

"It's all my fault," Guido went on. "You can only go so far with the seeds. I went too far. I took the biggest ones every year...ten, eleven years now. And then they go bad on me. Everything too big. That's why I got a mess this year."

"What's Santo going to do with the ashes?"

"I got 'em in there," Guido whispered, pointing to the shed. "Twenty-one boxes full. Plenty."

He collared and drew me close. "The sonofabitch doesn't want to trade. I told him fifty seeds for one full box, and he says no deal."

"For ashes?"

He pointed his stick at me. "What do you mean just ashes, boy? You never see chickens any more, and how many people you see got stoves with ashes in them? That Bruno is lucky he listened to me about that stove. Nobody's got ashes any more."

And though Bruno violated the lease and a half-dozen city codes, Bruno had no heating bill.

"What's in it for Santo, Nonno?"

"He just wants to show me up. Just once he wants to tell everyone he beat the old man. I told him: Give me some seeds this year and I'll die for you in the fall. Then you can have my ashes for the spring. You dig me in the ground and I make you the nicest tomatoes you ever saw. But he says no, he's gonna make tomatoes all himself. The sonofabitch. I say let him rot."

Bruno came out. "You can stay here all night if you want," he said to Guido, "but don't forget Nonna's all alone." Then he turned to me. "And don't forget to lock the door."

"I don't like it there," Guido said after Bruno left us alone. "It smells funny in that new place."

"But Nonna will worry about you. You know how she is."

"I stay away for her sake," the old man said. "You think I'm going to live forever? She's gotta get used to spending some time alone."

I offered him my arm but he turned away. I knew he would fall to brooding before getting up, that it would be useless trying to hurry him. "We'll have to go in a few minutes," I said.

"If I'm lucky I'll go in the ground first."

I went into the store, sat in Bruno's chair, and tried reading a biography of Heine that Markels left behind. The words made no sense.

Guido, still unmoved, did not blink when I returned to him. A cold breeze had begun to stir. "Nonno, you ready to go?"

His eyes ignored me.

"You'll catch cold out here."

"Don't tell me about cold." He pointed with his stick to the bare spot of ground where the fig tree once stood. "You dig a hole six feet deep right over there, and then you come and give me a hand. I'll go with you then."

"Nonno," I said, "it's getting dark. Everybody's waiting for you."

"You all go to hell," he said. "Tonight I stay here."

"You mean inside – in Bruno's place?"

"No, right here."

I called Mamma and told her he wouldn't budge.

"I don't know what I'm going to do," she said. "I just don't know. Your father can't talk to his own father any more. It's like they're not father and son."

She arrived in half an hour, my father standing behind her with his hat in his hands. The three of us surrounded the old man and showered down reasons and pleas, but he sat on his crate unmoved, silent and serene.

"You'll be the death of me yet," Mamma said, wringing her hands.

"Papa," my father said, "Sal will just have to pick you up and carry you home."

"You all go to hell," the old man said.

We were about to give up when we heard a shuffling of feet behind the fence. "Guido," said a voice through a crack between the boards. "Guido, you go home to your wife."

Guido jerked his head up and pointed his stick at me. "You go look for a job? Then you go home to that wife of yours right away. You're no good to her. You understand?"

Abruptly he pushed himself up, offered me his arm, and with a glance toward the fence allowed me to lead him away.

"Who was that?" Papa asked.

"Donna Anna," Mamma replied. "The one who lives back there. The crazy one. The witch."

4. *"Yes, thank you, you're welcome, please, pasta, pizza, to fly, farewell."*

Witch. Mamma whispered, hissed the word as she led Guido toward the door. There was contempt in it and a dread as old as ruined monasteries on worn Italian mountainsides.

"What do you mean 'witch'?" Witches were old hags, and there were a few left in the neighborhood – leering from windows of run-down apartment buildings on hot summer nights, blocking aisles of busses and supermarkets, their hair wrapped in babushkas, eyes intense and dark, breaths reeking of garlic, dresses dirtied by dust and sweat.

"Just what I said," she replied. "Witch. Don't you know what a witch is? Don't you believe in anything any more? They can give you the Evil Eye."

If I knew what was good for me, I'd better believe. As Guido stepped forward I said nothing, turning away as Mamma kept staring at me. Finally she let me off the hook and preached to Guido instead.

"You stay away from her. You're not getting any younger, you know, and you don't want to throw your soul away after you work so hard to get this far."

Guido, pretending he didn't quite hear, winked as he brushed past me through the door. "Lose my soul, she says. Yep, I've lost my ass in this place."

I made the mistake of letting out a laugh.

"Don't you go laughing at me, you with your college degree!" Mamma screamed. "After all I do for you! I get no thanks from nobody here! Someday you'll be sorry you laughed at me!"

25

Her words were part of The Scream – the shrill rush of sound that cut through everything in its path like a siren slicing through a hurricane wind. Hysterical. I had used the word many times, thinking she's out of control, irrational, this woman my Mamma who is so clean, practical, responsible, moral, and full of beautiful song. Because she either screamed or sang. She sang, especially in my boyhood days, while she worked – melodies that floated out of windows into the streets below, all of them longing for something lost, some vision, dream or sea carrying her away to a beautiful place she never saw before, maybe the Old Country, San Giovanni and Serafina, her own mother who went back a long time ago and who never wrote, never wanted to return to America. Mamma sang while scrubbing the tub or washing the dishes, but she really let herself go over the ironing board, her hands unaware of the neatly pressed blouses and white shirts they were turning out. Mornings I waited for the songs to begin, knowing then was a good time to steal away unnoticed to the alley and streets.

The Scream always caught up with me, the reasons always the same. Where was I when she needed me to get something for her at the store? Why were my hands in my pockets when she was trying to talk to me? Why didn't I look her in the eye? Why was I never home, and where was I when it was time to eat? Didn't I like to eat – what was the matter with me? Was I sick? She slaved all day cooking for me, and now I looked sick again.

She never came after me – never walked the block or two to my haunts. She sent The Scream. From blocks, miles, a city away, her voice, desperate and shrill, sliced through sidewalks and streets and wound its way between houses and into alleys until it found me out.

Then too began the strangling slow burn in my chest. "Your Mommy's calling you," my friends laughed. I stifled breaths, ready to explode when I returned to the door of the four-room flat we called home.

For as long as I could remember this door had been the way into my home – a third-floor apartment on Third Street just three blocks from St. Paul's. The neighborhood was lined with row houses, all of them made of stone and brick fifty years ago, and all fronting the winters with hard unsmiling faces, their varnished hardwood interiors browned like antique photographs. Some of the units had small balconies. On summer evenings after the dishes were washed everyone crowded onto the balconies and watched the traffic below. When I was a teenager I still approached the balcony rail with some fear, Mamma's warnings that I someday would fall and kill myself shriller than the sounds of the distant whistle signaling every day at five that my father was released from another day at the factory.

In back of our place was a narrow yard too small and too public for a garden plot.

"All my life I work like a dog," Papa complained, "and when do I get a little piece of ground? A few beans, a little spinach, a couple carrots right out of the ground. Did you ever eat a carrot right out of the ground? I gotta go begging my own father for one. Or else I gotta go pay like everybody else a sack of money in the supermarket. You think food comes from supermarkets? You call that food what you get in there?"

Still every spring he planted a half-dozen tomatoes next to the alley fence, and woe to anyone who stepped on a leaf. An old garage dominated the yard, a shed for bicycles, old boards, car parts, tools. We spent time in the alley instead – kicking the can, chasing each other, nosing here and there like cats. Or we crossed to Jefferson Park on Third with its basketball hoop, monkey bars and swings, the statue of our third president tucked in a corner next to the drinking fountain. Here was enough grass to lay out a softball diamond facing Fourth. Right field was out because the swings were in the way, but anyone who hit the ball all the way to Fourth had a home run. And when a new left-handed kid showed up, he had to hit from the right side unless he was small. Pitchers had to dish the ball up slow and over somebody's teeshirt we called home. It was hard to strike out unless you were under ten. Once, with The Scream finding me just as the ball was floating in front of my face, I swung so hard I fell down.

So when the phone rang on a Saturday night and I heard the first word – "Sal?" – I moved the receiver two inches from my ear. "Sal, I had another terrible dream last night. Here I am all alone in my room, and suddenly my legs start to hurt. I look around for you but you're gone, and your father has a terrible face. He won't talk to me. He just stares at the wall like there's

27

something I don't see, and when I look he's gone, not even there any more. What does it all mean, these dreams I have? And why don't you please go to confession tonight."

I braced myself. "No, Mamma, I don't feel...the *need* right now."

"Ah," she said, her sigh releasing from her chest a history of miseries so deeply felt that she had to feel sorry for everyone at once, "What can I do? God knows I tried." She established the terms of her forgiveness before I could comment. "If you don't go to confession, then why don't you come over tonight. I made your favorite – *gnocchi*. I slaved all day. Bea says she never sees you anymore. Your own little sister, poor thing, will be here for a change."

"And you said yes, you'd go, just like that?" Sandy's eyes turned steel-grey as she spoke. When she's upset Sandy's softness turns sinewy. Like a ferret she attacks the soft underside with sharp claws. "You *know* we talked about going to a movie tonight. And you still said *yes* to your mommy-dear?"

"But we didn't make any final plans."

"So you made plans for both of us?"

"It's either confession or dinner at her place. She said I had to do one or the other. Do you want me to fess up to what we do in bed?"

"What does confession have to do with eating?"

She was too Protestant and American to understand certain things, so I had to explain.

"You can't eat after you come clean in front of the priest. Your soul would be like a white china dish stained with tomato sauce." I waited but she still looked straight through me. "There are two things God can't stand – dirty dishes is one of them."

I waited for her to ask about the other one.

"Dirty linen's the other," I said. "I did the laundry today."

She backed off and gave a little laugh. "You Catholics are really weird."

"Because we still believe in a few things a lot. You Methodists believe in everything, but everything's crewcut the same for you."

"I believe in getting along. And that's the only reason why I'll end up going to your mother's with you."

28

"You won't really have to be there heart and soul."

She came over and kissed me on the neck. "Then maybe I should go to the movie instead. By myself."

"No, you have to come. Your body is required."

"Why can't I do what I want?" she purred.

"Because you're my wife. You're family. Eating at my mother's is a required family activity."

Her eyes narrowed. "Just don't forget you owe me one."

She tried to give me another little kiss, but I turned away. Again I owed her one, one of too many favors to count, and another kiss would have added to the total for the day, week, year.

"Is there something special you want me to wear tonight?" she asked.

"It's a come-as-you-are."

"And how would you like me when I get to your mom's?"

"Naked," I said, hoping my little joke would be a way of kissing her in return. "That's the way I like you best."

It wasn't true. I liked her best when I saw her for the very first time sitting alone at a table in a crowded cafeteria. As soon as I caught a glimpse of her I couldn't stop myself. I turned my chair slightly, twisted myself toward her, and propped my book on the table so I could catch a full view of her when I peered over the page. She was in a white blouse and tight jeans that did justice to the contours of her body, but it was the way she sat – head and back held high, proud, eyes straight ahead, her left hand resting on her right forearm like a serpent sunning itself – that drew me to her. She was elegant, her lovely face, dark eyes and auburn hair made more beautiful by the way she carried herself. I had only one fear: Was she too tall?

She caught me in the act the first few times I gazed at her. And she was the first to smile two days later when we managed to end up sitting at the same table for lunch. "It was rather funny the way you were looking at me as if I was all there in that book in front of your nose. How do you manage to understand anything you read that way?"

"When a book is interesting," I replied, "I devote myself entirely to it."

For the next seven months I didn't try to understand what was happening. As we grew close I kept wanting to step back from her, gaze as she sat or walked or stood, arrest each new view of her in my mind. And as we became intimate, groping, tentative, nervous, fumbling, unsure what to do and how far to go, I was often at a loss for words. One night I got lucky with them.

"I like your perfume."

"I'm not wearing any," she said.

"Then I like the way you smell."

"And you like history? Why *history*, of all things?"

"I love old things."

"I like new ones," she replied. "I've been thinking about art – about making nice things."

"Then for sure we're a match. Art History."

The marriage took place right then, in those two happy words. We began holding hands in public, reading each other's books, talking about big ideas, big dreams. Art and History. Our solemn vow.

"What is she?" Mamma asked.

"A student like me."

"No, I mean what *is* she?"

"Methodist."

"Do they believe in going to church?"

"You ever going to bring her here so we can look at her?" my father asked.

"You're not going to get married in her church, Sal. Don't you even think about that. Don't expect me to watch my son married in some Protestant church."

"Marriage? Who's talking marriage? We're still in college."

"Watch what you do with her," my father said. "These American girls these days. You never know."

Mamma agreed. "You watch, she's going to hook him good."

She was just past twenty-one on our honeymoon night, and I was not yet twenty-three. At the altar I didn't hear myself say, "I do," and when I lifted the veil to kiss her I closed my eyes. "Art History," I whispered as we turned to walk the center aisle out of St. Paul's, and she squeezed my hand. That night, in a motel, she seemed awkward getting out of her

30

clothes. There were too many buttons and snaps, and I had a terrible time with the hook on her dress. I was trembling and didn't know what to do when finally she slipped her panties off. As she sat naked on the bed I stole a glance, but when she opened the covers to let me in I closed my eyes, taking her fragrance deeply in and seeing her again sitting at her table in the cafeteria, smiling when she caught me gazing at her over the top of my book.

Whatever was the title of that book, I wondered as I got on top of her.

Six years of marriage now, and no more holding hands unless Sandy takes hold and refuses to let me slip away. There's always a certain tension we can't explain, and so far way too little Art and History.

"What do you mean marry?" my father asked years ago when I broke the news. "How you two gonna live, pay any rent?"

"We'll get by."

I finished my degree but Sandy had to drop out to take waitressing jobs. "It would be real nice," she said, "if you did suppers. And frankly, I see so many dirty dishes they make me sick when I come home."

Before long we discovered each other's dirty underwear too. Our apartment had a small living room, a bedroom, and a kitchenette. I took odd jobs here and there, but managed to get fired or quit within a few weeks. No, every part of me – my mind, my nerves and blood – said no, I refuse to spend my life doing stupid useless things.

And she kept coming right out with it: "But what *are* you doing with your life?"

"History! I read, I study. I'm in the library a lot. I'm doing my part. What are you doing with *yours?*"

A few hours a week she spent on the living room sofa with a sketchpad. But she kept ripping things up.

"What do you mean where are we going?" I said as Sandy and I walked down the stairs. "We're going to my mother's for dinner."

"I know that Sal, and you know what I mean."

"You keep asking me that."

She took my hand as we walked. "We have to go somewhere, *do* something with our lives."

"We can go to the movie some other night. I already told you that."

"Maybe if we both work part time."

"I told you I'm *trying* to get a job. And it's not as if I haven't pumped my share of gas. I've had all kinds of crummy little jobs. Do you want me pumping gas again?"

"I'm sorry you think waitressing is a crummy little job."

"I never said that. We both need to find something worthwhile. I'm not just wasting my time. I study and read. Do you know how much history there is in the world, how many centuries are black holes to me?"

"You need a project."

"I need cash. Preferably in large amounts."

As Sandra imprisoned my hand I had an urge to tear away, escape to some old neighborhood haunt, a park bench, a coffeehouse table next to a window looking down on crowded sidewalks and streets.

"I think you're too self-absorbed," she said. "Don't be such a boy."

I made nothing of her comment, too taken by the form on the other side of the steet. She was tall, sure of herself, long light-brown hair, too classy for our neighborhood. I looked away, afraid Sandy would catch me in the act, and followed her reflection in a store window.

"You see something in her you like?" Sandy asked.

I quickly looked at my feet. "Who?"

"That one, across the street."

"We're married."

"Is that the way you look at me?"

"I look at you a lot of ways."

"You know her?"

"Nope. How would I?"

"Of course not," she said. "How *would* you? You don't know anything about us."

"And you don't know how long it took me," Mamma said as we stood in the doorway, her voice walking barefoot on broken glass as she took my jacket to the front closet. "I slaved all day. It would have been a shame. You don't know how much your sister Bea thinks about you. She didn't really come tonight like she said. And Bruno can't be here, poor thing. He slaves every night at that piano of his. I wish he'd get a job."

She took Sandy by the hand and led her to a high-backed chair in the living room. Mamma was a stout woman, sixty-three, her legs beginning to weigh her down and her body beginning to sag. Her face flexed like a muscle when she spoke.

"Sal says you had to change your plans. I know about that, and I know what it's like being young and going to a movie on a Saturday night. I used to be young too, you know." She always wore an apron, wiped her hands on it whenever she concluded a speech.

My father, slumped in his fat brown chair across from the television set, did not look up, even though there was no football game on tonight. He was stout but tough, his hands too thick. I knew he would require us to come to him.

"Papa," I said for both of us, "you're looking good."

"I'm getting old," he said tonelessly. His face wore its permanent complaint. He looked straight ahead, his silence demanding that we let him examine us.

I eased Sandy past him into the room. "Mamma might want a hand in the kitchen," I said.

Sandy gave me a bitter look he caught out of the corner of his eye. "Sure," she said as she sidled away.

I sat down across from him and waited for words. "You like retirement now?"

He stared straight ahead. "We never see you anymore."

Mamma got the white linen tablecloth from inside the trunk, the one, she reminded us, used at her own wedding forty-three years ago. She told us to sit at the table, then left us for the kitchen again. My father pulled himself up from his chair, descended the back stairs and reappeared with a gallon of red wine.

"You know he's too lazy to make wine anymore," Mamma teased as she entered the room again. "That's why he has to pay Giovanni ten dollars a gallon for it."

"Not true," he said. "Who can *afford* to make it anymore? The grapes are ten dollars a case."

33

Mamma dismissed him with a wave of her hand. "They were three dollars a case when you stopped making it. You wouldn't know *how* to make it anymore."

My father unscrewed the cap from the jug and brought his nose in close. "P. U.," he said as he nosed about. "I pay that sonofabitch ten dollars for *this*?"

He poured himself a big glass, then set the jug down. "You want some?" he said as he filled my glass.

Sandy came in and took the chair next to me. "Now you," he said, "you want some too?" Managing a polite half-smile, Sandy said no thanks. "Gloria! Get the girl some milk," he called across the room. "You people drink milk, don't you?"

Mamma appeared with a glassful of milk. She looked askance at Sandy. "Sal, will *you* help me carry things in?"

I waited too long for Sandy to stir, conveying to Mamma that I expected Sandy to get up. As I pushed away from the table I avoided Sandy's eyes.

Together Mamma and I brought the dishes in – a big salad of spinach and endive, broccoli in olive oil, a plateful of tomatoes sliced in half, and the long silver platter heaped high with *gnocchi*. "One more thing," Mamma said. She returned with the hot bread wrapped in a white linen towel, and placed it next to me. Before my father could reach over to it, I began cutting thick slices and passing them around. The last, biggest piece, my father harpooned with his fork.

I stood and raised my glass of wine. "A toast."

Pleased, Mamma looked up while I, holding the glass of wine on high, stood suspended between my words still making their rounds in the room and the speech required of me. I held my breath.

Mother, father, and wife: Let us drink to what we are, the twisting of selves into the tangle called family. One day, may we all find ourselves in a white hotel on a mountainside, all of us holding our breaths as we gaze at a sea bottomlessly blue. There, in that sea, may we see each other smiling – you, Papa, your hand unaware of itself stroking Sandy's arm, and Sandy thrilled by the feel of your rough flesh. And you and I, Mamma, may we also smile as we look at them, thinking of the night when I finally surrender myself to the plush pillows, lay my head in your lap, and let you stroke my brow with your worn loving hands. This toast I propose in the name of the father, mother, son, and daughter-in-law, Amen.

"Yes?" Mamma said. "We're waiting for your speech."

"I propose this toast to you, Mamma. To the wonderful meal you have made for us. *Salute.*"

I leaned toward the center of the table with my glass, motioning for Sandy and my father to lift theirs. As our three glasses, Sandy's still full of milk, stood poised ready to clink together, Mamma groped for something to join us with. Her hand found a butter knife.

"*Per cento anni,*" my father said.

Wine, milk and butter knife came together. "For a hundred years," I said.

"Now everybody pray," Mamma said, "and then we eat."

She raced through the Sign of the Cross, my father's hands reaching for fork and spoon before the words had their final say. "Amen," she said alone.

I knew she would get around to it. "You got a job yet?"

No. No job.

"Did you call Uncle Fred like I said?"

"No."

"Why not? He's your uncle."

"I don't want to work in a clothing store."

My father lifted his eyes to beseech heaven's help.

"I know you," Mamma laughed. "You don't like work."

"No, that's not it," Sandy said. "It's not worth it for him to work at certain jobs. The pay's not worth the trouble and time."

"He should do his time, work his way up," my father said.

"That's not it," Sandy tried again. "You don't understand. You see...it's not just the pay. It's the *kind* of work."

"Don't tell us we don't understand," Mamma said. "We are not dumb."

I leaned toward the *gnocchi*. "Your *gnocchi* is so good, Mamma. Can I have some more?"

"God bless, my boy. Here, eat." She filled my dish too full.

Sandy shrank into silence.

Mamma broke in. "You two got kids in mind someday?"

"Ha!" Papa said as he pushed a tomato slice into his mouth.

"Someday maybe," Sandy said, looking shyly up.

"Good, good," Mamma laughed. "You think about it more, and then you got to do something about it too, you know."

"How you going to support kids?"

"Off the fat of the land, Papa."

"I can't get them to come here once a week to eat. So I don't know what they want from me," Mamma said.

"Don't worry," I said. "And I'll take care of *you* when you want me to."

Sandy involuntarily lifted a brow and Papa snorted skeptically. "On your salary – or hers?" he asked.

"Paul, that's enough. You leave him alone now." Mamma put her arm around my shoulder. "Sal means well. Besides, we should be better off than we are now."

"You think it's my fault then?" My father let his fork fall loudly on his plate. "I didn't work hard enough all my life?"

"No, no, Papa. That's not it."

"I look at you, Sal, and I think, What's going to become of him? I work forty, fifty years and have nothing to show for it." His eyes accused.

"You two never have to worry," Mamma said, turning to Sandy. "This is always your home. If you need something from us."

I put my arm on Mamma's shoulders and drew her closer. She winced as she came near. "Ah, my back. I've got such a pain here...right here."

I ran my hand gently over the spot and she, suddenly relaxed, half-closed her eyes. "I think my son someday will be rich," she said when I stopped. "Then we won't have to live all crowded together here. Sandy, you ate everything on your dish. You so sorry you missed the movie now? You like my *gnocchi*, don't you?"

Sandy's smile, warming up to forgive, spread over her face.

"Bea's at a movie now," Mamma said. "With a boy."

"Is it Dylan," I asked, "Kate's brother?"

"He has hair down to his asshole," Papa said to the wall.

"This young generation...you know what I mean." Mamma's face showed resignation.

"He better respect her," my father said. "I'll break his bones."

"Sal, do you want some more?"

"My plate's still half-full, Mamma. I'll die if I eat all this. You trying to kill me?"

"I don't see why you worry about her so much," Sandy ventured. "Things are just different now, that's all."

"Ah, there are some things you're too young to understand," my mother said, not looking at her.

"Don't worry about us, Mamma."

"If I don't worry about you, who will?"

"And don't you see," Papa said, "we got nothing to leave behind – no savings, no house, no furniture worth a damn. Nothing. Fifty years of work and nothing to show for it."

"Not even grandpa's store. Is that what you mean?"

"Goddamned right, that's what I mean. At least that dump. Your Nonno works in that store all his life, and that was my work too until I was a married man."

A silence fell. My father lowered his eyes and looked away. He was next in line for the store, and I was after him. So he had failed us all.

"Papa," I asked, "Do you know this man Waldman – the one who took the store away from us?"

He shook his head as if he wanted to be free of the thought. "How the hell am I supposed to know? I never saw him. He sent a goddamned lawyer because he didn't have the guts to show his face."

"Where is he now?"

"How do I know? Over there in one of those houses on The Hill with nobody home. He's out strangling somebody else."

"Do you want more wine?" Mamma asked. A silence came down on us while she poured. Then quietly she spoke. "You know," she said looking at me, "it is not for us to take revenge. God will bring justice someday. That man will suffer in hell for what he did."

"I should find the sonofabitch and make sure he suffers a little right here," I said.

"Don't talk that way. If you talk that way you go to hell too."

"She's right," Sandy said. "You shouldn't talk that way."

"Why don't you all go to hell," Papa said.

Sandy shrank, still not used to the tough way my father talked.

Mamma held the platter up in front of my face again. "Does Sandy cook for you the way I do?"

"No thanks."

"I don't know, I don't know. You look so thin, so tired, Sal. And you don't work. I don't know why you should be getting so thin." She shook her head.

Sandy's eyes were angry and small. She wanted out.

No. I turned my back to her.

"I think we should be going," she said.

"You just got here," Mamma said. "You going to eat and run?"

"I'm very tired."

And how could I tell Sandy I was tired of being emotionally dishonest, of fending off the urge to push the chair back, the plate away and scream at them no, no, stop this nonsense; that no, I couldn't just leave, felt sorry for my mother, left behind to sleep away her self-pity into the night, that I was too certain my tough little dad would harden himself even more, my revolt justifying the cynicism he tests on me every chance he gets. Yes, no, I wanted to slam the door on them.

On Sandy too.

Because if I leave when she wants I lose out to her.

And she would want to get even by making love to me that night, while I was trying to conjure another glimpse of the woman we saw on the other side of the street today. Go ahead, I would say to myself, make love to me. Make me feel even worse. See if I care. I'd rather just fuck.

Mamma sighed again her weariest sigh. "Ah Sandy, you have to take care of Sal. I know what it's like to be tired. I know what it's like to want to go to bed and leave the dirty dishes in the sink."

"How would they know?" Papa accused. "Do they have a kid of their own? Leave them alone. Leave them go if they want to go."

Mamma got up and began gathering the dishes. Sandy, confused, looked at me. I nodded her toward Mamma, and in silence she got up and began clearing the table. Papa pushed himself away and took slow stiff steps to his favorite chair, sank down and stared at the wall to the left of the portrait of my great-grandfather Raphael, builder of cathedrals. I propped

38

my head on my hands and stared at the tablecloth while the women worked. I could hear Sandy scraping dishes clean and the water running to fill the sink.

Then Mamma's song began, a low hum stirring in some deep underground place, slowly rising, gaining strength and clarity as the song made itself at home. Papa, his body still stiff, stirred uncomfortably, and then Sandy, her apron still on, took a seat in the corner of the sofa across from him. As it rose the song hovered over us, filling the room like the aroma of coffee brewing fresh. Then out of the song words came forth, plaintive and full of the longing of lovers:

Mamma, son tanto felice
Chè io ritorno da te.
La mia canzone ti dice
Chè un bel giorno per me.

Mamma, solo per te
La mia canzone vola.
Mamma, sarai con me
Tu non sarai più sola.

Quanto ti voglio bene,
Queste parole d'amore
Chè ti sospira il mio cuore
Forse non s'usano più:

Mamma, ma la canzone
Mia più bella sei tu,
Sei tu la vita, e per la vita
Non ti lascio mai più.

She sang the chorus three times, and we waited as the melody glided upward like a dark bird. Then suddenly she appeared white-aproned in the kitchen door, a silver pot of coffee in hand. "Hey," she said, "who wants coffee now? Sal, you deadbeat you. Wake up or you'll end up like your father there. Sandy, would you get four cups? We gotta have some life around this place."

"What do the words mean?" Sandy asked me in a whisper.

"Something about mothers, I suppose. I lost out on all that. I used to look for places to hide whenever they started jabbering like that in front of my friends, only picked up a word here and there."

Yes, thank you, you're welcome, please, pasta, pizza, to fly, farewell.

5. *"Where in the hell have you been?"*

In bed she turned her back, wanting me to curl my leg over her thigh. As the minutes passed I shifted first an arm and then a leg, but she drew away, curled up into herself. I don't know how long I waited before I dared approach her again. When I tapped her on the shoulder like someone knocking quietly on a door, she did not respond.

I disentangled myself and stared at the ceiling, aware of her faint fragrance in the bed. I did not understand: Why, if I loved her, did I want to be free? Why, when any attractive woman walked by, did I suddenly want to disengage myself from my wife, at least become invisible so I could follow the stranger, and God knows where, how far?

I shrank from the words that followed like an inevitable *non sequitur*: You don't really love me.

Let me count the ways.

Go ahead, try.

All right, but don't expect me to say what I really mean right off the top of my head.

Try the bottom of your heart.

Alright, then, but don't expect poetry. First, I have this feeling for you. It's steady and deep – and it'll be there 'til death do us part.

Trite.

And I think you're intelligent, honest, compassionate, generous, kind....

Boring. Do you still find me sexy?

Yes, I really do.

Then what's so hot about that stranger across the street? Answer me that.

I have no intention of ever abandoning you.

You would have gone with her.

No. It was just a physical thing.

Hearts made of stone, do-do ah, do-do ah.

Next to me on the pillow her face was serene, the gentle contours of her belly and thigh half-exposed, one hand resting on her left breast. My eyes had hands in them as they wandered over her smooth spaces. Beautiful, her body's form.

So many of them beautiful – the strangers on the street, the ones in the ads, posters and magazines, the Hollywood types. All those dim-witted salesgirls showing their bodies and smiles to everyone, even me.

How do you know they're dimwits? Have you ever talked to them? Do you know what they're really like?

No.

Do you want to talk to them?

Yes.

Ha! I knew it! I know why you can't look me in the eye.

She was still asleep, her head turned away, her body as cool and white as a statue in a museum, nothing moving but the slow rise and fall of her chest. I feasted my eyes on her, suddenly aroused, but when I put my hand on her thigh she rolled away, covering herself with the blanket again.

The bell of St. Paul's sounded three times before I slipped out of bed and dressed myself. My father always slept like a stone, and he knew the one reason why I didn't sleep right: If I ever got a job I also would be too tired to stay awake.

I opened the door to the cool smell of silent streets, the sidewalks, the old brick buildings that seemed to have a cold sweat on them. The city turned in its sleep, as if driven by the inexorable hum of a giant turbine deep underground. I stepped onto the sidewalk just in time to avoid a car that wheeled around the corner and blasted past. I took careful steps, turned right down Grand and in a few minutes found myself standing at the base of St. Paul's. I ran my hand over the stones, marveling at their rough massiveness, how difficult it must have been to drag them from some quarry by horse and cart. Above, against the drift of passing clouds luminous in the night sky, the campanile seemed to circle and sway dizzily.

How carefully had each stone been put in its place, how delicately balanced one by one?

I walked south along Grand to the lower part of town, a neighborhood of huddled stores, most of them boarded up. Once upon a time my kind of old neighborhood, full of people strolling by, shopkeepers standing in doorways when business was slow, mothers walking hand-in-hand with children distracted by some new thing in a store window, old men on streetcorners arguing about the weather, baseball and politics; and boys weaving in and out of the sidewalk traffic so girls would see how wonderful they were. All that noise and activity gone now, nothing left but empty sidewalks and stores, here and there a yellow light shining dimly through drawn shades in an upstairs window, and the slogans of sex and disgust painted on walls. At the end of the block a black woman sat head-in-hands on the curb. *"Loro,"* Guido called them. *Them.* Beware of *Them,* the blacks moving in with their old sofas and lamps, their ragged mattresses and box springs and stares, this sullen people from a time so lost in space our Old World seemed new.

I crossed to avoid her and turned left to Twenty-Second Street South, a street dirty, defeated, hopeless like the black woman still in view, lifting her head to follow me. I hurried away from her gaze, walked several blocks, and turned a corner again. Here and there gaps appeared between buildings where bulldozers had done their work.

I hurried to an intersection, hoping to get a glimpse of the dome of St. Paul's. But it was nowhere in view. Here I was, on the corner of Twenty-Second and Stanford, streets no longer familiar to me. In my mind I looked down on a map, saw the city's grid of streets and then myself, a dot standing alone, not sure which way to walk. A sudden fear seized me as I reached to see if my wallet was where it was supposed to be.

I turned the next corner and came face-to-face with a stranger lighting a cigarette. He was leaning against a lamppost, stoop-shouldered, sporting trim white pants and a slick gem-studded shirt, his face twisted, his frizzed Afro hair dyed orange. Then I saw his painted lips and shirt bulging with big breasts, and his eyes following me as I picked up my pace.

He laughed as I broke into a run, my legs going numb as I slowed to a walk. I kept walking in streets that looked alike – desolate, broken, dangerous. Then suddenly I found myself facing an unlit dead-end. Below, bounded by a chain-link fence, the freeway wound its way, and in the haze a mile or two to my left across the freeway the dome and campanile of St. Paul's were visible against a streak of light beginning to break through the night sky. Home was somewhere over there, near that big dark thing.

Dawn had arrived when I found myself standing in front of Guido's old store. It was dark inside. Across the street, within reach of Bruno's arms, Kate and her revolution slept. Kate, opinionated Kate – sure of everything, convinced that a proletariat rebellion was historically inevitable after a general collapse that would wipe everything away, even the most massive stones at the foundation of St. Paul's. Kate, always so full of history lessons climaxed by the triumph of her beloved proles – the factory workers, secretaries, blacks, Hispanics, waitresses, a few journalists, and all housewives. But never me. Kate, lean good-looking Kate, in love with my little brother Bruno, a pudgy kid whose only sense of how to make history advance was to spend days and nights trying to get notes to do their sad wild dance beautifully enough in his mind, then convince himself it was time to make them stand still on a page. Bruno and Kate, Art and History all over again, trying to work out their twisted relationship. Pity poor Bruno. When the Revolution arrived would Kate, armed to the teeth with I-told-you-sos, defend the barricades without him? Would Bruno be in the way then, swept to one side like bourgeois debris, doomed to humming his tunes while hiding under some weary socialist's bed?

I turned my nose up at Kate's headquarters and walked on.

Only a few doors from Guido's old store I faced another sign of the times. Hanging askew on the door of Danko's shop – the place where Bruno had discovered his piano – was a simple hand-painted sign: "FOR SALE."

My heart sank. This, the only shop still alive on the block. I pressed closer to the glass, tried to see in. Against the dim outline of old chairs, tables, clocks, and odds and ends heaped here and there I saw nothing but my own face looking back at me.

Danko, skinny and crewcut, always wearing a leather apron with tools hanging from loops. His wife Rosi, squat and round-faced, her smile decades younger than she really was. This couple who arrived in the neighborhood in 1947, taking the shop over from a widowed Pole. "From Slovakia," Danko said. "We had to hide. You wouldn't believe. We got out just in time – 1941." Danko, always in the back of his store stripping away old paint, gluing the broken leg of a chair, sanding a tabletop smooth as baby skin. His shop was crowded with old stuff – picture frames, candlesticks, desks, chairs, staircase railings, brass doorknobs, hinges, handles, porcelain bowls, books, crocks. Things – all of them charming or unusual or one-of-a-kind or handmade or beautiful. All of them worth passing on. "You look all you want," he would say without taking his eyes from his work. "I see you like to look. I think you maybe got a pretty good eye. You find anything nice and then we talk about how much."

A pretty good eye but no money to buy. Danko's shop, full of history, old-fashioned stuff, the things that survived other people's lives. What would it be like doing what Danko did – salvaging a nice piece from a garage sale or dump, polishing, repairing, restoring it to life, passing it on? Danko and Rosi had made it, gotten by since 1947, almost thirty years. Why not pass the store on to someone with a pretty good eye? And no money to buy.

Who had money these days? Waldman, whoever he was. He had confiscated Guido's old place and God knows what else. And as soon as he saw the sign he would buy Danko's too.

No. I would return as soon as Danko opened his door. Maybe he would teach me about old things, porcelain, china, furniture. And maybe he would wait, save the place for me. Maybe I could get the money somewhere, somehow.

"Out early this morning?" Markels, the collar of his wool overcoat turned up, suddenly was standing next to me. His eyes were weary, red from too much drinking or too little sleep.

"I couldn't sleep."

He nodded. "Morning's the best time."

Together we walked. We passed Guido's old store without looking in, then another two blocks, listening to the city come to life. When we stopped at an intersection to let a car pass, he finally spoke. "Come on over to my place. I'll put some coffee on."

His was a small third-floor apartment three blocks from St. Paul's, cramped and dusty, the curtains grey, the walls lined with old books he had hauled back from Guido's place. Books everywhere, on shelves made of planks and bricks, piles stacked high on the floor. He started brewing coffee on an old stove while I looked down on the streets below, the dome of St. Paul's visible over the rooftops to my right.

We broke the silence by playing an old game.

"I'm thinking of a book," he began, "that sold more copies before the middle of this century than any other but the Bible."

I ventured one of my guesses. *A Message to Garcia.*

He slowly shook his head. "A pamphlet, not a book, but you've got the idea. So now I'm thinking of another one, a novel by a great Russian, a book about a man whose self-spite undermined the premises of modern scientific pragmatism."

"Tolstoy."

No. Wrong again.

"Now please tell me who the great Jew was, the one reviled as much as he has been revered."

"Ah, that's Jesus," I said. "He's one of ours."

Markels laughed as he poured coffee for me. "Try Freud. And then tell me why you're walking the streets in the middle of night? Good men aren't supposed to leave their wives alone in their beds at night."

"Then I am not a good man."

"Thank goodness."

"You've seen the sign in Danko's shop?"

Markels nodded. "He's one of the last of the good ones left."

"You were the last one in our place until Bruno moved in."

"Your brother is a good one too – and I see he's still there."

I nodded. "He's at his music day and night."

"That's good."

"And you, what happened to you?"

"I'm not a businessman," Markels said with a twist of his neck. "There were some books I would never sell, and nobody would dream of buying most of them. And the rent kept going up, and then they beat me up. No way to get by doing that.

Here I have a nice view of the streets below. Warm in winter, maybe too warm."

"How do you...eat?"

"Food stamps."

He got up, circled the room, his head lowered and his hands behind his back. This was the professor again, seeing ideas as if they were houses in a neighborhood he was walking through. "In my intro course I used to take an hour to explain how one word altered the course of history. That one word was a preposition, and prepositions, you know, are serfs in the kingdom of language, little words that serve the bigger, more important ones. Do you remember what that one word was – that one serf that sealed the fate of millions of people for centuries to come?"

He looked up at me and waited for an answer.

"*Among*. That was the word. *Among*."

I had not had his introductory course.

"In the year 325 the Church Fathers met at Nicea. To figure themselves out, what they were going to do with their lives, what rules they were going to make everyone else obey. On pain of death and eternal damnation. For they were afraid of death and needed something more than the rumors they'd heard about Jesus, really afraid because these rumors might only be truth.

"So what's wrong with the truth?" I asked.

"If the rumors were truth, then Christ was real, like one of them, nothing much more, and if he was like them then he too was afraid of death. So their task was to convert the rumors to pure story, for a story is easier to believe than any truth. Then they had to nail that story down and force a simple confession from it. It didn't matter what the confession was. It only mattered that something be confessed, something simple enough to memorize. Once they had that they had something manageable to give them a solid grip on reality, and they didn't have to be afraid of dying any more."

He paused, turned away to the wall.

"The Nicene Creed. All neatly wrapped up in that. Something simple and short, easy for the urchins in schools to memorize, something tidier than all the rumors coming and going as if nobody owned the place. Nobody, you know, likes an untidy story, one that doesn't have a clear plot, nice morals, and happy ending."

"Yes, I see," I chimed, not sure where he was leading me.

"And that's when they argued about two words. *Among* and *by*. They finally decided Christ was killed *among* the Romans. Right then and there they concluded he was not killed *by* the Romans."

He turned to me. I nodded as if I understood.

"You don't understand, do you?"

I shrugged.

"I'm a Jew. Christ was crucified under Pontius Pilate, not *by* him. The Romans didn't kill Jesus. I did. *All* my people did."

"And that's why you were dismissed from your professor's job?"

He laughed – not at my question but at some distant absurdity affronting him. "That would have been reason enough. A few of my lectures attracted the attention of some of my distinguished colleagues who let it be known that what I said to students was extraordinary. They didn't stop whispering even when the books appeared proving me right. And they really went limp when a few of my true-believing students complained. He's a Jew, they said. Look at him, that hair he never combs, his shirt hanging out the way he does, in all those dumps along Second Street, bars, maybe even whorehouses now and then. What right has he to teach Christianity to anyone?"

He sat down, brought himself in close. "Yes, that would have been reason enough. I made a man of their god, thereby killing him. It never occurred to them they should thank me for it – since they believe they're saved by his death." He came closer, whispered. "They said I was corrupting young girls. And a few said it was boys, but they only whispered that so everybody would be sure to hear."

I backed off with a laugh. "So you screwed a co-ed?"

"They were right about her – and I told them that. I made love to her. And there was more than one. They nailed me because I actually did what a lot of them wanted to do to her."

He got up and walked to the tallest bookshelf in the room. For a minute he scanned the top rows of books. Then he let his head hang and stood in silence, his back to me. A truck horn blared outside the window. "I was looking for *The City of God*. But maybe that should wait for another time."

He poured more coffee in my cup. "We'll miss our dear old Danko, will we not?"

"If Danko sells, Bruno will be the only one left on that side of the street."

"Who owns your old store now?"

"I'm not sure. Someone named Waldman. Does the name ring a bell?"

"This Waldman bell is not for me to ring. You own a degree in history. Maybe you should find out who he is and ring his bell yourself." He walked to the window and looked out. "I know an old fart, a Russian Jew who likes to talk. He knew Waldman from way back."

"What's his name?"

"Rostopov. Joseph. Corner of Fifth and Saxon Street – upstairs. But nobody believes what he says."

"Why not?"

"He doesn't lie. But would you believe someone who says he's a communist and a Christian too?"

"I don't know what to believe any more."

Markels smiled. "Then maybe you should move in here with me."

I didn't know what story Sandy would believe about my being AWOL from bed. As I walked home past St. Paul's people were beginning to come out from the early morning Mass, smiling when they emerged into the Sunday sun. Most walked away from Tommy, the toothless newspaperman who stood at the curb flashing the latest headline at people coming out. Isabel Peron was back in power in Argentina, and the teacher's union in New York City agreed to dig into its pension funds to save the city's schools. In Italy legislators were incensed that the president had broken his traditional silence to complain about corruption and inefficiency. And on this day that the Lord had made few were buying the news.

Tommy positioned himself in front of me. As I was rummaging in my pocket for some change, I froze. In the main cathedral portal, Mamma, her eyes adjusting to the light, was looking my way. I hadn't shaved and was still in Saturday's clothes. Quickly I turned, hunched my shoulders, and sauntered across the street to my left. When I dared to look back Mamma was safely on the sidewalk leading home. Then I became aware of a woman watching me. She was on the curb, smiling as if she knew more than I did. Slender, dark-haired, wearing a dark blue dress. She abruptly turned when she saw me return her gaze.

Sandy was sitting over an empty coffee mug when I got home. "Where in the hell have you been?"

6. *"God, what a lovely woman the stranger was."*

There was a time when she would have wanted to help me make sense of things. Now I had to apologize. "Some weird things started going through my mind. I couldn't sleep, went out for fresh air, and ended up walking the streets. It all looks so different when everyone's asleep. And Danko's is for sale – the junk shop down the street from Guido's place."

She sorted through everything I said and found nothing true enough, nothing of use.

"And you won't believe. The sun's coming up and I run into Markels. My old professor, the one who started the bookstore at Guido's place before Bruno moved in? I took you to one of his classes."

She looked up, more interested now.

"And we had coffee at his place – not far from here – and he talked and talked. I learn about stuff from him."

"Stuff?"

"Would you believe, the Nicene Creed. You wouldn't believe what he knows, all the fine points."

"And you're trying to catch up." Her words accused.

"The bad news is that Danko is selling out. What'll happen now to Guido's place? What would Bruno do if someone tore down the whole block?"

"Bruno would have to get a real job."

"What if we bought Danko's place?"

"Buy?"

I asked her if she wanted to picnic that afternoon in the Old River Park. There was one special grassy bank, not far from downtown, where I had played as a boy. And it was already mid-October, so there wasn't much time.

51

She had things to do around the house.

So I went to the park by myself and spent the afternoon with a book about heroes and history. Plato, Jesus, Michaelangelo, Hitler, Marx – Products of their Environment. Merely names that managed to surface and survive the glacial advance of cultures that ground millions of other identities into dust? Or Prime Movers, the true engineers of events, saviors and destroyers of the world? The question was as big as my name, Salvatore. Still with me was the dim hum of the city at night, that huge turbine grinding away on its own underneath the streets, and it was such a beautiful day I couldn't keep my eyes on the page. Now and then I put my hands behind my head and watched myself scan the lawns, for someone interesting and beautiful to come my way.

Later, at dinner, Sandy was silent and sad. "Should we go see the movie we missed last night?" I asked.

"No," she said, "it's already too late."

The next morning I stayed in bed until Sandy left for work. I took an hour to read the morning paper, turning to the help wanted ads as a last resort. President Ford and Congress had swung a deal to provide trade benefits to the U.S.S.R., and the Watergate trial was grinding on. Inflation was up again and so was the price of oil. More of the same old stuff. I could be a clerk in a hardware store, a bartender, waiter or shoe salesman. I could sell door-to-door or over the phone, and if I was ambitious, had a car, and was willing to be on the road perpetually leading away from home toward some distant California fault, I would be a success in six short months. I could be a police officer too, but I would have to pass the test. And if I was young and willing to smile my way to the top, I could be assistant manager in a new hamburger palace going up a half-mile from St. Paul's.

I threw the paper on the floor and closed my eyes. What would it smell like to be a cop? Like Franco's Bakery, that used to be a few doors down from Guido's store, the first place every morning to open up? Franco – whatever happened to him, his pastries and bread, the aroma that disappeared with him when he left the old neighborhood? Or did cops smell like the fragrance that spread through Guido's place whenever Rosina had a big pot of spaghetti sauce simmering on the stove upstairs? Things were better when I was a boy. I could stay overnight at Guido's store. "Why not?" Papa would say. "He's got to learn what it means to work." I used to wake to the sound of dishes, to Rosina's quiet slow steps from table to sink, to Guido pushing back his chair and walking downstairs to unlock the door, to the fresh morning air stirring with the scent of apples and oranges stacked in pyramids below. I used to eat hungrily and then run downstairs, always checking the brown brine in the olive barrels next to the meat case and the penny candy behind the glass in front of the cash register. "Fix the shelves, fix the shelves," Guido winked when he caught me looking too long. Then I would stack boxes and cans in rows until the store's two aisles stood at attention like troops on parade. From outside Guido, next to his open crates of fruits and vegetables facing the sidewalk and the summer sun, would nod his okay for me to raid the candy shelves. Until the cold arrived the door stood open all day long. Cars inched by, faces inside looking here and there, and women, shopping bags in hand, stopped at Guido's to discuss the weather, their trouble for the day, and the price of pears. "I'm almost giving them away," he told those who came in the late afternoon. "Why don't you come early and get the best?"

At twilight we moved everything inside, restocked the shelves and swept the floor. Finally he poured the change on the counter and together we stacked the coins in piles of ten, and we counted it twice.

Yes, things were better when I was a boy, but not just because I was a boy.

I decided to try it out. I had pumped gas, delivered laundry and sold credit cards over the phone. Why not be a clerk in a hardware store? Besides, Guido's was on the way.

From the sidewalk I could see Bruno at his piano again. Bruno – dark and too round, too soft, the boy still visible in the lines of his face – clumsily bent over a page full of notes that looked like dozens of small stray cats skittering every which way. This brother I had bullied as a boy, whom women found handsome and mysterious, seemed to be fading prematurely toward middle age, taking on the drabness that came over the store when Guido was coaxed out to live a half-mile away. The drabness was in Bruno's clothes, his posture and smile – all but his eyes, intense, a bit crazed by what they saw in the music he was always making in his mind.

I pressed up close to the window, never doubting my right to intrude. The store was still more mine than his, and not because of order of birth. It did not matter that I, big brother, had been in Guido's store first. What mattered was that I was the first to make it a second home.

"Do you think you can share this joint for an hour or so?" I asked as I walked in on him. "I just want to get off my feet – brought the paper along to look at some ads."

He turned to the keyboard and ran his fingers wildly up and down. Then suddenly he stopped. "I'm expecting Kate any minute now."

"Whatever turns off your metronome," I said with a smirk.

I found an old chair and put the morning paper up between him and myself, staring right through the news about dirty little wars in Africa and Latin America. I knew too much about these wars – the names of a few of the bad and good guys involved – and nothing at all. I thanked my stars again that Bruno and I had escaped Vietnam – Bruno especially, who seemed so unfit for any strife, whose head danced in a musical fog through all the troubled years, and who managed to disappear whenever Kate marched and preached and raved about the evils of imperialism, never letting me forget how corrupt my own merely liberal views were. And she was always outrageously right – informed, logical, "scientifically historical" – always standing back, hands on hips, waiting for me to confess my political sins. And Bruno bugged me too, his refusal to pay any attention to our arguments, let alone to what was going on in the world.

I turned the newspaper at an angle so Bruno would have to see me. He made no sounds, sat, waited. Then in a fit of impatience he got up and circled the stove.

I put the paper down. "What's wrong?"

"Nothing. Nothing." He turned his back to me, as if ashamed. Then he sat down and stared out the window.

"My, isn't this a cozy way for the brothers Grimm to start the day?"

Katherine Sweeny, slender and twenty-five and neither soft-spoken nor soft, stood hip-cocked just inside the door. In her tight denim jeans and flannel shirt she looked sexy, stylish, and tough. She had a lovely face – dark brows, smooth skin, and high cheekbones that gave her a haughty air, her looks much too attractive for the sharp-edged opinions that put people off. She had a sneer in her voice.

"In one corner we have the Artist, brooding over notes that one day will make freeway traffic sound like the music of the spheres, and in the other Mr. Philosopher, the one whose real work in the world is the production of more words."

Bruno turned slightly, gave her a sardonic glance, and returned to his wooden chair.

"And you," I said, "have decided that right here is the best place to change the world."

"Maybe not the right place, but certainly the right time. Isn't 1976 just around the bend? Maybe now's a good time to remember back a couple hundred years."

"Maybe you can set up your guillotine next to the piano here."

"Ah no, I wouldn't want to intrude on your right to life, liberty, and property."

"You forget, comrade Kate, that we don't own this place. We just pay our squatter's rent like all your other unblessed workers of the world."

"Three-quarters of a century you pay and pay and you still don't own the place. Tsk, tsk. It must be you don't deserve to own the place. Maybe you should ask your overlords what you can kiss next. Or maybe you don't work hard enough."

"Someday, comrade Kate, the store will be ours."

"Oh really, if you work hard enough?"

"That's right, Kate. Work will set you free. Isn't that your party line?"

She flashed her hip at me and walked to Bruno, who had turned his back to both of us. Damn him, I thought. Why doesn't he pipe up just once? A slow burn started in me when Kate spread her hands on his shoulders, massaged a moment with her fingers, bent down, whispered to him and kissed him on the ear. Reluctantly he put his pencil down and let his head relax against her waist.

"Where you playing tonight?" I broke in.

"Near the river. Some joint. Stephanie's, I think."

"It's where working people go." Kate let her words dig in. "Not far from here."

I spoke past her. "I'd like to listen to your new stuff. Maybe I'll come out tonight."

"Oh, and you'll buy all the drinks?" Kate said.

"Leave him alone," Bruno snapped. "Sometimes you two make me sick. Sometimes I wish you'd leave me alone."

"And I suppose that means me too!" she said, raising her voice. "Goddamn you two! Coming into this place when the two of you are here is like..."

"Trying to marry into the family," I said.

"Marry? What makes you think I'd stoop to marrying?"

"You don't believe in marriage? What about stooping? Do you stoop now and then – in the position of your choice?"

"Bruno, why don't you shut this sex fiend brother of yours up? If you want to see me I'll be across the street." She took loud strides toward the door and slammed it so hard behind her that it bounced open again. Then her head appeared in the door. "See you at seven – like I said."

In the silence Bruno and I looked at each other. "She'll be ready at six for you," I said.

Bruno nodded but didn't smile. "You should hear this thing I'm working on, mainly blues, but there's this wild part underneath that just takes off."

I spoke before a silence could come between us again. "You know, I don't know how you get on. You play your piano in those joints three nights a week. How much do they pay you? Twenty-five dollars a night? You have to eat, you have to heat this place and pay the rent, you have some fun now and then, see a movie, have a drink. I don't know how you make it doing what you do."

Bruno looked up at me and stroked his chin. "I get by."

"And what do you see in that woman across the street? Oh yes, sex. I know, I know. But what else?"

"She's a puritan."

"Like her politics. So what do you see in her?"

"She's got lots going for her."

"Yes, opinions, politics. And you've got as much politics as that piano. I don't understand."

"It's more than just opinions."

"You mean a certain disdain for what you do all day? You can see what she's after, can't you? She wants to take you across the street, drag you away from your piano, take you out there..."

"Where the trouble is?"

"Yes. You know she doesn't believe in what you're doing."

"So what? Neither do a lot of the people I play for."

"And that doesn't bother you?"

"Only when I take the time."

"What bothers you?"

The silence fell, Bruno averting his eyes from me as if searching for a way to escape. "You mean what bothers me right now?"

"Yes."

"Right now you're bothering me," he said. "Would you please go away. I want to work."

Bruno was playing by the time I got to the door. I closed it carefully behind, as if trying to seal him off from the noise of traffic on the street.

The door to Danko's was open. Danko was in back – I could see him holding something up to the light. I cleared my throat to announce my presence, and he came forward when he saw who it was.

"Come to buy the place?" he said with a wink.

"Now or never?"

"Six months. By then I gotta be out of here."

My heart sank. "You mean the place is sold?"

"Oh no," he laughed, "not so fast. I put the sign up only three days ago. No, not sold, but I'm out in six months. I got a new place in Florida. These old bones..." he screwed his wrist and elbow around, "...can take one more winter here, no more. The bones want sun. I need a little cash for the place down there."

I suddenly found myself on his side. "No offers yet?"

He laughed again. "An offer yes, but nothing I can take serious. He offered me half. I told him I thought my price was fair and he just walked out."

"Anybody I know?"

"No. Probably not serious. Didn't look at any of the stuff in the place."

"A young man?"

"About your age."

Not Waldman then. "Do you mind me asking how much?"

"I think I said thirty-five dollars, didn't I? That cup you wanted to buy for Christmas last year, and everything's up now with inflation, you know. That cup was a while ago. Still, for you the price is the same, maybe less."

"No, I mean the price for the store."

"Oh..." His eyes opened wide. "Can you believe forty-one thousand? I need thirty-three-five hundred for my new place in Florida. That's why."

"It seems a little high...these days."

He looked at me closely, searchingly. "You really interested?"

He knew. "I'd like to learn how you do these things."

"You have six months to learn. Free. Here – from me. You really want to buy?"

I nodded a helpless little nod. I wanted to tell him I'd be the best helper he ever had, that I'd buy everything with the store, not change a thing and keep calling it Danko's Shop.

"But you got any money?"

"No, not enough."

"You get a loan then – at the bank?"

"Yes, maybe, a loan." A sudden hope surged through me. "Would you...keep the place, I mean save it for me? In case someone else comes in, I mean, and wants to buy? You'll let me know?"

He put his hand on my shoulder. "If you want this place it's yours. You are a good boy – a good family. Guido gave me more tomatoes than I can eat. You got plenty of time – six months. I let you know."

He took my hand and we shook on it.

"Now you want to buy that cup for that nice wife of yours? If you don't get it for her, give it to my girl. Thirty-six years we been married next month."

I had twenty-two cents in my pocket, one penny more than a cup of coffee would cost. "Not now," I said, "because pretty soon everything here will be mine."

Danko's wife came down from the apartment above. She stood in the doorway at the foot of the stairs watching us, wiping her hands on her apron. She was smiling as if I were the son she never had.

And wouldn't she be proud of me, I thought as I left Danko's shop, if I were the owner of this store some day? I saw Sandy smile and approve, and then I saw another woman standing at the bus stop across the street. Very pretty, somebody I maybe had seen before. Danko's wife saw me gazing at her. God, what a lovely woman the stranger was.

7. *"...someday, someday, someday before Guido died, I would hand him the deed to the old grocery store."*

She was gone before I got a really good look at her. For a moment I stood there wondering. What was she doing in my neighborhood? Why had I never seen her before? Could we sit down together and talk, maybe someplace where we'd be lost in the crowd? I loved the way she carried herself with purpose and confidence. And what a lovely face – perhaps clear blue eyes looking out from behind dark brows, an enticing curl to her lip when she smiled, maybe a small beauty mark on her left cheek.

The bus went east on Second, so I hurried that way too, looking for her. Then a car squealed its tires and another bus bullied its way toward the curb. I gave up. She was gone, lost in the confusion of noise, and suddenly I found myself standing at a familiar place, the steps of the public library.

What the hell, I said to myself. The hardware store will have to wait. What do I know about hardware anyway?

I glanced at my watch – 10:36 – then at the pigeons huddled atop the columns supporting the pediment and porch. Down the walls, bare except for three rows of windows, rain had stained the stones into the greyed appearance of antiquity. As I walked up the steps Athena, Apollo, and their retinue of heroes sculpted into the pediment turned away indifferently from me, their hard serene eyes gazing into the space somewhere between the traffic moiling below and the distant clouds. Athena and Apollo – I looked up at them again before I entered the shadow of the porch. Athena, warrior and woman at once, her masculine toughness draped in a graceful gown. And Apollo, feminine in his muscular nakedness. Neither of

61

them showing the face or form of any of the white marble
Marys on the side-altars of St. Paul's – except for the eyes, the
blank hard sadness of their eyes.

I had never felt at home here. Heels clacked on cold floors,
so I always watched my step, and the spaces were wide: Long
oak tables in rows with wide aisles between; thousands of
books arranged on perfectly ordered shelves, the rows of
books tidy but asymmetrical, their backs turned to those
wandering by as if contemptuous of those unimpressed by
their place in history. I expected to see Markels facing the
shelves, the grey of his wild hair, his shirt hanging out, a thick
tome open in his hand.

Only the reading room made me feel comfortable, the
sculptures between windows reminding me of the monuments
behind the choir of St. Paul's. Carpeted and lined with
cushioned chairs, its quiet moved into me. Again I surveyed
the books lining the shelves, my common sense rebelling
against the feeling that the past they represented must have
been a better, more beautiful time. I arbitrarily picked out two
books and put one under each arm.˙

As I turned I surprised a librarian on her knees reshelving
books. She was middle-aged, pretty, maybe a bit heavy in the
hips. "Are you looking for something special?" she asked as
she lifted her eyeglasses onto her hair.

"Just browsing." I was embarrassed, troubled to think she
might conclude I was an idler. "But I wonder if you could help
me find something out about a certain man."

"What is his name?"

"Waldman."

"Have your tried any of the biographical indexes in the
reference room? What was his first name and when did he
live?"

"I don't know his first name, but I think he's still alive."

"And what is he noted for?"

"He's...a businessman."

Her face disapproved. "We'll have to try the reference
room."

She led the way, as if suddenly curious, and together we
searched the shelves. I first picked out a thick green book
entitled *Who's Who in the Midwest*. No Waldman. On the shelf

above I found the *Who's Who in America* volumes. In a minute I found an entry:

WALDMAN. ADOLPH, *Peter. b. Koenigsburg, Prussia, Germany, July 5. 1901. Came to U. S. 1913; student Missionary Inst., Selinsgrove PA; A. B. Wittenberg Coll., Springfield 0.; elected Chief Jefferson, Brotherhood of the Union, 1917; Society of Friends,1918; IWW; Corporal U. S. Army 1922, honorable discharge; Desk boy, District Mgr. of sales, St. Louis Post Dispatch, 1925; President, United Bath Co., St. Paul, Minn. 1928; Deacon, First United Presbyterian Church, Fort Dodge, Kan., 1929; President, Northwoods Lumber, 1932; Knights of Columbus, 1933; Chmn. of Board, United Magazines Corp., Northwest Machine Corp., 1935; Public Works Project, 1936; Elder, Church of Latter Day Saints, Salt Lake, Utah, 1939; Candidate for U. S. Congress (Rep., Nev.) 1940; Europe Development and Reconstruction, 1945; Western Aircraft and Tool, 1946; Pres. Beaux Arts Assoc. 1950; Pres. Pacific Wines, 1950; Pres. Hollywood Prod. Inc. 1950; Chmn. of Board, Southwest General Corp., 1951; Retired, 1952; Chmn. Philanthropic Association of America, 1952; South African Pretorians, 1952. Unmarried.*

Could this be my Waldman, the one whose name appeared on the rental invoices Guido received every month, the one Guido said lived in one of the old houses on The Hill? Or could the signature on the letters be Waldman's son's? "Unmarried." Waldman's son – illegitimate? Was this my Waldman or some strange surrogate for the man who lived behind St. Paul's?

I looked around for help. The librarian was gone. I read the notice again, tried to imagine the progress of Waldman's pilgrimage from place to place, from enterprise to enterprise, each one bigger than the last, the art and philanthropy, final touches to the picture of a full rounded life, the movements always sporadically west, then part-way back. And the varieties of religious – what? – credentials.

This, then, was a successful American way of life.

I weighed the volume I was holding in my hand, the flesh and blood life of a man reduced to a recipe. Waldman – a vague fascinating someone about whom I now had a few facts.

But what to make of them? I folded the corner of the page and put the volume back, ran my eyes along the shelf, and paged through every volume that seemed promising. But there was nothing more about Adolph Peter Waldman.

The librarian stood behind me again. "How you doing?"

"I think I've found my man," I said as I placed a volume back on the shelf. She smiled in a way that showed no further interest in me. As she walked away I looked around the room to see if there might be some other woman glancing my way.

At the front door of the library a thought caught up with me. I charged back up the stairs past the librarian, who slowed me to a walk with one hard stare.

I found the book with Waldman's life in it and turned to the title page. "Published 1962." Thirteen years between then and now. Nothing on him since 1952. He would be seventy-five years old. But between 1962 and now he would have had thirteen years in which to get lost, disappear, maybe die in that house of his on The Hill.

I knew vaguely which way to go – past St. Paul's and the rectory, onto the narrow circular streets leading to the ridges of The Hill, the grand houses there, hidden under venerable oaks and elms, less than a mile away from Guido's old store lost in the streets below.

The sky was overcast by the time I found Waldman's house. Leaning slightly askew, it rose out of ground covered by shrubs gone wild, the large 'W" embroidered in bronze on the iron gate of the front portal providing the only passage through the stone wall surrounding the estate.

I backed away from the gate, found a grassy incline from which to see more of the house.

Stone. Heavy grey stone, greyer than St. Paul's, stone hauled up the hill by horsepower and men. Hard, grave, unyielding stone. Dense with centuries of history, a history so fossilized it would not endure trafficking with less substantial stuff, all the suburbs made of sticks that the huffing and puffing of some wolf developer could easily blow away.

There was a light visible in a small window high in a turret to the left of the porch, a glow staring dimly into the western sky like a yellow eye in a great stone face. I strained to find some motion, some clue in it, some glimpse of this man so distant and so large and small as to exact a monthly rent from men as shrivelled as Guido. The window had nothing to show.

I reviewed again and tried to summarize. First common labor in a factory, then Bancroft and Sons, whatever that was. Desk boy, United Bath Company, lumber, United Magazines, Northwest Machines, politics, Public Works Project, aircraft, wine, motion pictures – a life concluded by his becoming Chairman of the Board of Southwest General and a South African Pretorian, whatever that was. And like his businesses, his beliefs seemed to cross his life like freeways cutting broad swaths through old city neighborhoods. Waldman must have had the missionary urge as a young man, and then a Quaker urge in time for the first Great War, an urge weak enough to allow him to serve in the army after the war. Wittenburg had to be a Lutheran college, and yet he somehow had it in him to become Presbyterian deacon, Knight of Columbus and Mormon elder. The man, then, had no beliefs or somehow managed to live with them all. Was his life boundlessly unscrupulous, or was it an incoherent pilgrimage toward some shrine, perhaps this house on The Hill?

Politics, foreign relations, European reconstruction, beaux arts and philanthropy. Was Waldman's life entirely out of control?

And if Waldman was not in control, then who was? Or, worse yet, what was? And if no one or nothing, then...

Then systems were not systematic, all bodies drifting, waiting for a chance door to open or close on them. Then bathtubs, lumber, machines, foreign relations, beaux arts, movies and wines had nothing to do with one another except their coincidental existence side-by-side and struggle to exist, like daydreamers walking down the same street on their way to pointless jobs. The American Dream. The American Way of Life.

Within an hour I found myself inside the hardware store. When a smiling man told me the position had just been filled, I secretly smiled an I-told-you-so to myself as a slow burn began flaring inside my head and gut. Not sure which way to turn, I stood on the sidewalk watching cars, busses, an old woman hobbling along on a cane. A car squealed around the corner, radio blaring, and passed within two feet of me.

Then something in me screamed. All these god-damned jobs could go to hell! I would find out everything about Waldman and his schemes. I would get next month's rental invoice from Bruno, would put it in my fist and shake that fist in front of Waldman's face, or somebody's face. I someday would buy Danko's shop, and someday, someday, someday before Guido died, I would hand him the deed to the old grocery store.

8. *"But I'm honey," she said to him. "I taste very good without you."*

The corner of Saxon and Fifth. Rusoff. Rominoff. Raskolnikov. Something like that. A Russian Christian communist who liked to talk, who knows Waldman from way back.

The corner of Saxon and Fifth. I walked into my boyhood here. On one corner a movie theater, an elegant palace with gilded frills that curled along ceilings and walls until they met a big Wurlitzer set like a throne in the center of the back balcony. I watched movies there, awed by the spectacles and colors on the screen that made life in the streets seem small, slow, and drab. I never heard the old organ played though I remember standing with a crowd gathered to watch workmen take it out piece by piece. We tried to get inside, and somebody asked the workmen if we could help smash the organ apart.

The old theater showed sex movies now, all its windows that curved into a wide vestibule under the marquee painted green. Across the street to the left was a place I remembered as a Five-and-Ten, its windows now full of records and radios. To its left was a brown brick building, the curtain in its window open far enough to show a sign made of small red bulbs blinking JESUS SAVES at the sex movie theater directly across the street.

Everything looked different, worse. Shopowners had come and gone, half of them losers within a year or two, most of their shops boarded up. In upstairs apartments dim windows looked down on the streets below, most of the windows bare, a few showing a greyed curtain or half-drawn shade.

67

The corner of Saxon and Fifth. There were no apartments above the theater or bank, but behind me, above the gospel church, a face ducked behind a curtain when I glanced up. I found a door and three mailboxes at the foot of the stairs, the name "Rostopov" scrawled on one.

He was standing in the doorway when I reached the top of the steps.

"I watch you down there," he said. "You maybe looking for somebody here?"

"Adolph Waldman. Professor Markels said you could tell me about him."

He gave a little laugh as he stepped aside. "Waldman, eh? I see you never heard about the fool, what he said to them after the men almost beat him to death."

"Fool?"

"You should thank God all the lights were on, the fool said to the men with the sticks. Otherwise I maybe find someplace to hide."

Rostopov laughed and laughed. He could have been sixty or eighty years old. He was stooped and walked with small careful steps, but his arms, shoulders and neck were sinewy, still showing the shape of a lean hard-working life. His eyes, deep-set behind bushy brows, seemed indifferent to what was in front of them, but his words came forth from his small round chest with surprising force.

"So the old Jew sent you here."

He stepped aside and showed me to a seat in a small area that doubled as a kitchen and living room. He said nothing as he put water on to boil. At long last he set a cup of tea in my hands and sat on a rocker near a window looking down on the street.

"My name is Sal Amato."

"Ah yes, yes, a student of Professor Markels. You writing a little history?"

"I'm giving it some thought." My words, once spoken, suddenly made the notion seem real. "Waldman interests me."

"You know where he is," Rostopov said, pointing toward The Hill. "Over there, rotting away in that little castle of his. In some window looking down on the little paradise in back."

"I know the place."

"But you don't know him. And now you want to write our little history."

Our? "Yes, my interest is mainly historical. It goes way back. I have good reason to believe that Waldman cheated my grandfather out of the family business – years ago, Depression times."

"Ah yes," Rostopov nodded, as if he knew. He shifted away from me and gazed out the window again.

"There was a peasant once, Nesterka. Six children but no land. Nothing to eat but bark and snow and too afraid to steal. So what does he do? He calls his children to him, put a harness on his cart, and goes out. In the world he finds a man lying on the road. A man with no feet begging him, 'Put me on your cart. I have no feet.' 'Look at my miserable horse,' Nesterka says, 'and my children starving to death.' 'Please,' said the man with no feet. So for him Nesterka made room on the cart. 'Now,' said the man with no feet, 'let's throw dice to see who the eldest brother will be.' And the footless man, he won the roll of the dice.

"Now Waldman, he sees me standing on the street, walks up to my face. Coffee you want? We go for coffee on Twenty-Third Street. Was I German too? I know only a few English words. No, I am Russian. Thank you, goodbye, hello, yes, please. He paid for the coffee, everything. He said to visit him, a little room not far away on Twenty-First."

Rostopov turned and confronted me with eyes that were suddenly alive, circling as they searched for my motive.

"So you want to know about him, what it was like to be him inside? You see, we never got married, really. Neither of us. No good wife. That is why everything has gone so wrong. Do you see?"

"I don't think I understand."

"Then listen to me a little more with your ears. Nights I go to his place. Do I want to get ahead in America? He has cards with words on them. I have to learn one hundred words every week, not one word less. Fifty-two hundred words in one year, he says at the end of ten days, like he is counting dollars already in the bank. He is working a little job here or there like me, my brother, but he has words and I have hello, please, yes, goodbye. And one night he opens a Bible in front of my nose. 'This is the Word of God,' he says. 'Do you believe?' Yes, I believe, but I want to go back to Leningrad because here it was all wrong too, but there we had some hope, people we know. And one night I use the word. 'Socialist?' I see his face now, all confused. If I said to him 'crocodile' it would be the same. No difference to him. I tell him not to make fun, the socialism is no joke with me.

"So Nesterka, all loaded down, he came with his children to a village. 'Go see if we can spend the night in that house,' the footless man says to him. Nesterka finds an old woman in the house. 'Please, please, a room,' he says to her, but she says no. 'Go back to the old hag,' said the footless man, and use new words. Tell her I am the son of a king from a faraway land.' Nesterka looked at his children and the man with no feet and took pity on all. He said son of a king from a faraway land, and the old woman, what do you think, she falls on her knees and kisses his hand. 'My husband is out stealing,' she said, 'and with him he has our two sons. So you put your children under the table where they belong.' But the footless man he wanted to sit next to the stove. There he could keep warm and dip his spoon into her bowl of soup.

"So that's how it goes," Rostopov said with a smirk. He pulled himself up from the rocker, stood by the window, and looked out. From where I sat I could see the bulbs in the window of the gospel church, Jesus blinking at a few people walking by. At the far end of Fifth the avenue widened and went downhill toward the river, offering a view of downtown skyscrapers against a grey sky.

"I sit up here," Rostopov began again, "and watch the people, and if you ask they all give you a reason why. They all say I go where I want, even if they go to work. Now me, I find myself in New York right off the boat almost fifty-five years ago and all I know is yes, thank you, hello, goodbye, please. All the streets somebody else made, and I am just one little man, looking up and not believing my eyes, everything confused. I had a woman in Leningrad and she said no – that's all. So what the hell, I pack a bag and go. Why this way or that? Because I have a little money for the train, beause the street from the train to the boat is there already made for me. Because my Sonya fifty-five years ago said no in my face. You see her now – all wrinkled up, fat like a cow, her babushka a rag on her head."

He whispered as he leaned toward me. "It is Waldman's story, this. I said no to him – I want to go back to Leningrad. And later he said no to me.

"Sure, I found a woman here, but already she has twenty-six years. Then one night your Mr. Waldman he's in front of my door knocking to get in. And there she is half-naked on my bed. Three hours I have to beg her to get that way, and she's twenty-six years. But he won't leave us go. I open the door and he gives a dirty look at her sitting on the chair. 'Who is she?' he says. 'You get her out of here.' I say no and he grabs my shirt. 'I come all the way to tell you,' he says. 'I believe like you now. Like you always said. It's not right the way things are. We must change things now.'

"Can you believe – in a couple months he's a socialist, no, a communist, a crocodile. When is the next meeting, he says, what do I think about this or that, when will the revolution start, and will the unions really come in, and the girl gets tired sitting on the chair so she takes her coat and goes away. Good riddance he says after she's out the door.

"Waldman. You go figure it out. We meet in a bar or coffee shop, or I go to his room. Every word is unions, revolution, workers' party, and one night he says to me what's wrong, don't you believe any more? Maybe, he says, I spend too much time with that girl. Did I not get rid of her yet? I go away to Detroit, then to Minnesota, the Iron Range, and when I come back in October, 1923, I ask around for him and nobody knows.

"So that's how it goes. In Russia there was a poor peasant once. In a big log a nice rabbit is hiding in there. 'I'll kill it with a stick,' to himself he said, 'and sell it for thirty kopeks. Then I'll buy a sow and she'll have ten piglets and the pigs will all grow up and have fifteen pigs more. Then I'll kill them all, sell the meat, get married, and have six sons. My wife will cook, the sons will plow the fields with the laborers, and I will sit in the window and smoke.

"You got to get in with them, Waldman says to me just before I go to Detroit. From inside bring them down. But inside it is hard to get with no job. We all need a job, so I go here and there – from Mr. Ford's coke ovens to Ohio, back to Detroit. Tool and die, assembly line, janitor, open hearth – who remembers any more? And your Mr. Waldman, where is he? What do you expect? We lose each other looking for a job. America is too big. Sooner or later in America everybody gets lost."

He went to the stove for more tea, mumbling to himself and letting out a little laugh as he poured more into my cup. When he resumed talking he had taken his seat by the window again, his back half-turned to me.

"How many years we are lost this way – fifteen I could say, who remembers any more? Then I see him again – in 1941. He is in a car and I call to him. He tells me to visit him. Do I need a job?"

"He was rich by then – suddenly rich. He cheated my grandfather Guido, you know. Did you ask him about that, ask him how he got so rich?"

"The money?" Rostopov turned and grinned at me. "He found a rabbit hiding in a log."

"But how did he get his money?"

"The rabbit he killed with a stick. Easy to make switches after that."

"Switches? For what?"

"For everything."

"Everything?"

"Everything – cars, lamps, furnaces, everything."

"Switches?"

"Easy then to do bathtubs, life insurance, airplane parts."

"But how?"

"What do you mean how? How. If there is a rabbit stuck in a log, what would you do? He had all the words he needed to talk sweet. The rabbit said yes, came out by herself. And the stick he had in his hand."

Rostopov fell silent as he gazed at the street below. I could see him standing apart from himself, watching scenes from his own life appear and disappear, he reduced to old man sitting in his chair by the window, the one looking out, seeing and not seeing a few souls walking past the blinking Jesus on the building below. How had his fate – his place by the window here and now – been turned out? And how had Waldman turned out so different?

I had an urge to interrupt his reverie. Was it a question of character? I'd had all I could take of a certain type – the consistently consistent one full of passionate intensity for some narrow belief, fanatic whose quest for purity concluded in the construction of gulags and concentration camps designed to purge the earth of the impure, all those ordinary ones, inconsistently consistent or consistently inconsistent, whose devotions were uneven and unreliable, and dull enough, like mine. Was Waldman truly extraordinary, inconsistently inconsistent? No, impossible. Character could not exist outside some parameters. Even madness had its peculiar behaviors, forms, and names.

"Did he ever want to go back to Germany – back home to his roots?"

"Never," Rostopov said.

Rostopov's certainty on this point slammed a door on both of us. In a certain sense Rostopov still lived there, in Russia, with the peasant named Nesterka, the footless man, and the creature who killed the rabbit with the stick. And I had Guido and Rosina, Mamma's bread and song, and St. Paul's, the vision, however gone wrong, brought across the sea by an architect from France and the Raphael still in my blood.

"Then what did he want out of life?"

Rostopov shrugged, didn't know. "The house? In 1941 it was still new. He had that. But it was not that. 'Everything's going to hell,' he said to me. He lost an election – somewhere in the west. Gone all the time, was tired of being away. Told me to sit down, eat something with him. Told me I worked too hard. Did I want a new job?"

"Butler."

"Gardener. Half an acre he has in back. He has a wall in back of the house – eight foot high made of granite that came in a special train. He told me to make a little paradise back there – just tell him what I need to make it look nice. A little grass, a few trees. That was my job, he said. A little paradise in back for him."

"So you built his little paradise in back?"

Rostopov gave me a hard stare. "The war. You young ones maybe do not remember the war. I said no to him, and he said are you a nigger now? You don't want to work? Or maybe you're really a Jew? All you want to do is sit there and watch it come in?"

Rostopov smiled as he leaned toward me. "I go ahead and ask him what I do not ask many years ago. I ask him to marry me."

"Marry you?"

"I am no different, I say to him, still the same crocodile. Why don't you want to marry a crocodile? You laugh, but I use logic on him. We could start a new life, work together, both of us put coal in the stove. But he says no, never, it is too late now, he is too far gone. So I tell him watch out, the bishop will move in and marry you instead."

"Bishop?"

"The one from the big Roman church. His buddy, his friend, the one who came to the house all the time, dragging his skirt on the floor. Waldman took him around, showed him the windows, the tile on the floor, the wallpaper, all those nice things. The slope of the roof."

I tried to recall the dates in the library notices. I was sure about the Lutheranism, that it came first. Presbyterian. Mormon. Some Quakerism that must have quietly abandoned him when he was still young.

"He was a Knight of Columbus, in the thirties, I think."

"Who knows what he was? Democrat, Republican. He wanted to be a congressman. Why not a senator someday? Why not pope, build his own church?"

"You haven't talked to him since that time?"

Rostopov shook his head. "You know," he said, "there was a turnip once who bragged to everyone. 'I taste very good with honey.' When he came to where honey was, he said the same thing to her. 'But I'm honey,' she said back to him. 'I taste very good without you.'"

9. *"Did he say he was going to heaven?" Mamma asked.*

When I emerged from Rostopov's I walked several blocks and found myself standing on a freeway overpass, cars rounding a bend in the distance, an incessant stream racing past buildings and billboards crowding in on the freeway walls.

> Made you look,
> Made you look,
> Made you buy
> A penny book.

In my pocket less than a dollar in change. What will a penny buy? Waldman, ·counter of Rostopov's words, piling words up like shiny new cents. How many would Rostopov have to learn before Waldman had enough? The city seemed endless, its cars streaming out to flood fresh green fields, distant suburbs with names too new to be on maps, all these places different and all the same. When – where – would it all end? Did Waldman have any city limits to his life?

I began walking toward home. I should have something ready for Sandy, some pasta or rice, a nice salad with fresh greens. She would not be happy if I didn't have something waiting on the table for her.

She wasn't home. On the floor next to the bed she had left her dress and underwear in a heap. I picked up her clothes, piled them in the closet, and put some water on to boil. I was sitting with the newspaper when the phone rang. I let it ring three times, each ring an alarm, a warning, bad news.

"Sal? Is that you, Sal? Oh Sal," Mamma cried. "Sal, what are you doing there? A nightmare is coming true."

There was an ambulance outside the house and a few people standing across the street. The ones who mattered were inside: Bruno on the couch; next to him Sandy, staring hard at me; Mamma, sitting on the edge of Papa's chair, her eyes swollen and red; Beatrice, slender and pale, little sister, teenager; even Kate, in jeans and flannel shirt; and in the corner, silent in straight wooden chairs, Guido and Rosina, showing not anger, acceptance, or tears, their faces saying only that it was useless to weep or speak, that there was nothing to do but wait. They were next.

"Don't go in there," Bea said as I headed for the bedroom door.

I went down on one knee next to Mamma's chair, gathering her in as she began to sob, afraid she might see I was not weeping with her. I looked over my shoulder at Bruno, but he turned away.

"Where were you?" Sandy said. "We had no way of knowing where you were."

Just out, I said to myself, just out.

"But you don't always die from a heart attack, do you?" Bea managed to ask all of us before she broke down again.

"Your mother wanted me to call the Bishop. Some priest is in there with Doctor Gigante," Sandy quietly said. "We called and he came right away. We decided it was better for the priest to give your father the last rites now."

My mouth went dry. "It's that bad?"

"Is the Bishop here yet?" Mamma asked as she lifted her head from my shoulder. "Is he coming soon?"

"There, there, Mom. Don't worry. He'll be here soon enough," Bea said as she came over and threw her arms around Mamma.

"When did it happen?" I asked.

"About an hour and a half ago," Sandy whispered as if we were forbidden to talk.

"He was watching the game," Mamma said. "I was in the kitchen. Something happened in the game and he yelled. Then he called out to me – but I didn't go right away. How was I supposed to know? Then I saw him – right there on the floor, holding his chest, and his legs jerking." She buried her hands in her face, then looked up accusingly. "I tried calling you. I tried over and over, but you never picked up the phone."

"There, there," Bea said.

Bruno, his head in his hands, still said nothing at all.

Kate got up. "He led a good life, Mrs. Amato."

I jumped her. "You think what's happening in that bedroom is a class action? It's my father in there! Of course he led a good life!"

"Sal!" Sandy snapped.

"Can't you two beat on each other some other time?" said Bea.

"Let's not argue," said Kate, backing away. "I was only trying to help. I have nothing but the highest respect for a man who has worked like he has all his life."

The Dignity of Labor. Still harping on the theme. At me. What about labor that brought no dignity? How much dignity did Papa feel dragging himself home from the factory?

I nodded at Kate, expecting an answer from her.

"What did the doctor say?" I asked Bruno.

"To him it looks like a breakdown of the heart," said Mamma.

Breakdown of the heart. The title of a song.

"He doesn't want to move him," Kate said. "He says the strain – we should wait. It could be just a matter of time."

"No it won't!" I said. "You just wait and see!" I stared into space, seeing the five, ten or twenty years Papa might still have lived. There, against the background of stars, all years and decades looked like the same senseless moments in the night, my own remaining thirty, forty or fifty years dots among the rest. The thought gave me a momentary consolation, but I backed off from it when I returned my gaze to the bedroom door: In there Papa was staring at the most terrible dot of all.

"Did he ask...for me?"

Bruno shook his head no.

"Did the Bishop actually say he would come?" Mamma asked again.

"I talked to his secretary myself," Sandy said.

"Maybe I should call again," said Mamma.

"We were all in there together – before you arrived," Bruno broke in, "but he didn't move, except his eyes. His eyes went from one of us to the next."

"He never spoke?"

"Not a word. His eyes were there, his mind, but his body was somewhere else. No voice, no words, nothing. Just his eyes."

"His soul," Mamma said with a sign.

We all turned at the sound of the bedroom door opening. The priest came out first, his left hand twitching nervously. Behind him, hat in hand, followed the doctor, a small balding man in brown who let the priest lead the way.

"Tell us something," Mamma said.

"He's ready. He's confessed his sins and wants to go to heaven. He'll rest in peace. He's in God's hands now."

"I've done everything I can, Missus. I gave him a shot. That should relax him a little bit." Dr. Gigante put his hat on and sat at the kitchen table, one knee pointing toward the door.

"There's nothing more you can do? Take him to the hospital?"

The doctor shrugged apologetically. "I wouldn't move him now. He's calm. In a while we'll know better what to do with him."

"Is there a Salvatore here?" the priest asked.

Everyone looked at me.

"He wants to talk to you. You better go in right away."

The dread came all at once. If all of us could have sat around his bed I would have escaped. One by one we could have taken our turns saying our last words to him, words that would rush from our hearts, insisting that we loved and honored him, our words final oaths of allegiance carefully packaged and wrapped like presents he could carry away to his new home. But to be alone with him was another thing. If it did not demand a summing up, it did require a final say. Papa had already paid his bill to the priest, the confession owed for a lifetime, grudgingly handed over at last. So what would be left for Papa to give to me? Nothing. He would want to be repaid, would try to conclude my life in there, not his own, use the hour of his death to bring me around to his way of life.

They saw me hesitate. They had paid their respects, had escaped until now. The priest, his summons to the condemned prisoner served, stepped aside for me to pass to the death chamber under my own power.

I brushed past the priest to the bedroom door and opened it, leaving it slightly ajar.

I saw first the small lamp on the table next to the bed, its yellow light dimming the faded flowers on the wallpaper covering the room. Next to the lamp was a small photo of the two of them – Mom and Dad, maybe thirty years younger, smiling at the camera. On the wall in front of the bed was a small brown portrait of Raphael, his stone house and the hills of San Giovanni in the background, and above the mahogany headboard an unsmiling Jesus and a pale Mary looking blankly down. Beneath the Jesus Papa, his head turned up to the ceiling and his eyes open and unmoved, lay in the yellow light of the table lamp.

I went down on one knee next to the bed. "Papa..."

I found no other word. Tears came and I began repeating the word – "Papa...Papa...Papa..." – until it got lost as I buried my face in my hands. Then words and thoughts got all mixed up. It's all my fault, I heard myself say: My fault I wasn't home when Mamma called, my fault I was not here when your heart failed, my fault we said so little to each other all our lives, that you droned your life away in the factory for us, that you came and went each day in your sullenness – my fault you are dying now before me, helpless. My fault that everything is my fault.

I lifted my head to face him again and found nothing but the sunken eyes and rigid jaw. A sudden fear: Maybe he was dead. I watched for breaths, relieved when I saw the slight rise and fall of the blanket over his chest.

"Sal." He called my name out of a distant dream.

My hand found his, rough and thick. "Don't worry, you'll be okay, Papa."

"Sal..."

"Yes, Papa?"

"Sal, where were you?"

"I'm here, Papa. I'm here."

He lay unmoved while I gazed at his face. He had kept too many silences all my life, required me, required all of us, to imagine his words and read his heart. I remember lying in bed mornings as he prepared for work, his feet shuffling along the kitchen floor as if already wearied from another dreary day at the factory, the clatter of a pot or pan in the kitchen sink, the sound of Mamma's voice making small talk, asking questions, and, long and arbitrary, the silences afterward.

I pressed his hand, trying to make him hear. Then he moved – a leg at first. With a sigh full of reluctance, he turned on his side toward me, lifted his head close to my face, and propped it on an elbow. The light, hitting him from behind, created a musty halo around his head. He squinted, searching for me.

"Sal?"

"Yes, Papa."

"Sal? I had a heart attack."

I waited.

"Goddamn, you wouldn't believe what it's like."

"Ssh." No taking the name of the Lord in vain.

"It hurt like a sonofabitching little virgin whore. Like a big alligator got it in its teeth, squeezed like hell, and tried to swallow me whole."

"Oh, Jesus, Papa, Christ Jesus."

"I say to myself this is it. I'm gone for sure."

No, please no.

"And I said I got nothing to show for it."

No, you were a workingman. You built America.

"I thought of you. I thought, Christ, I'll die from this before I get a chance to say anything to you. Are you listening to me?"

Then for the first time it occurred to me that maybe a true confession would come forth – a statement merely, sufficient but short, admitting to some insufficiency, a final declaration of his failure to live up to some dream.

"Tell me what, Papa?"

"What you gotta do."

He moved his head closer to my face, his eyes searching, fighting the light.

"This country is a mess. Just look what they did to me. No control. Everything is a mess."

"Yes, Papa."

"You gotta promise me one thing."

"Yes, Papa."

80

"Your Nonno and Nonna – they'll never see the inside of an old people's home. Promise me."

"Yes, Papa."

"And something else. You don't go chasing around other girls. You understand?"

I waited too long. "Yes, Papa, I promise."

"Good," he said as if a deal had been struck. "You'll see how everything works out. That wife Sandy of yours will pay you back for that. She'll let your Mamma live in her house. She'll owe it to you, just like God owes a place in heaven to sinners who go straight."

"Yes, Papa."

"Now," he concluded, "put out that goddamned light. It's shining right in my eyes."

He let his head down softly and turned away from me. Once again there was silence, and again I could not see his eyes. Could this, then, be his last will and testament? All his strength saved up, squeezed tight like a muscle, into these last few minutes with me, all so the baton, in a last dramatic lunge, was passed on from father to son? The baton – it seemed so unsubstantial, so light.

Suddenly, he gave a long low-pitched moan, and his body, convulsed in pain, shrank toward the wall next to the bed.

"Oh God!" I screamed as I ran out of the room.

Outside, they all waited huddled around the door, their eyes big with fear.

"Did the Bishop really say he would be here?" I caught Mamma shouting at Sandy just as I came out. I wanted to run out of the place, but Bruno grabbed my arm.

Kate pushed forward. "What did he say?"

"Did he say he was going to heaven?" Mamma asked.

10. *"Honor thy father and mother. It is the Sixth Commandment of the Lord."*

At midnight Mamma, under the influence of a strong pill, settled into a quiet sobbing that ebbed toward hopelessness. As if aware that dying was a private affair, she surrendered when I told her she could not sleep in her – his – bed. I waited for her eyelids to close, then led her into the bedroom that used to be mine.

The peace came only when she was safely asleep. I breathed it deeply in even as I sensed the smell of death in the living room – an odor that clung to the old curtains and rug and especially to the sofa that for years had faced Papa's chair. Some things never changed – the lumps in the cushions, the plastic slipcovers over the arms. Within a minute I began dozing off, leaving behind the voice whispering that I had no right to peace tonight, that I had not shed enough tears, that even on a bed as brutal as the old sofa it wasn't fair to escape Papa's suffering.

There are some things, I answered back, for which I am not responsible. I may have touched, or failed to touch, my father's life, but I did not make his death. I let weariness speak for me, let it conclude my case.

I awoke once in the middle of the night, lifting my head like a small animal on a highway interrupted by headlights bearing down on it. Something was terribly wrong. Papa had worked all his life and had nothing to show for it. Why nothing? How many years had he worked at the plant? Thirty-three, or just short of that. And his wages all those years? When I was a boy he brought home seventy-five dollars a week. There was a union in the plant, thank goodness, so his salary went up like everything else. Let's say at least five dollars an hour for the last twenty years. At the very least. Forty hours a week, fifty weeks a year. Five times four. Again times five. Then the total times two. Two hundred. Now the zeroes. Two thousand, twenty, two hundred thousand. Two million? No, too much, not possible. Too many zeroes to make any sense. What did it all come to? Divided into twenty years. Minus the food, of course, the clothing and rent, and the TV set and the Compton Encyclopedia set Mamma bought for me behind his back. And taxes, insurance, all the wine. And we – I say we because Sandy suddenly was there too, figuring it all out with paper and pen – didn't include the early years, the lean ones that brought in the seventy-five dollars a week.

There had to be something left over for us.

But Mamma should have all that. She worked so hard all her life, with never a moment's rest.

And how old was she? Her shoulders seem to be slumping so, and her eyes glazed, worn out.

But there would be Bruno and Bea. What about their share?

Let's say twenty – no ten – thousand dollars left over in the end.

And if we sold the furniture, dishes, the encyclopedia set?

We'd have to pay someone to cart it all away. And we'd have to pay someone to take Papa away. Do you think it's cheap to die today?

Wouldn't insurance pay for all that?

What if it did? And what if Bruno and Bea and Rosina and Guido refused to touch a penny of it? What if there were ten thousand dollars for us alone?

I'd have the down payment and then more. For Danko's store. I'd be able to borrow the rest. And never in a thousand years would I ever let some junk man haul this furniture away. I'd fix it all up myself, make Papa's chair my own in the store.

Sure, sure. I like to hear you talk. I like to hear you make excuses for getting money that doesn't belong to you, money your father worked a Christ's age for in a goddamned filthy factory.

Okay, okay, it's all yours. Keep the goddamned money for yourself. I just want some peace in this house.

I tried figuring the zeroes one more time, but nothing ever came out right. His dying was not my fault and there was nothing I could do. He had squeezed promises out of me, and I gave back the answers he had to have. The promises would have to take care of themselves. He never took care of himself. He came home every evening, took a bath in four inches of water, stuffed himself at the table, and sat in front of the television set until he fell asleep. He never did anything but bring the paycheck home and set it on the kitchen table every Friday night. He let himself die in the factory and cursed the lazy ones who refused to die with him. "My son, The Bum." Because I didn't want to end up like him. And now, soon, he will be gone. This is what he earns in the end. Maybe he reaped what he sowed.

And maybe I will be free of him at last.

The next morning when the ambulance returned to take him to the hospital I whispered farewell through tears I couldn't stop. His eyes seemed hollow and black, his mouth open, his face shrinking into his jaw. Dr. Gigante only shook his head. It would only be a matter of time – God only knew.

The hours slumped with us as we waited at the hospital, Mamma refusing to abandon her place next to his bed until the doctor made me take her home. I was eager to get out of the place – even welcomed the stink of traffic on the streets when I led her to the bus. After the third day I waited at home all morning for the news, but he was still the same. Then all the days started looking the same, my morning trips to the hospital with Mamma, hours spent next to Papa's bed, waiting for him to stir, say something to us, afternoons in the apartment again waiting for the phone to ring. On the seventh day the phone rang in the middle of the night. He had just been rushed into surgery.

Dr. Gigante shook his head sadly for a week after that. Every morning I dropped Mamma off at the hospital, explaining that I had to look for work. I spent hours walking in the streets, brooding, cursing, rushing home to clean the apartment before Sandy got home from work.

One night just before midnight the phone rang.

"We have to thank God with all our heart," Mamma said in a wavering voice. "He's coming soon."

"What?"

"They say your father's coming home in a week."

He ended up where I had left him so many times before – on the chair in front of the TV, but this time smelling of bandages and gauze, a wry curl on his lip as he searched the channels for another football game.

"A bypass," Mamma explained again and again as if she couldn't believe her own words. "They call it a bypass. See, they took veins from the legs," she said as she turned his leg to the light, "and they put them in his heart. It's a miracle. I took some of the bandages off today."

"Bullshit miracle," Papa said. "If you stood on these legs in the factory for thirty-three years, your goddamned veins would be like lead pipes."

Mamma grabbed my wrist. "It's a miracle. I made a deal with God. I said, If You give me his life, I will do whatever You say."

"Help me move this leg," Papa mumbled, "I'm getting a sore on my ass."

"God said yes, it's a deal," Mamma explained as she adjusted the pillow under his knee. "He said one way I could pay for my sins is by taking care of you."

My father groaned. "Not too hard right there with your hand. You're breaking my hip."

When she went to the kitchen to put the coffee on, I faced him alone again. "Papa," I began, "you sure had us scared."

"You thought the old mule was used up?"

I managed a smile.

"But you found out."

"What do you mean?"

"What do you mean what do I mean? Somebody's gotta get things done. That's what I mean. You don't think I'd leave your mother all alone? You got a job yet?"

"I've got a few leads."

"Leads. Don't talk to me about leads. Where you gonna lead? You still got a milk moustache and nice clean hands. What do you know about work? You ain't even forgot the Old Way because you ain't never learned something new. Your Nonno – he knows. But he's a hundred now, talks like he's losing his mind. If I was sure he could have taught you the right way, I would've said to hell with it all, I'm getting out of here once and for all."

"So what's the right way?"

"The Old Way."

His way.

"Tell me then."

"When the son doesn't listen – it's finished. Kaput. And there's something worse."

"I'm listening, Papa."

"You can't leave a woman alone. It's no good. You gotta have something for her, or else who's going to take care of her? Something to pass on, you understand?"

"I understand, Papa." Something to pass on, something of genuine worth. Guido's old store.

"That's why you gotta have some kind of work, so you got something to pass on."

To your son The Bum. Your job in the factory. You want me to go down there today and knock on the gate, tell them I'm Paul Amato's son, that he's passing his wonderful work on to me, yes, thank you, please.

"And there's something else."

He strained to inch himself closer to me.

"What do you do with that wife of yours? I mean, maybe she's too tired when she gets home from work. That's what I don't understand. You gotta get going. You're almost thirty years old. You gotta have a son."

"Yes, Papa. We already have a name picked out." I smiled as I fixed another pillow behind his head, enjoying every moment of my delicious lie.

"Oh yeh?"

"Yeh, Arturo." Art.

"I don't know about a name like that," he said as he turned his head to the wall. "I used to know somebody with that name, but good thing he wasn't in our family. And there's a lot of things you don't understand, you with your college degree."

"Yes, Papa."

"Girls. I don't think you know how they are."

"You're right, Papa. Them I really don't understand."

"I see you don't know. Because it's like your Nonno told me. *La natura* has two parts to it. The beast and the saint. These are the parts. Did you know that?"

"No, yes Papa."

"The man, he is the beast, and the woman is the saint. The man is the flesh, the woman the soul. So when they get married they fight."

"But Papa, that means if you had died, the world would have had one less beast in it." I sent a triumphant little smile toward him. "And I don't think that's right."

"Sure, you can look at it that way too if you want. If I'm gone, what the hell. God alone can judge me on that. But don't forget – when I'm gone that means the world will be heavier by one saint."

"You mean...?"

"Your Mamma.."

A beast of burden, this saint, lumbering on under her load.

He paused, turned toward me again, then looked around the room. "The world is full of beasts. Nobody, not even a saint, can resist."

"But you said, Papa, that you are a beast. Why do you think you are a beast?"

The question, as if coming from behind, sent a shiver of perplexity through him. The color suddenly left his face, and his hands, clasped together on a blanket covering his lap, went limp. Slowly he lifted the blanket from his lap and left his legs, their scars still red, exposed. He allowed his eyes to wander over himself. "Look," he said, "look at me, this thing of flesh. A wreck."

"A man."

"A beast."

"My Papa," I said as I returned the blanket to his lap once more.

The next evening we were all there again – Guido, Rosina, Bruno, Beatrice, Sandy and Kate. Papa was feeling worse, didn't want to get out of bed. Mamma was in the kitchen getting dinner ready with Kate, while the rest of us were in Papa's room, crowded around his bed.

Sandy was sullenly furious with me. Because when she came home the breakfast dishes were still in the sink, and I wanted to make love. No, she was tired and wanted to eat. I took my pants off and began washing the dishes, saying please, please, I want you, I need you, I love you very much.

What did you do all day? she asked. I was in the library again, looking up some stuff. Stuff? Yes, stuff. Stuff about Waldman, the man who is screwing Guido to the wall. What does he have to do with anything? Maybe everything, I said. He's an interesting character. Character? So what? What did you find out about him? Nothing new, really, about him, but I found a lot of books about cathedrals. Interesting books, one in particular called *The Gothic Image* by a man named Mâle. Full of illustrations, explanations, diagrams. The cathedral at Chartres, a small town in France – that's the main one, the one that took two hundred years to build. From the book I could see how beautiful it is. They named it after Mary, Notre Dame. Some day in spring we should go to her, spend a few weeks in Paris first, making love, walking the boulevards, sitting in the outdoor cafes watching people on the streets. Are you sure you don't want to make love right now?

And what did I accomplish today? Accomplish? Nothing. Notre Dame of Chartres is beautiful, that's all. That's what I accomplished today.

And okay, okay, so you don't want to make love. Do you want to screw? Yes, she said, I want to screw, but first I want to eat. But Honey, I feel stupid standing at the sink with my pants off, my little dragon just hanging there useless, depressed. You really want to screw – you mean *screw?* I mean, we're nowhere near ready to eat – no leftovers in the fridge and the hamburger frozen hard as a rock. What do you expect me to do next? Let me finish washing the dishes at least.

And thank goodness the phone rang and Mamma said why don't you two come over here to eat. Papa's feeling worse, and hurry up.

"Then screw me now," Sandy said. "Hurry up, screw me now."

I said no, not now, better not be late when Mamma calls, not with my father the way he is.

"It's no good," Guido said when he saw Papa on the bed. "Look at him there. It's not natural when the father lives longer than the son. It's against the laws of nature and God. That's why nobody should be a soldier and go to war."

"Bah!" Rosina said contemptuously. "Look who talks! To me he looks better than you."

"I'm not on no train headed for the graveyard yet," Papa said.

Guido jabbed the air with his stick. "You got to thank Mussolini for doing one thing over there. Me – I never would have voted for him, but before he came in nobody waited in line. When a train stopped, everybody tried to get on at once. Nobody could get off. At least we got a little law and order over there. All the trains ran on time, and everybody waited in line. I'm just waiting for the next train to come for me. That's all Mussolini was good for – the trains."

"Nonno," I said, "you're not going anywhere. Mussolini died thirty years ago. According to everything I've read, Italy's a mess."

"Like here," Papa broke in. "Everybody's a crook."

"Frank Sinatra too," Bea said. "His friends are in the Mafia."

Guido shook his head. "Everybody knows he was in on it – he killed Kennedy. What a disgrace."

"But Nonno," said Bea, "he can really sing. You can't take that away from him."

"Use your head, girl. His song don't make no sense if he's a cheap crook like he is. Besides, someday you go over there, to San Giovanni. You see for yourself. On any street there's ten boys who can sing just as good, and two or three more who make him sound like a dying fish."

"Like all that stupid music you hear on the radio today." I targeted Bea's boyfriend Dylan with my words.

"A lot of it's really great!" Bea shot back.

"Sal, leave her alone!"

"I'm not picking on her. I was just trying to make a comment on the general culture, the trash..."

"Why don't you ask Bruno about music, Mr. Genius?" Bea said, her face turning pink.

"Huh?" Bruno looked the other way.

"I agree with Nonno," I said. "Sinatra's got nothing special. He was just in the right place at the right time."

Sandy looked at the floor when she spoke. "But maybe he worked his way up."

I nailed her with a stare. "Yeh, screwing everybody on the way to the top."

"There you go criticizing again," said Bea.

"Nobody asks me," Rosina broke in, "but to me the Beatles – I think it's just noise. I want to close the window."

Papa stirred and turned on his side toward the wall. "Young people got no respect over here."

"Me," Guido said, "I want to go back to Italy as soon as I can. And I ain't coming back here no more."

"But Nonno, you came here as a boy. It's been eighty years. Maybe everything is different there now."

"I keep it all here," he said, tapping the side of his head. "You think I forget? I remember it, even the things I did wrong."

"You?"

His lips curled into a smile. "Every day. Lots of little things. Heh, heh. I remember one day. We had a little shack for the goats. My mamma was gone, so I had Aunt Lizetta looking after me. Lizetta made me go in with the goats. 'Go in there,' she said, 'and close the door. You go in there and stay in the dark.' She chased me there with a big stick. 'If I was your mamma,' she said when I was in the shack, 'I would make you stay in the pig pen because you are such a dirty pig.'

"So I stayed with the goats – an hour, maybe two, I don't know. I did not mind at first but after a while I began wishing my papa was home. He would have let me out, beat me on the behind once or twice, and be done with it.

"Well, Lizetta called out after a long, long time. 'Come to the kitchen.' She told me to sit in a chair and shut up. I sat with my hands folded like a saint until she finished with the dishes. Then she wiped her hands and sat on a chair. That damned stick again was always in her hand.

"'I'm sorry,' I said to her."

"'Be quiet,' Lizetta said. 'and listen to me.'

"'There was a woman I once knew. She lived alone in a house just outside San Giovanni, and she was like a saint. Her name was Maria. Her husband died just two years after they were married. After a son was born, this woman started going in the church three times a day. If there was someone hungry, it was she who left a loaf of bread. If someone was ill, she was the nurse, the one who went to the church in the middle of the day to pray. She was poor, but her son she fed and clothed better than any boy in San Giovanni, and at the age of seven he was the priest's favorite boy. As the wind carried word of her good works from town to town, she became known as Maria the Good. I have peace in my mind, said Maria, all these years.'

"'But then one day Maria became pale. She said hard words to an old woman on the piazza, and everyone knew there was something wrong. Things got worse and worse with her. Her dress was no longer clean, and no light shined off her forehead like it did. She began smelling very bad, did nothing for the poor and sick, and one night her son ran away to a city in the north. Before long a young girl accused Maria of giving her the Evil Eye, and a young man staying up all night to watch the moon said he saw her in the sky flying. Then everyone closed their hearts to her and she never came out during the day.

"'One night I was scared but I went to her house. I went near like a cat, looked in a window, and saw her lying in bed half-awake. I went in to her. "Donna Maria," I said, "what has come over you? What has taken possession of your soul?î

"'At first she did not want to speak, but I coaxed her on. "The Devil," she said at last. "The Devil came into my house."'

At this Guido stopped and shifted in his chair, reaching down to scratch his leg with his cane. "I can't scratch the thing," he said. "I want to scratch, but I'm afraid the old thing will bleed."

"But what happened?" I asked.

"Hold your horse while I rub my leg. The story has not yet begun."

Mamma called from the kitchen. The spaghetti was going into the pot, so we had to get ready to eat. The aroma of her sauce, rich and thick, was spreading through the room. And she had baked her bread.

"Donna Maria was close to death," Guido said, "but could not die until she told my aunt Lizetta how the Devil came to possess her soul. The story Donna Maria told is true. Nobody lies while waiting in line for the train destined for the Great Beyond."

I nodded. Papa was watching me.

92

"The Devil," Guido went on, "entered the house through a crack in the wall."

And the crack was just over the hearth where Donna Maria kept a big pot of soup. She was not sure, but she believed the Devil hid in the fire, until one night the fire went out. Then the Devil had nowhere to go. When she was out giving food to the poor the Devil looked everywhere for a place to hide. Finally, he spotted a small bottle of oil on the shelf. When Donna Maria came back, she knew something was wrong. Her son Giovanni pointed a finger at her and laughed. He laughed and laughed until he fell asleep. Then, in the middle of the night, a strange odor filled the room – at once sweet and bitter-sour. Donna Maria arose, put on her dress and shawl, and started searching the house. Finally she found the bottle of oil, the odor the Devil could not hide coming from there. In the candlelight she saw a yellow swirl like an eel swimming inside. Right away she pressed the lid on tight and put it high on a shelf.

The next morning when Giovanni awoke she was still dressed and awake. 'My son,' she said, 'this bottle of oil is rancid and stale. Take it to the outskirts of the village where the garbage is burned, and throw the bottle away.' 'But why not pour the oil out?' Giovanni asked. 'Because the bottle is spoiled, unclean. Nothing will clean it now. Be sure to break it on a rock as you pitch it in the fire. Promise you will do that.' 'I promise,' Giovanni said. Only then would she hand it to him.

Giovanni put the bottle in his pocket, careless as he tripped through the village toward the fire. Halfway there he suddenly began to laugh. And the laughter, it seemed, came from the pocket where the little Devil in the bottle was stored. He stopped under an old fig tree, looked around to see if anyone watched, and pulled the bottle out. At once he was overcome by the sweetest smell, and his head began to spin. In the sun the bottle gleamed, brilliant colors shining inside of it.

Quickly he buried it deep in his pocket again, took a crooked way back to the village, and spent an hour laughing with the lazy bums on the piazza. Then he returned home to his mamma.

'Did you destroy the bottle?' she asked.

The boy lied. 'It burned with the strangest flame,' he said, 'all red and blue, orange, and green.'

'That's good,' she said.

Giovanni hid the bottle in his bed. In the middle of the night he lifted the covers over his head and breathed the sweet smell in. The odors began to make him drunk, and then he could not sleep the rest of the night.

On the third day he looked tired. 'What ails you, my son?' asked Donna Maria. But he would say nothing. He only gave a little sad laugh. Then that night, in the middle of a dream, Donna Maria smelled the Devil again. She looked everywhere, tearing things off shelves in her fear of the thing.

'Did you?' she screamed at the boy, 'did you destroy the bottle like I told you to do?'

The boy, scared, said yes. But she could see something wrong in his face, so she made him get on his knees in front of her. 'Now I ask you again, in the name of the Virgin and the Savior of Mankind himself: Did you break the bottle like you said?'

And the boy, making a little laugh, said yes.

From the little laugh she could tell he was lying again. 'If your papa were alive I would have him beat the Devil out of you,' she screamed at him. Then she picked up a stick and started hitting him. He covered himself with his arms, but when the blows began falling on him like stones he began dodging about the room. Suddenly he ran for his bed, with her still after him. As he yanked the blanket from his bed to cover his head, the bottle fell on the floor and the oil spilled out. Donna Maria gave out a cry and in one motion brought the stick down with all of her might on the bottle.

When the boy saw the bottle broken to bits he had only one word in him. 'Whore!' he screamed at her, and he ran from her sight. He disappeared from the house and was never heard of again, though the priest said he had gone to Milan and given himself to all the evil in that city. It was on that night that Donna Maria changed her ways. She got on her knees and scrubbed and scrubbed, but the smell never went out of her house.

"That's the end of my story," Guido said. He sat back, relieved, as if he had unburdened himself, an embarrassment lurking on his face. "That's the story Donna Maria told Lizetta. Every word is true."

"Yes," I said, "but I don't get it."

Papa sat up straight, his finger raised to instruct. "Its meaning is clear. It is a story about the power of the beast, how you got to keep it out of your house."

Just then Mamma and Kate came into the room. "Sal," Kate said, "dinner's ready. Will you give me a hand? He's got to eat something to keep up his strength."

"Oh Mother of God," Mamma whispered as she crossed herself, watching Kate and me lift Papa out of bed.

Papa wouldn't let the story get away from him. "No," he went on, "it is a story about how to keep your wife from going crazy on you. Sal, you remember the promise you made on that night when the doctor said I would not see the light of day ever again. Honor thy father and mother. It is the Sixth Commandment of the Lord."

11. *...her leg twitched, but she didn't wake up.*

After dinner Papa fell asleep in his chair, his posture still upright after his head circled a moment and sank to one side. While I sat in the living room with him, Mamma finished the dishes. "I get so tired these days," she announced, wiping her hands. "I'm going to bed early tonight."

"And so am I," Sandy said.

"I'll stay up with him, Mamma. Why don't you get a little rest tonight."

Even after I was sure he was asleep, I did not dare turn the TV off. I had seen him jerk himself awake as if guarding his program in his sleep, secretly waiting for me to steal it away. When a commercial broke in I turned the volume off but left the pictures free to flicker in front of his face.

He didn't stir as I settled myself on the sofa again, silence settling in the room like heavy dust. For long minutes we shared nothing but our slow breathing, his broken by fits and starts. Any moment now, any minute, day, or year – his last fit and start.

I was looking at his face, slumped toward me, when I became aware of the other presence in the room. Looking down on me from the wall, its glass reflecting the flittings of the television screen, was Raphael, great-grandfather. All my life this portrait, his brown unsmiling face lifelike compared to the smaller one fronting my parents' bed, had hung on the wall in this room. Careful not to make a noise, I arose to take a closer look.

His eyes, brown and deep, followed me as I crossed to fix the blanket over Papa's knees, not letting go of me as they took in a vision at once future and past. Raphael was looking across a vast expanse of sea, and there, below the distant haze of a purple-mountain majesty, he saw many San Giovannis, busy towns crowded with brown stone houses, markets and piazzas, here and there a palace, tower, and church rising above red tile roofs, all huddled in the lap of green meadows and hills.

He must have been past sixty when the portrait was made. His wrinkles were deep, but nothing sagged on a face hardened by a jaw as determined as his eyes. It was a lean face that had weathered sun and wind, as rough as hands accustomed to handling marble and stone.

Guido. Guido had Raphael's face, the same forehead and eyes, but more oval and small. And Papa had Guido's eyes, though not as sharp or dark. And his face was longer, sad like Rosina's. More like mine. I came from Papa, from Guido and Raphael, this line of men, and Bruno did too, though he had more of Guido in him.

But who was Raphael's wife? Did she also have an oval face? Why no picture of her? Banished no doubt because she had run away with a lover to France. And who were Mamma's parents? Her father had died in Chicago more than twenty years ago, and her mother, Nonna Serafina, who went back to Italy right after the funeral, was still alive. Why no picture of them in the house?

I turned as Papa stirred uneasily in his sleep. Raphael was the most handsome of all, still present in Papa's face. I imagined Mamma at nineteen, hair jet-black and breasts firm, her smile big and shy as she tried not to notice my father looking at her. She was beautiful then. What was Guido thinking when my father won her away from a family of jealous and possessive men?

And Beatrice – the youngest one, pale and almost blond, no trace of my mother in her, no Rosina anywhere. That blond in our blood, like a streak on a map flowing down, an invasion from the barbarian north now suddenly present here, in America. Bea the youngest, newest one. Outsider – where, who, did she come from? She could have been Sandy's child in another few years. My sister a daughter, forbidden fruit of America. From the time she turned twelve she had sent quivers through me every time we brushed past each other in the house.

And Sandy, the greatest outsider of them all.

I remember the first mention of marriage in the house, my father saying no, though it was Mamma who put him up to it. They wanted to pair me with a distant cousin, grand-daughter of the man who fought hardest to keep Mamma away from my dad. I saw this girl many times. She was lovely but too dark, too familiar and shrill.

"You can't marry cousins," I protested. "That's the way you get monster-kids."

"She's not really a cousin," Papa said. "She's Italian. Where you going now?" I remember him saying as I got up and headed toward the door.

"Out."

"Where out?"

"Just out." To look at other girls, strangers on the sidewalks, so many of them lovely, mysterious, impossible. I wanted to do nothing more than gaze at them – no, not touch or even speak, only gaze and wonder at the strange unfamiliar beauty that was alluring, intimidating, and physical.

Not one word more was said about my dark-skinned cousin, but I saw my father eyeing Sandy the first time I brought her home, stealing long looks at her legs, breasts and ass. "Where did you pick her up?" he winked when she turned her back. "On the streets?"

I lied. "No, in St. Paul's. We happened to be next to each other kneeling in a pew."

"At least she's Catholic."

"No, she was just looking around."

"And who the hell turned the TV off?" Papa said as he jerked himself awake. "Goddamn, my legs hurt. Will you turn that goddamned thing off and help me to bed?"

Again the city at night, noisy engines on all sides, groaning under some weight, all sounds metallic, even the tread of tires on concrete. In the distance a siren, somebody injured, perhaps on the way to a hurried and noisy death while lights stole the glances of people speeding by, all the garish flashings resolved high over rooftops into a dim glow beneath overhanging clouds.

I paused in front of St. Paul's, situating myself squarely in front of its main portals before letting my eyes move up along its broad forehead to the spires that turned dizzily against the movement of passing clouds. Why this thing here and now? In an ancient time, when men piled stones to make ziggurats so they could climb toward the stars and talk more directly to gods of the sky, yes, this would have made sense. But gods of the sky were all greyly God now, a vaguely brooding forehead indifferent to the girlish skin-and-bones man who writhed his three hours on the cross, unable to imagine how the centuries would dress his agents in black gowns and business suits, proper uniforms for those accustomed to winning friends and influencing solid citizens sold on life insurance as a way of life. Build a monument to God, Father or Son, the way the people of Chartres chipped away at realizing their dream of heaven in the middle of their town? Are you kidding me? Heaven, God, Jesus. Hell no. All they could come up with was Paul.

My father Paul, who is on earth, hallowed be his name.

So why bother at all? Because, well...it's been done before, this sort of thing. Then why do it again? Because it's what they do.

Who?

Them. The bishops, priests, popes – celibates wanting to marry themselves to a monument that can be at once a trophy, a palace, and a tomb.

So that people will wander by, wonder and gaze at a strange unfamiliar beauty at once alluring, intimidating, and physical.

So that Art, by virtue of the power vested in itself, will command the attention, respect, and obedience of those subjected to its influence. So that people may be beguiled into Belief.

And St. Paul's somehow went wrong, did not live up to Raphael's dream. Still, how grand it was, so strangely out of place in a landscape of dull grids broken by freeways and factories; and how singular, like the widow alone in a pew fingering beads along her lips. How wonderful – all this energy serving that solitary widow, her prayer a vapor absorbed by the mass and gravity of the stone. Alluring, the symmetries suggested but deliberately unrealized, the spires of unequal height and girth, the brilliant hues of stained glass set in the walls of these man-made caves, candles flickering in darkness full of the fragrance of incense and dank odor of stones. Strange and wonderful, this place that somehow went wrong.

A shiver ran through me as I stood before this monument to Vanity and Belief, and the shiver turned to terror as a car squealed around the corner close enough for me to feel its cold breath.

I hurried home, suddenly afraid of everything along the way.

From the street I could see that the only light still on was the small table lamp in the living room. I tiptoed up the stairs, sure that Sandy would wake up when I opened the door. The bedroom was full of the warm fragrance of her body. She stirred as I undressed, turning away from my small noises toward the light that fell on her from the living room.

Slanting in through the door the light softened her face. As I lay down next to her I saw how sleep had relaxed her tired and taut face. In the past year work had stolen the softness from her eyes and leisure from her lips. Everything seemed smaller, tight like a spring. But here again was the woman who was my wife – composed, absorbed by a dream I wanted to disturb because I was jealous, wanted in. Yet how could anyone not pity the weakness and vulnerability of her sleeping form, the very softness I wanted to own and protect?

Was there some way I could make love to her without waking her up, so that in the morning she would sit up in bed and stretch her arms out with a smile on her face? "Was that you last night?" she would ask, and I would turn coyly away with my response: "Maybe, maybe not."

She stiffened when I ran a finger along her neck, and I quickly pulled back from her. I listened until I was sure her breathing was regular and calm, then ran my hand lightly over her hip. Yes, lovely, and here she was right next to me in bed, though the bone under the curve of her flesh seemed too angular, too visible inside the sheet of skin covering her flank. All those shrunken bodies in concentration camps.

Do you or do you not want to make love?

She covered her shoulder with the blanket, yawned, and turned away from me.

So you just want to screw.

Yes, why not sometimes yes. Slam, bam, thank you Sam. Or Sal. Or somebody, anybody, some stranger perhaps. She wanted it.

I threw my arm over her and closed my eyes, letting them walk past me on parade: The women, auburn-haired, blond, tall and short, all of them attractive enough to make me want to follow them, feast on them with my eyes, my mouth.

She let out a deep breath when I threw my leg over hers. I was thinking of our wedding night. "Ten years from now," she asked, "will I still be able to turn you on? I mean, if I were coming out of some shop on a crowded street and you were just walking along, would you stop to look at me, I mean cross the street?" "Oh baby," I replied, "are you kidding me?" I ran my tongue along her arm, feeling it go dry as I reached her shoulder blade. She turned to face me, still ashamed, covering her breasts with the sheet. "Well?" On the ceiling where I was searching for words the paint was chipped near a hairline crack. "Look at me," I said, sliding the sheet away from her. She put her hands behind her head as she relaxed, and I took the fragrance of the bed deeply in. "From out of this breast all sorts of creeping things come forth – toads, lizards, snakes, scorpions." Her eyes narrowed, confused. "What damned fullness," I whispered. "See all the browns and blacks, even touches of red, how sun-shined and scaly I am. Do you think you'll be able to put up with this in ten more years?" "Yum," she said as she reached up to pull me down on her, "you're such a brat."

We did it again and again that night, my eyes closed to what seemed the incredible: Her body right there in the same bed, but not her body any more, the one I looked at and longed for when I held, kissed, followed her across a crowded room, and certainly not suddenly one, mystically joined, with mine. On that night and in the privacy behind eyes closed tight, other women were walking in and out of my secret room. And when I dared to open my eyes I saw that hers were also closed tight.

"Sandy," I whispered, "do you want to screw?"

"Huh?" she said, pulling the blanket under her chin. "Why don't you ever turn off the light before you come to bed?"

"Do you want to screw?"

"Huh? Sure, go ahead."

Who should I be, I thought: Tom, Dick, Harry, Pete, Joe, Sam, Sal? Sal, some other Sal, one better than the one next to her. She deserved at least that, some stranger she can meet all over again. For what? Love. Call it that, and call me Sal when we're done.

"Do you really want to make love?" I whispered again, pressing in on her.

"Just don't wake me up," she mumbled, not opening her eyes.

"Think of a name," I whispered. "Any name. Somebody good."

"Huh?"

George, Clarence, Pierre, Byron, Horace, Joe, Martin, Adolph.

Waldman. Why not him too? Once upon a time Waldman had to be young, perhaps handsome or charming, maybe not one to endure women with words but able to attract them with perhaps his shy and quiet ways. Maybe he really was the artist type, until something twisted him into somebody else. Why could I not be Waldman for Sandy now, owner of X number of shops on Second and Third, harvester of forests, maker of bathtubs, of switches for everything, czar of a private empire stretching from the neighborhood to the westside factories and warehouses and then onto the freeways curving out of the city toward suburban fields? You want to screw? Let's screw someone else then, both of us close our eyes and screw our way out of this bed, beyond Guido's old store and freeways and suburban lawns right into some stormy sea. Tonight let's screw our way right into Africa. Pretoria.

And let's make a little deal. You can screw anybody that comes to mind. But remember, it's tit for tat. You have to cut me some slack, let me pick out one of those who keeps walking down the street. What do you say? A deal? You said it yourself. You just want to screw.

And God you're so beautiful still.

As I reached down and kissed her lips, her leg twitched but she didn't wake up.

12. *Dead? "Yes" I said, enjoying the little lie I told as I brushed past the bishop out the door. "But he put up a hell of a fight."*

When the phone's ringing woke me up, Sandy was already gone.

Mamma's voice: "Sal, I want you to go to him, the Bishop. I want you to find out why he didn't show up when your father almost died. I don't understand why he didn't come."

"Don't you think, Mamma, that you should talk to him yourself?"

"Sal, you talk better than me. You got a college degree. What good is all the money we spent if you can't talk for your father and me?"

"But what do you want me to say?"

"Edna Conklin says he didn't do the Christian thing."

"Who's Edna Conklin?"

"She's my new friend I have. I met her in the supermarket. She wants to know if the Bishop is really Christian like he says. She says why didn't he come that night. And I had another terrible dream. You and me and your sister Bea, we're all in church, and I'm thinking here he is, such a good boy. Then Bea is at the communion rail ready to take Communion and she has her eyes closed and her tongue out, and a man stands up all dressed in black and points a finger at me. Right away you have a heart attack right in your bed. You can't breathe and you start walking to her with your arms out, and you fall like a rag in her lap. I scream, thinking where's the Bishop again. So I push you away from Bea and we both run out of there."

"Did I live?"

"Don't make fun of me, Sal. That was a real dream, and sometimes you don't know what dreams mean about what's coming next. And that Bishop never came. So I want you to go ask him what's wrong, and you call me right away when you get back."

I'd had an egg and two slices of toast, but the coffee pot was dirty in the sink. Again a dirty coffee pot. And dirty dishes all over the place. Every day a hundred little objects – forks, spoons, platters, cups, bowls, pots and pans – to clear from the table to the sink, scrub clean, dry, put back in place. Thousands of small wearying steps from table to sink to refrigerator to cupboard to table to sink, little circles making the rounds from breakfast to lunch to dinner to breakfast again. Woman's work, every day everywhere in the world. Here now it was my work, part of my deal with Sandy because she brought the real money in. Dull futile work if eating was a chore – if, as Nonno complained, we ate in order to work.

I craved my coffee, but how long could I put up with this? No, the dirty coffee pot would have to wait this time, and I'd do without.

It was a few minutes before ten when I found myself in front of Guido's place, an ad for a cabinet-maker's assistant stuffed in my coat pocket. I didn't need to open the door to know that Bruno had just put a fresh pot of coffee on.

"The coffee's free today," he said as I walked in. He was not at the piano. He was sitting in his chair, Kate standing next to him, their cups empty and their faces down.

"It's too early in the morning for you two to be falling out of love," I said as I stood across from them. I tossed my words onto the floor, half-hoping she'd pick them up and start a little fight. But she smiled. "We were just talking, and you look a little down yourself."

I found a chair.

"How's Dad?" Bruno asked.

I didn't know. Better, I supposed.

"What will your mother do if he dies?" Kate asked. "That's what we were talking about before you came."

"We were talking about a lot of things," Bruno corrected her.

"Marriage and money. Hot topics these days. Like violence and sex."

"Bruno's thinking of leaving."

"You mean here, the old store?"

"Bruno's thinking of leaving the city."

"To go – where? Both of you – together?"

She smiled again, amused and sad. "My work is here. I'll be staying here."

"I guess I don't understand what's going on."

"We're not sure we do either," Kate said. "It's just that Bruno isn't sure this is the best place to work."

"You mean the old store? What's wrong with Guido's old store? There's plenty of room here. What else do you want?"

Bruno turned away.

"He gets twenty-five dollars a night for playing – sometimes only three nights a week."

"But you get by, Bruno, don't you? You just want to get by. You just want to get by so you can keep working here."

"I get by."

"So what's the problem?"

He had picked up my father's habit of silent suffering and complaint. I saw that Kate was going to speak for him, explain what he maybe couldn't understand.

"Someone tried to break in last night."

"Here?"

"Second time in two months."

"But why? Who?"

"Bruno didn't catch the name."

"What did he want?"

Bruno shrugged. "Money."

"Bruno had the shit scared out of him. The guy had a gun."

"Did you get a good look at him?"

"Bruno says he was maybe eighteen, twenty years old. A dirty leather jacket..."

"He was black, wasn't he?" I said.

Kate stiffened. "No need to bring race into it. Somebody obviously without a job. Somebody who..."

"He scared the shit out of me," Bruno said. "I couldn't do anything."

"So now you're going to just pick up and go?"

"Sal's right, Bruno. We can't run away."

"Go where?" I asked.

"Someplace."

Kate turned away, trying to hold back tears.

"But if you went away, what would Mamma say?"

That was exactly the question I asked myself as I stood at the door of the rectory behind St. Paul's. Though it was a stone house not much different than the lesser mansions on The Hill, the rectory got lost like some paltry garage in the shadow of the cathedral itself. If it was convenient to imagine St. Paul's as God's actual residence, it was also easy to think of the rectory as elegant enough to exempt priests from the payment of light and water bills.

The woman who answered the door seemed attractive and smart. She looked me up and down with intense blue eyes, and her voice had a sassy edge. She was in her late thirties, the sheen of young beauty gone from all but her eyes, darker colors and lines beginning to show on her face. A lovely face I wanted to touch.

"The Bishop is a busy man," she informed me through a half-opened door. "You can try him later if you want. What brings you here?"

I tested her. "A very hard matter," I said. "A spiritual problem."

She ignored my comment and left me standing there. She returned a minute later. "He's in his office now. You're welcome to wait. Please come in and sit."

As she led the way into an antechamber, I couldn't take my eyes from her. She walked with a confidence that put me on edge, distanced me. She obviously knew what she wanted and knew something about us, males. "I'm Sonia," she said as she showed me to a chair, a caned highback more elaborately embroidered than the upholstered ones carefully situated around the room. Sonia exited, leaving me alone to take in the furnishings. Small orientals covered the floor, each surrounding an intricate Persian that dominated the room, and centered on the Persian was a table inlaid with mother-of-pearl. Looking down from panelled walls were the visages of bishops, all six of them portrayed in oils and framed in gold leaf. Visible in the background of each portrait was detail depicting a chronology of American history. Just to the left of the door the chronology began with the story of a missionary priest preaching to an Indian child. The chronology ended just to my right with a portrait of the most austere face in the room, his determination relieved, behind his left shoulder, by a bright suggestion of Christ hovering over the dome of St. Paul's, the entire hill on which the cathedral was built floating in haze rising from silver smokestacks in the city below. Next to this picture was a space left vacant for a concluding scene.

I was looking at some lovely leather-bound books when Sonia reappeared in the door, hands on hips. She looked at me in silence, then crossed toward the Bishop's door. I knew, from the way she glared, that the books were not to be touched.

"So what do you make of the portraits?" the Bishop said as he closed his office door and showed me to a chair. Bishop James was smaller than he appeared when I first saw him nodding approval after Mass on the steps of St. Paul's. He had thin well-polished hair and a narrow dark face. He might have been seventy, his voice, nostalgic and correct, showing not age but reverence for a former, more formal time. As he took a seat behind a large antique desk, he revealed a monkish balding spot on the back of his head.

"So, a matter of the spirit, you say?"

I gave him a courteous nod.

"You are, I presume, Gloria Amato's son. Fortunate indeed to have a mother like her, if she serves her family the way she has served the church. I can't help but wonder: Did you ever get your college degree?"

"Yes, Father. City University."

"Your course of studies?"

"History."

The Bishop lifted a brow. "History. Not much of that around these days. So few bothering themselves with it you would think it didn't really exist any more. How did you ever find your way to it?"

"By accident, I suppose. Fell into it. Woke up one day and found myself...there was a certain professor who..."

"Gave you a line, yes, pulled you out of your intellectual confusion, and here you are. Your mother, you know, she also was your guide, not merely in those usual motherish ways. She had many little things to say about you – how you might one day turn out. She was always very concerned about that."

"Well, here I am, turned out."

"Not exactly according to plan."

"Her plan?"

"You might say ours. She had her heart set on your becoming a priest."

"And I went wrong instead."

"You went to City University. We both had in mind a solid Catholic university. We assumed everything would follow from that. Your mother was convinced there was something special about you."

I gave a cynical laugh. "My name means Savior."

"Oh yes, of course. That's a nice connection. Maybe you would have made a good priest."

"I'm afraid, Father, that I'm just short of being a bum."

He leaned back in his chair and put his hands behind his head. "Money can do that to a man. That was the sticking point between your mother and me. How much that solid Catholic education would cost. It would have wiped your mother's savings out. You went to City University instead, and now here you are."

"Up to my ears in history. And with no real job."

"You might have had one here one day." He smiled. "And perhaps your mother was right about your extraordinary abilities. The portraits in the other room, for example. Perhaps one day you would have been there too, hanging on that wall."

He got up from his desk and signaled for me to follow him to the portraits. We gazed at them a long moment before he spoke again.

"You shouldn't like them too much. If you really look you'll see a certain sameness there – an excessive, almost acrylic, ambiance that makes the history of this region seem garish and obvious. And the poor bishops hardly seem equal to it – they all have such a grim Protestant look to them. It's all really my fault. I made a mistake commissioning them from a man I did not know. His samples were outstanding, but I did not know the man himself. That makes a difference, you know, in how the art turns out."

He stepped back to get a better look. "And that is, of course, neither here nor there. They're impressive, some would say spectacular. Those six men filling the room with their faces and watching us all with those eyes. They absolutely require your attention – for a time. But when you pass by them every day for a year, five, twenty years, their true colors begin to show."

He turned toward me again. "And as a student of history, you should know how art lies."

"I'm not sure what you mean."

"Proportion and space – structure and design. How for the sake of something attractive we betray what is. For example, these pictures here. Six of them, all equal in size, all in their way symmetrical. All telling one part of the history of this bishopric. And yet the parts of that history were not equal. One of those, for example, was bishop for less than six months, another only four years."

I smiled. "Aren't all men created equal – in the sight of God?"

Bishop James treated my comment as if it didn't exist. "And there is a vacant space, the one near the door – obviously reserved for me. Did you know that I have been bishop here since 1957? The Lord has seen fit to keep me his bishop longer than anyone but my immediate predecessor."

He paused, smiling as if lost in memories. "You can't tell that, can you, from those pictures there. Nor can you really tell what they did or did not do, their works. Influence – a nice word. Like history, whatever that is. You'd say history is the net, wouldn't you, what we get caught up in, or the events that somehow get caught – like fish we have names for. I'd say history is the holes in the net, everything that gets through. Maybe you can see why my wish is to be able to choose the man who paints my portrait one day. That way maybe my image would get caught in the net, and I'd be able to disappear from history, as we all ought."

He ushered me back to my chair.

"Forgive my rambling, my philosophic bent. When you read a bit you end up talking to yourself. It's nice to have someone else on the other end. My rambling interrupts the story you want me to hear, but it's so seldom I get a chance to carry on with someone who's also read a few books."

He gave a little laugh as he sat down again. "Now what can I do for you, my son?"

I didn't know what he could do for me, so I blurted it out. "Do you know a man named Waldman?"

The Bishop turned his eyebrow up and gave the name a long thought. "The name rings no bell of mine." He turned his head up and ran the name through one more time. "In what connection?"

"If you don't know the man I suppose it really doesn't matter at all."

"A matter of the spirit. Is your concern with this man a spiritual concern?"

"Yes, strictly speaking. Are not all matters spiritual?"

He lifted his brow again. "All, my son? Are matters of the flesh also spiritual? I was under the impression that notions like that were silently prohibited even in public institutions of higher learning."

"Then let's call it a family concern."

"Ah yes, go on."

I threw out a net. "I'm writing a short history – a simple record – of our family. I found an old box of letters my great-grandfather left behind. They fascinated me."

"You speak Italian?"

"No, but I manage to get the gist."

"Good for you."

"I took to interviewing my grandfather and grandmother – just letting them talk about the Old Country, their coming here."

"They must have wonderful stories to tell."

"That's exactly it. They went through so much that I – my generation, I mean – will never know about. I want to get it down, a record, something to pass on."

"And someday a book."

"I hadn't thought of that really."

"You ought to," he smiled. "There might be a little market for that kind of thing."

I congratulated myself for my little lie, the family history pulled out of my hat. And suddenly my little lie became a project again, something to do. There was a story to discover and tell, one as big as Guido, his store, Waldman. Bigger than Raphael and Vente. If there was, as the Bishop claimed, no connection between himself and Waldman, there was even more to know. Who was the bishop Rostopov told me about, the one who visited Waldman in his house? It could not have been Bishop James.

"So how can I help this little history along?" he asked, glancing at a wristwatch up his sleeve. It was obviously time to get down to hard spiritual business as usual.

"There is a point," I began, "where my history gets hung up. Call it tangled in the strings of the net – a time when something important happened to turn my family's fortunes back, snare them, Father, so that I perhaps was never able to become the priest you and my mother wanted me to be."

"That is quite vague, and I don't know what all that has to do with this office."

"I had a great-grandfather who was called over to this country to work on St. Paul's."

"Oh? Yes, go on."

"He was a stoneworker, a craftsman and architect, they say one of the best in Italy. He came here with a French architect named Pierre Vente. Both of them were commissioned by the bishop here to build St. Paul's."

"That would have been long before me. St. Paul's was built under Bishop Oliver."

"What concerns me is why my great-grandfather and the Frenchman didn't get a chance to see the cathedral through."

The bishop dismissed my comment with his hand.

"Does that really matter? The great cathedrals took hundreds of years to build. No workman had a chance to see a cathedral through from start to finish."

"But Father, Emile Mâle in his distinguished book says that the cathedral teaches us to respect any kind of work."

He smiled and settled back in his chair. "So they did require you to read a few books. But do you remember that Mâle also tells us that another lesson she teaches is not to expect riches from manual labor, that work is but an instrument of man's inner perfection?"

"She? You mean St. Paul's."

"In a manner of speaking, yes. And of course why not St. Paul? Can you think of anyone who did more to build the Church?"

"My great-grandfather Raphael certainly never got much of a chance."

"He was dismissed. What do you expect?"

He had jumped too hastily to that. "Dismissed for what? That's what I'd like to know."

"We all want to know. The cathedral shows what we know. But The Church also teaches us to disconnect knowledge from fame. I take it that your great-grandfather is not a famous man."

"What happened to my great-grandfather has something to do with the cathedral itself, its structure and design."

The bishop laughed. "You're not trying to tell me the thing is going to fall down on my head. It wasn't ladies who built St. Paul's. It was built by solid, God-fearing men, and it's as solid, my son, as the Rock of Gibraltar."

"No, that's not it. There was an argument over design. That's what I'm trying to find out."

"I think the design of St. Paul's will do. St. Paul's is one of the greatest cathedrals in America." He looked again at his wrist, making his impatience obvious.

"Do you have any idea why my great-grandfather was, as you put it, dismissed?"

"No. And I fail to see any reason for a fuss."

"You have church records?"

"We have archives, and of course a parish log. Ordinary stuff, but not open to the laity."

"Not even for historical research?"

"Of course not. We have historians. Yours is a family history, not a legitimate history of our church. As such it is quite irrelevant to our ministry."

"But if one were to do, let's say, a political history?"

He snapped. "The church takes no political positions. Our stands on matters controversial stem from our teachings. I, personally, abhor politics. When Sonia informed me of your visit, she said you had a spiritual matter to discuss. I assume we have not touched that matter yet." His face softened into a smile. "Shall we proceed to what troubles you spiritually?"

He had me. "I'm troubled only by what seems a black mark on my family's past."

"I see," he said, rising. "You are Italian. It's only natural that family be important to you. That I can understand, as you no doubt can comprehend that your personal queries about family are not a matter of the church's spiritual concern."

With his right hand he instructed me to rise. The interview was done.

114

Sonia waited for us at the door, her eyes avoiding mine. At a signal from the bishop she opened the door to let me out.

"I'm sorry I can be of no more use to you," he said. "We have our policies, and even I have my conditions of employment."

He extended a hand. "Besides, I know you will remember who you are. Gloria Amato's son. You have a wonderful mother, a true child of the Lord. And given that fact you should rest easy about your past. Give her my blessing."

Sonia caught me looking at her again.

"But my mother has a question for you too," I said as the bishop and I stood face-to-face at the door.

"Oh?"

"She wonders why you didn't come when she called."

"I didn't come?"

"To my father's deathbed."

The bishop seemed confused. He looked to Sonia for help, but she turned away. "Did you forget a call?" With his eyes he accused her of making a mistake. "I have no recollection. And your father – he's dead?"

Dead? "Yes," I said, enjoying the little lie I told as I brushed past the bishop out the door. "But he put up a hell of a fight."

13. *What's wrong with me? I asked myself. I'm a married man. Why am I doing this?*

I could not help looking back – no more than Sonia, mistress of the rectory, could keep herself from gazing at me. She smiled as she caught me in the act of stealing my little glimpse, a smile full of knowledge and confidence. She knew something – maybe why I couldn't help looking at her. Why was I looking at her? She was beautiful in a strange permanent way. But what could I do with her, with it, that strange, useless, and inaccessible beauty of hers? Nothing but gaze when I was sure she wasn't watching me.

I saw us together at a table in a small restaurant. She was telling me about the bishop, her former life, lovers, travels, dreams, what moved her to her rectory life. How unusual or wild she was, her ambitions and fantasies. Raphael, the bishop's nemesis, came to mind, and Raphael's wanton wife, the one who took the opera singer as lover and ran away. Who was she and where did she end up? Suddenly I wanted to know her too, find a portrait or photograph, read her eyes, the curl of her smile, the lines on her face.

And Waldman – how many Sonias in Waldman's life? He too had his past, perhaps the least interesting facts recorded in the parish logs and histories forgotten in the basement of the rectory. Waldman, as if already dead, entombed at the base of the bishop's actual residence, with Sonia brushing by, lifting her eyes as she opened into her sly, knowing smile. Did Waldman have enough passion to desire someone like her, or enough mind to conjure a grand conspiracy? Or was he just another landlord exercising his American right to keep raising Guido's rent?

What I could do to undo Waldman's greed? Get a job. Because in America I could be anything I dared to be. Doctor, lawyer, Indian chief. Do anything anyone asked me to do. Yes sir, you say you want me to hand you the goddamned screwdriver? Yes sir, one goddamned screwdriver coming right up. Yes, please, thank you. Was there any work that could compel me the way Sonia did – make me want to keep coming back, yearning to discover and do more with it? Raphael's Sonias – who were they? Maybe only one, the wife he lost, woman who maybe one night disappeared in a dream when he lost the argument over the design of St. Paul's.

I already had a beautiful woman, a wife. What more did I want? A job. Quit your whining about work, your dream. Just get a job. I rummaged in my pocket for the help wanted ad. Cabinet-maker's assistant. 357 Third.

I stayed on Grand and turned left on Third, checking a few addresses along the way. The afternoon sun made no sense. The rectory, its plush fabrics and dark colors, had taken me into another, older time. There was a sense of Europe there, of Sonia and late autumn and its cool winds, the opulence of a palace occupied by a solitaire given to brooding over life, seemingly uninterested in, even unaware of, the presence of a woman in his house. But here on Grand the street was full of cars, each driver sitting alone behind the wheel, each waiting for a light to turn green. Was it noon, three, or five o'clock? I kept looking for someone I knew, and I was desperate for a clock.

I was directly across from Sonsalla's Dress House when I first caught a glimpse of her. She was inside the shop, walking toward the back. Then, as if she knew she was being watched, she turned and paused to ask herself if she had seen me before. That is exactly what I asked her with my look, which glanced off her before I could be sure of anything. Her dress was blue, her body like Sandy's, but she had long black hair that shimmered in the flat fluorescent light.

I crossed the street and entered the store, pausing for a moment just inside. She turned left toward a row of skirts, and with her back turned began trying a few against herself. In the mirror over the door I saw the store clerk – a short balding man of fifty – watching me from the back. I found myself between a row of houserobes and evening gowns. The clerk, craning his neck to peer at me from the end of the row, retreated as he saw me studying the robes. I no longer could see the woman in blue, but there was a faint scent of perfume in the air. I kept an eye on the door.

I made my way slowly from robe to robe, hoping she would work her way around to my row. Maybe come up from behind, take me by surprise, she the one to smile, the first to speak. "Something for your wife? Here's one she would adore." She would hand the robe, the green velour, to the clerk suddenly all smiles. "Please gift-wrap it," she would say, but I would insist on paying for everything. She would lead the way out and we would walk to a small restaurant three blocks away. "And what's your name?" she would ask at the end of our day.

I came to the end of the row of robes and knew I had to make a move, turn toward the lingerie, maybe retreat toward the door and cut her off. I chose to retreat, noting the clerk's head suddenly bobbing to watch my moves. I hesitated in front of a rack of skirts.

"May I help you?" He had taken a different aisle and come up on me from behind, his back to the door.

"Just looking." I heard soft footfalls at the back of the store.

"You were interested in a robe..." He glanced at my left hand in search of a wedding band, "for a wife?"

"Ah yes," I said, catching a glimpse of the woman walking toward the front, "that would be nice."

He caught me by the elbow and led me toward his robes. Over my shoulder I saw her pause at the front door, throw me a backward glance, and go out.

"Do you have a color or size in mind?"

I slipped my arm away from his. She had paused on the sidewalk one more time as if trying to make up her mind. Then she walked away to my left and disappeared.

"We have these in velour – on special this week."

"Nice and soft," I said. "How much?"

"They run anywhere from thirty to eighty-nine."

"Oh I'm sorry," I said. "There must be some mistake. I really have no money at all." I put both my hands in my pants pockets and pulled them inside out. "And my wife is very, very tall."

I ran out of the store. But the woman was gone, and I had no idea which way she had turned, no hope of following her. I stayed on Third and walked a half-mile. At the corner of Third and Front I discovered that my right pocket was still hanging out like an old sock. In my fist was the newspaper ad. I checked it again and found a number over a door. I had walked past the place by two blocks.

The man who met me at the door had a ruddy oval face. "I'm Rochelle," he said, "Terry Rochelle." I had found my way through two sets of doors leading into an old brick warehouse showing no sign of life. "So you want a job?" Rochelle asked out of a permanent smile. "You know you're not the only one these days."

He showed me into a small area crowded with wood-working tools, a sawdust film covering everything. Pausing before a big table saw, he handed me a white-grained scrap of wood he had picked up from the floor. "Do you know what this is?"

I ran my fingers over it. "Not sure."

"You ever built a cabinet before?"

I saw an unfinished one in the center of the room, and had an urge to run my hands over the freshly sanded wood. "No, can't really say I have."

"You ever worked with wood?"

I shrugged in defeat.

"I mean as a boy – you ever build a car out of an orange crate?"

No. "I wanted to once. Had a lot of crates in back of my grandfather's grocery store." They smelled sour and sweet. "I tore them apart, did some hammering and sawing, but can't say much ever came of it."

"Why not?"

"I never could find wheels."

Rochelle laughed. "Yep, never enough wheels. I had two sets of beauts once, but I needed an axle for one. You ever try to drill holes through steel rod a half-inch thick?"

"How'd you do it?"

"My old man's hand drill. But then I said the hell with it. I put the wheels on anyway and let her roll until the damn things just wobbled and fell off. Then I just put them on and started all over again."

"Ever thought of sticking bubble gum on the axle ends?"

Rochelle laughed. "Now there's an idea for you. That stuff turned into steel after a few chews, didn't it?"

He walked me around the shop, saying little as he led me from workbench to workbench, six of them beneath the windows along the walls and a seventh in the center of the room. I could see him watching me all the time, looking for clues.

"You want to learn a trade?" he asked as he sat on a corner of a workbench.

I ran my hand again along the smooth surface of the piece of wood he had handed me. "I've thought about owning a little shop of my own – you know, restore old furniture in the back, make a few things now and then."

He laughed. "You want to find out what's under the varnish and veneer."

"I'd like to learn about wood."

"You're holding a piece of white oak. You come back tomorrow at lunch. To be honest I got to tell you there's another boy coming back tomorrow at nine. He maybe wants the job pretty bad, and he got here first. But you come and we'll see."

The next morning I was up earlier than usual. When I told Sandy there was hope for a job she shrugged. She left before we had much chance to talk. On my way downtown I detoured past Danko's shop, pressing up close to the window to see in. He was in back, examining the leg of an old chair.

I again found an empty booth facing the sidewalk in Darby's, the coffee shop across from Sonsalla's Dress House. Faces gave me strange hostile glances as they passed, one reminding me of the dark-haired woman in blue. Did Sonia ever get out of the rectory, come this way? And Rochelle. I liked the man, his perpetual smile. Lesson number one, white oak, an ABC of wood. And what reason would the woman in blue have for returning to Sonsalla's shop? She had made her tour and decided not to buy. Today she would be looking somewhere else. I was wasting my time.

The waitress returned to fill my cup. She was tall and blond, not yet twenty, her face pouting and broken out. I wanted to ask her what was wrong but thought better of it, covering my cup with my hand when she offered more. She turned away angry without saying a word. It was then I saw she could be pretty too. Ten minutes later I tried to catch her eye – even lifted my cup – but she pretended not to see.

What would Rochelle pay? I sat in the coffee shop an hour and a half. The blond waitress was gone, and a stout woman of thirty-five, her hair piled high on her head, took her place. Across the street a few women came and went from Sonsalla's shop.

Then the clerk came out of Sonsalla's shop, rolling his shirtsleeves up and propping himself on one leg against the front window of the store. He smiled and nodded to a few pedestrians, but otherwise he looked straight ahead at the traffic passing by, content to bask in the late morning sun.

There would be no job for me. When I met with Rochelle he would apologize and give me the word. That would be that. The coffee was tasteless and weak, but I needed something to keep me awake.

The clerk turned his head, straining to see down the street. On the sidewalk, thirty feet to his left, a woman in a yellow coat was walking away. A horn sounded but she ignored it and walked on.

I fumbled in my pocket for the two quarters I had taken off the dresser before I left. The new waitress smiled as I pulled them out, and she started toward me with her coffee pot. I slipped one of the quarters next to my cup and rushed out of the place.

I caught a glimpse of the yellow coat as I turned left down the street. I crossed in the middle to get a better look, dodging a car that refused to wait for me.

A bus pulled up. I found the quarter in my left pocket, and, clutching it tight in my fist, waited my turn to board. Near the back I found an empty seat on the sidewalk side, brushing past an old woman to sit down.

The bus jerked into motion, carrying me past faces I could not clearly see. The driver stopped twice in the first half mile, but then passed the next two stops because no one was waiting there. Suddenly we were crossing the freeway to the north side. I was at least three miles from home. "Stop!" I yelled as I stood. "I want out!"

It was past noon by the time I made my way back to Third. I had tried hitching a ride, but no one would stop.

"It's almost one," Rochelle said when I walked into the shop. "I thought we said noon."

I thought of two lies. "I'm sorry," I said.

"Have you ever worked with a lathe? A radial arm? You ever work with a router before?"

No. No. No.

"How far did you go in school?"

"BA in history."

He suddenly smiled more broadly. "Married?"

"Yes."

"Kids?"

"No."

He shrugged. The bad news was next. "The other boy came back and I offered him the job. But he needs another day to give it some thought."

He sized me up one more time. "You know," he said, "it would be just you and me eight hours a day in this place. Do you think you could handle it?"

"I think I could, sir."

"You could teach me a little history," he laughed. "I was lousy in it when I was a kid." He picked up a scrap of dark wood from the floor and handed it to me. "Now what do you think of that?"

"Mahogany."

"Walnut." His smile slipped away from him. "I remember when there were walnut trees everywhere in these parts. Can't find them now. I hear tell of a man who had an acre or two, went dancing on a Saturday night. When he came back someone had lifted a fat walnut tree right out of his yard – two men sawed the thing off at the base, clipped its wings, threw some chains on, and a helicopter just flew off with the log. Three minutes flat and the job was done."

I looked again at the piece he had handed me, ran my fingers over it, then brought it close to my nose. An acrid smell.

"You know," he went on, "I wouldn't want my helper running off on me after a couple of weeks. I had three other boys in here – taught them all I know – and all of them took off on me. One of them was no good – I could see that after a week. But the other two were good boys. Who knows if one of them would have taken over some day."

123

"Your boys went into another line of work?"

"Oh no," he said, his smile full of apologies. "I never had any kids. Now you come tomorrow again at noon. One way or another I'll show you around some more."

"I could see it in his eyes," I told Sandy that night. "He wanted to hire me."

"So you'll have a job if this other guy turns it down?"

"And we could save a few bucks."

"I doubt it."

"We'd both have jobs."

"Not the way our money disappears. Look in the jelly jar some time – our life savings in there, what's left of my tips."

I knew what was not in the jelly jar.

"And your mother called just before you got home. She wants to know what the bishop said."

The next morning I took three dimes from the jelly jar and made up my mind not to be late for Rochelle. As I entered his shop just before noon he was looking over the shoulder of a darkskinned boy, no older than sixteen, as the boy drew some lines along the edge of a square. My stomach sank.

"Come with me," Rochelle said, his smile suddenly dulled when he looked up. He led me through a door to the back of the shop. In one corner was an old roll-top covered with papers and dust, and across from it a small workbench under a long window letting in a streak of light. On the bench were small clamps and wood-carving knives and other tools I had never seen before. Hanging above it like chickens stripped clean were three violins.

He closed the door and offered me a seat next to the desk. "Look here," he said, rolling his seat to the workbench before turning to face me. "Look at this wonderful stuff." He held before me a piece of wood a foot and a half long and six inches wide. "It arrived in the mail just yesterday. What do you think this is?"

I shrugged. Nothing much mattered any more.

"Maple." His eyes widened.

"I was going to say maple."

"Two hundred years old." He handed it to me carefully as if it would break. I ran my hand over it and put it to my nose.

"No," he said, "this wood you put to your ear."

I pressed it close the same way I used to cup big seashells around my ear. "It isn't fair, is it?" I said.

"What isn't fair?"

"That this piece of wood should live to be two hundred years old."

"And who knows how long the violin will survive."

"That'll be even more unfair."

He laughed. "I'll hide my name on the inside of the violin. Then when a great sea rolls over downtown somebody being swept away will grab for it."

"And on that piece of driftwood will be the name Rochelle."

He gave a sharp nod. "You betcha!"

"So you sneak back here to make violins when you should be making cabinets?"

"My father-in-law did it all his life – even after he came here from Germany. I learned from him when his sons were killed in the war. He told me about the maple trees – the same ones the family had been turning into violins four hundred years ago. You can't just start with any piece of wood. The wood has to be dried for longer than you or I will live."

"You get the wood from Germany?"

"Only a few there do it any more. I can have all I want for the money I pay. In an old barn full of maple logs my grandfather cut down when he was a boy there is the whole string section of a symphony orchestra."

I felt useless and ashamed. "You'll teach your new boy to make violins?"

He nodded and turned away. "At first just how to make cabinets, the use of tools and machines, all about wood. We'll see. Then maybe I'll turn him loose here, in the back room, show him the way."

He got up and led me to the door. "I had to show you the violins, and you have to forgive me for not offering you the job."

"If he doesn't work out you'll give me a call?"

"We'll give him a good long chance," Rochelle said, giving me his hand. "I suppose we have to hope he works out."

"I'd still like to learn about the properties of wood."

"You come visit me."

125

It was hot when I hit the street again, so I carried my jacket under my arm. Not yet one and nowhere to go. I walked along Grand until I came to Sonsalla's again. I looked in and saw the clerk showing a dress to a smart-looking lady with greying hair, then crossed the street and looked inside Darby's coffee shop. The tall blond-haired waitress was on duty again, her hair, stringy and unwashed, falling in front of her face. I still had dimes from the jelly jar.

She came right over with her coffee pot. "How nice of you," I said.

With her free hand she brushed the hair from her face. "I remember you," she said, her face tired as if she had been up all night.

"And I haven't forgotten you."

She gave me a crooked smile, turned on one heel and walked away, throwing me a glance as she tossed her hair back. She avoided my gaze, even when filling my cup again, and I kept challenging her, following her as she went from booth to booth.

Finally I caught her looking at me. She opened into a smile as my eye caught hers, and she held her gaze on me until I shied away. The next thing I knew she was standing over me again.

"Geez mister, you must have a rich old aunt." She tried to fill my cup again, but I warded her off. "Don't you work for a living like the rest of us?"

"Do I look like somebody with a rich old aunt?"

"Maybe. What do you do?"

"I own a shop."

"That's nice," she nodded. "Real nice. What kind of shop?"

"It's antiques – old furniture and stuff."

"Old stuff?" She looked disappointed.

"Yup, my brother works for me."

"I'd like to see your place sometime."

"And I'd like to see yours."

She blushed, then left me to wait on somebody else. I hid the three dimes next to my coffee cup and quickly slipped out before she turned around. What's wrong with me, I asked myself. I'm a married man. Why am I doing this?

14. *"Is the bread ready yet, Mamma?"*

I ran most of the way home.

A half-hour to tidy up. When the dishes and counters were clean I ran the vacuum over the floors. And everything had to be put away before Sandy walked in the door. At five before six I put fresh coffee on. She would take her shoes off and lie back, and I would rub her feet.

By six she had not arrived. I found a couple pork chops in the freezer and put some pasta on to boil. By ten after six I decided to do everything right – a fresh salad and a pesto sauce. Ice cream, frozen raspberries and whipping cream, but no bread and only one bottle of Coke. If she were late enough I would have everything ready on time – the pots and pans all put away, the table set, the pork and pasta warming on the stove. But we would have to do without the bread.

By seven I finished with the pots and pans. I went to the bathroom to wash my hands again and saw the day's growth of beard shadowing my face. I brushed my teeth, and decided to shower and shave. I dressed, turned some Mozart on, and settled back with a book.

The phone was ringing when Sandy walked in the door.

"Sal? Have you forgotten about me, Sal?"

"No, Mamma, I have not forgotten you."

"Why don't you ever show your face over here? Why don't you call?"

Sandy was lost behind two grocery bags. "Sal, give me a hand with these, will you?"

"Don't you have a dime for a telephone call?"

"Sal, would you give me a hand?"

"Would you come over tomorrow first thing to see your poor father, Sal? And I want to know what the bishop said. You promise me you'll come?"

"I promise, Mamma."

127

"I don't forget, Sal. Remember that."

Sandy paused before the table and turned toward me with a smile. "Look," she said as she rummaged through the bags. She pulled out a loaf of French bread and a bottle of wine.

"Chablis?"

"Moselle."

"A little too light for pork, but better than one bottle of Coke."

She surveyed the room, nodding approval at my work. "What's the matter with you? You been fooling around on me?"

I looked at my wrist. "Look how late. I thought maybe you've been fooling around on me."

"I'm sorry," she said.

"For fooling around – or not fooling around?"

She abruptly turned away. "I suppose you didn't get the job."

"Let's eat."

I lit the candles and pulled out her chair, and later that night she led me to the bed. "I thought I was the host tonight," I said as she began unbuttoning my shirt.

"Allow me," she said, her fingers trembling the way they did on our wedding night.

She asked no questions about Rochelle until I was almost asleep. "He was a nice man," I said, "and he gave me some hope – if the other guy doesn't work out for him. And he suggested I hang around the shop, maybe pick up a few skills from him."

She didn't seem interested.

I told her about the violins, but again she had little to say. "I don't suppose making kitchen cabinets – or violins – is what I have my heart set on anyway."

"What do you have your heart set on?"

"I suppose it's Danko's place. Don't ask me why. No good reason – silly, impractical. But I see myself there."

"As long as you have your heart set."

Just before she fell asleep I turned toward her again. "I have my heart set on one more thing. A couple days ago I saw a robe that would have looked wonderful on you. It was blue – soft velour. I saw it in a window on Third."

"Sonsalla's place?"

"Yes."

"That's funny," she said. "I was just in there yesterday."

The last few leaves were falling off the trees in Jefferson Park. I put the collar of my jacket up around my ears and sat on a bench. Twenty yards to my left a little boy about ten was throwing a rubber ball in the air and trying to hit it with the handle of a broom. When he hit the ball he ran to imagined bases, rounding all four before chasing the ball down and bringing it back home. I watched him win game after game until he hit the ball into a pile of leaves and couldn't find it any more. The trees were mainly maples, but I couldn't name any other type of tree in the park.

When the boy found his ball again I walked over to see Mamma.

The door was opened by an unfamiliar face. "This is Edna Conklin, my new friend," Mamma said. "And this," she said taking my hand, "is my oldest boy, Salvatore."

"Close the door," Papa said from his chair. "You're letting in all the air."

Edna Conklin walked with an uncertain step full of vague pain. She was perhaps forty, suspicious of me even after Mamma took my hand to let me in. She had a tiny waist and big firm breasts that the rest of her frame, slender and angular, seemed too frail to support. When younger she must have been stunning, too innocent to know why men were always looking at her, too shy to do anything but tiptoe around in the world apologizing with weak smiles for being so obviously present in it. Her face was still remarkably pretty, but too many years of suntanning had made her skin leathery. Her lips tightened when she smiled, her unmoving eyes those of a woman who had made up her mind.

I sensed immediately that Papa, more than half-turned toward the TV set, was trying not to look at her.

"I met Edna at the supermarket and the next morning here she was right at the front door," Mamma said. "She was just here one day like an angel and asked if she could help me get through the day. That was right after your father's heart was bypassed, and I started to cry and she came back again and helped me do things, and we talked and talked."

129

Mamma took my coat and put it on the bed in my old room. Then she took me by the hand into the kitchen with her. "She never asked for anything in return, did you Edna? She helped me take care of your father when no one was around, and now I'm teaching her to make bread."

"Your mother's bread is so good," Edna said with a shy quiver in her voice. "I like it better than the store-bought kind."

"Would someone get me the goddamned paper," my father called from the other room. "Can you believe they're blacking out this week's game?"

"That's terrible," Edna said as she turned to get the paper for him. "I really wanted to see that game."

Mamma began softening the yeast. In a tub she poured a bag of flour, making a crater in the middle of the heap. "Now," she said to Edna looking on, "you add the water."

"How much water, Sister Glo?"

"Until it starts feeling good." Mamma plunged her hands into the flour. A fine white dust began to cover the table and drift to the floor as she worked the dough. "You better put an apron on, Edna. You put an apron on I'll let you try."

"How's Papa?" I asked.

"Oh he's fine, just fine. He gets up all by himself these days. He wants me to get him one of those remote controls. Now Edna, you be sure your hands are clean."

Edna ran her hands under the water in the kitchen sink. Mamma turned the dough over and over, her forearms muscular like those of a woman rubbing clothes by hand on a washboard.

"Here Edna, you try it now."

Edna hesitated, her face suddenly confused as she gazed at the sticky mass. Slowly she slipped her hands in, a smile coming to her face as she squeezed it a few minutes and tried to turn it over. Suddenly she pulled her hands out and began wiping her fingers clean.

"You have to keep at it, Mrs. Conklin," I said. "Keep working it until it gets stiff."

She looked over her shoulder as she slipped her hands in again.

"Do you think now maybe it's fun?" Mamma asked as if she didn't know.

"I don't know," Edna said. "It's something new for me."

Mamma wiped her fingers off while Edna worked the dough. She came in close to me, whispering so my father wouldn't hear. "What did the bishop say?"

"What do you expect, Mamma – for him to confess he did something wrong? Nothing. That's what he said."

Mamma and Edna exchanged a glance.

"But what did he say?"

"He said he's a very busy man. He said when you called – or when somebody called – about Papa, his housekeeper answered the phone. He said she never told him about the call."

She wiped her hands. "I don't understand."

"You don't believe what a bishop says?"

"No," said Edna looking up. "Some people are used to the lie."

"Did you talk to the housekeeper?"

"Yes."

"And what was she like?"

I saw her again as I did when leaving the rectory. If we had been alone anywhere – in a parked car, her room, a dark corner of the rectory – I would have been afraid of what we might do. "She seemed like a housekeeper, Mamma."

"Did she get the message?"

"She says she forgot."

"How could she forget?" Edna chimed, looking straight ahead.

"I didn't ask. I suppose housekeepers forget."

"You see," Mamma said, "Edna doesn't believe the way we do. She's a Protestant."

"Pentacostal," Edna corrected her.

"And she believes the bishop is the Anti-Christ."

"Not the Anti-Christ," Edna said, "a prefiguration of the Anti-Christ, like the Bible says."

"What do you think about that, Sal?"

"I don't know, Mamma. I don't know much about that kind of thing."

"You have a college degree and she knows all about the Bible and you don't? Sometimes I don't know what's the matter with you."

"Can I wash the dishes?"

She made way for me to squeeze between her and Edna to the sink piled high with dishes. "That would be nice, Sal. You know, it's a shame. I never got to them last night. If you would do the pots and pans, I can help Edna with her bread."

I began clearing everything to one side of the sink, glad to be free of them as Edna, gazing at her hands sticky with dough, tried to explain the Anti-Christ. From the corner of my eye I saw my father pull himself up, limp to the television set, and turn to a game show. Then he backed away out of view into his chair. I turned the hot water faucet all the way on, glad to hear the water, loud and clear, drown out Edna's talk. Rochelle's face kept smiling at me, and again I saw the lady in blue glancing back as she walked away from Sonsalla's. I let the water run until the sink was filled.

"So you don't believe in the Virgin Mary?" Mamma asked Edna with some disbelief. I turned my back to them and began scrubbing a pan.

"It's not that she wasn't a virgin, Gloria. It's that she wasn't a saint."

"But what's the difference?"

"You say Jesus was born of a virgin because he was perfect and clean. Isn't that right?"

"That's what we believe."

"But that doesn't give your people a right to treat her like God."

"What do you mean like God?" Mamma protested.

"Don't you pray to her when you say your rosary?"

Mamma had no answer to that.

"And don't you kneel down in front of statues of her?"

Edna backed away from the bread dough, a little curl of triumph on her face.

"Do you remember, Gloria, what God did to the Jews who worshipped the golden calf? He punished them full score. He did it because the calf was an idol, Satan's thing. God killed the Jews because the golden calf was a prefiguration of the devil, the whore of Babylon. Satan can do anything. He built the Tower of Babel and the Kingdom of Hell. He's the architect of lies and can fool people into thinking he can walk on water if he wanted to."

"But what about the time Our Lord cast the demons out?"

"That was another prefiguration."

"What did it mean?"

"It means that when a man is possessed there's a beast in him. The devil is a beast of cunning and art. He knows how to assume many forms. A part of the Anti-Christ comes into a man and fills him up. When Jesus casts the demons out, the demons come out of the man's mouth."

I tried to make a lot of noise rinsing the pot, hoping Papa would come to the kitchen to complain about the noise and tell Edna Conklin where to go.

"You read the Bible every day?" Mamma asked.

"And I love it," Edna said. "I take Bible study class."

"One thing I've always wanted to know," Mamma began again. "It's about when Jesus changed the water into wine."

"It's another prefiguration," Edna said. "It's Isaac and Abraham. It's all in the Bible like God said. God can do anything He wants."

"I don't know where you get all these things," Mamma said as she turned the dough out of the tub onto the kitchen table. "They never told us any of these things."

"I'm not going to say anything more about that," Edna replied. "Sometimes certain people don't want to teach certain things. But some things you can see with your own two eyes."

"Like what you told me about what came out of your husband's mouth just before he died?"

"Yes, the words, the words, the things that came out."

"Do you think he went to hell?"

"I'm not the one to judge," Edna said, lifting her eyes. "All I know is what the Bible says. We all sin and come short of his glory, praise the Lord. And that's why praying to Mary is wrong."

As I dried the pots and pans Edna was still trying to scrape the flour paste from her fingers. Mamma was shaping the dough into loaves and covering them with the white blanket she used for making bread. I drained the sink and began filling it again with water for the dishes left over from the night before. Flour had settled everywhere, a fine dust on the stove and counter top.

"Bravo!" Mamma said. "You finished the pots and pans."

"And I'll do the dishes next."

"No, no, no, no." She began ushering me out of the kitchen. "You did enough for one day."

133

"But Mamma," I complained, "the job is only half-done."

"Do as I say. This is not work for you."

I squeezed past Edna Conklin, not wanting to touch her anywhere. She smiled as I passed and I averted my eyes from her breasts. When my father saw me come from the kitchen toward him, he gave a look that said he was disgusted with all of us. From the kitchen I heard Mamma say to Edna, "He's such a good boy, that Sal my son."

"And how are your legs, Papa?"

"Sonofabitches."

I walked past him to the portrait of Raphael, his face handsome as ever, his eyes unmoved as they gazed beyond us all.

"It looks like Mamma has a new friend."

Papa gave me the Evil Eye.

"But maybe it's good for her – someone new to talk to, I mean."

"She's full of crap – with that Bible of hers."

"I suppose she's lonely. Her husband just died."

"Just look at her," my father said with contempt. "You see her wearing any black? She'll have herself another man in a couple of months."

I wanted to tell him about Rochelle, but I steered away from any talk about jobs. "It's getting cold. What does the paper say?"

"It says they're going to put something in Jefferson Park."

"What do you mean put something in?"

"Jefferson Park. The city council sold it last night – to some company. They say they got to do something with it, put something in. There you have it." He threw the paper into my lap.

"But what are they trying to put in?"

"How do I know if they don't know. Jobs, that's what. They say we gotta have jobs. You got a job?"

No.

"Well, there you have it. Maybe they're going to make a job for you."

So I can be across the street and come home for lunch every day.

He signaled for me to turn the television off. Then he swung himself toward the window and gazed out. I could see the tops of trees, a few leaves yellow and orange dangling from branches almost bare.

"Didn't anyone complain?" I asked.

"It says there was a group that signed a petition. What do I know about it?"

"Did it give names – Kate's name, Bruno's girl?"

"I didn't see any names. I don't even know what the hell her last name is. And why should she complain? What business is it of hers?"

"Because of the park. Do you want to look out the window at something like a lot full of used cars the rest of your life?"

He raised his voice so the women in the kitchen turned their heads toward us. "Why in the hell should you care? You got no job. You got a college degree and if you want they'll make you a boss in the car dealership, so why the hell should you care?"

I let him see me slowly clench my fist. I bolted up, walked to the window and calmed myself.

Mamma stuck her head in the room. "Sal, you two want some fresh bread?" She waited a moment, but when neither of us looked her way she returned to the kitchen.

"You know, Sal," he began in a mild voice, "our people came here to this country to get out of the jungle, and we worked like animals all our lives. We came because we didn't have washing machines and cars, because we were tired of living from hand to mouth, because we worked in the fields all our lives."

"So you don't want a park across the street?"

"A park is trees and grass. You going to eat trees and grass?"

"You don't want my kids playing in the park?"

"Your kids," he smiled. "You're going to have a kid? You show me first and we worry about it after that."

"So you really don't want the park?"

"You're wrong again. I want the park. The park was a nice place. I walked through the park every day for thirty-five years on my way to the factory. I like the park more than you like the park, but I got a helluva lot to lose if they don't put jobs in there."

I wanted to say the leaves shining yellow and orange in the late autumn sun.

"Something I gotta put up with because I'm the one who's going to have to live right here the rest of my life looking at them."

Little kids screaming as they run the bases, right field always out.

"Something I hope you and your family will have enough money to move away from."

You, Papa, you.

"I don't really think you really know about them. Your little sister Bea, for example, she used to hang around in that park half the night. And now where is she? Do you ever see her in this house even to say hello? She thinks she's a bigshot college girl, out somewhere all night long, and what can I do? How do you know she's not out with one of them."

"Them? What are you talking about, Papa?"

"Niggers, that's what. Niggers. You just wait and see. This neighborhood will be full of niggers if somebody don't do something soon."

He fell into a silence he would not let me intrude upon. What good would it do to walk him once more through my tirades on the history of slavery, the urbanization and alienation of blacks, the institutionalization of racism? He had heard my history lessons enough times, and he had his standard response: "They're lazy. Why don't they work like everybody else? If they don't like it here, why don't they go back where they come from?" He was born an American who eventually had nowhere to go but the factory, now and then making long leaps to a San Giovanni never seen, an Old Country glimpsed only in the faces of those already beginning to forget. Who were the heroes of his Old Way? Frank Sinatra, Vince Lombardi, and Al Capone: They did it their way, and winning was the only thing. Guido, on the other hand, had crossed as a boy, the old fig tree carried here from San Giovanni always full of the delicious dreams of childhood, dreams that looked good enough when the produce in his store smelled pungent and fresh, its colors those of a garden landscape left behind. And across from me, his eyes dreamy and bitter, Raphael had come as a man wanting to transplant not a fig tree but a monument able to pull all eyes toward itself, provide a center powerful enough to focus and give beautiful shape to the level gravity of the American plain. Though crossed in his attempt, Raphael was father of us all. Now what could he do but keep contemplating how the opportunity was lost, and keep looking down with pity at what his children were becoming in America?

My father and I looked at each other in silence until he closed his eyes and drifted toward sleep. I saw him there in his darkness, crouching in fear as he made his way from alley to alley, his heart drumming and terrified of Them.

The aroma of Mamma's bread was filling the room. Feeling a sudden urge, I walked to the bathroom, Mamma leaning toward me as I passed the kitchen door. "The bread will be done in ten minutes, and I'm putting new coffee on."

Edna Conklin smiled as I passed.

I sat down on the toilet and let my head rest in my hands. When I thought I had stayed too long, I flushed and washed my hands with soap. I did everything quietly, accustomed now to tiptoeing in my old house.

I heard the two women whispering as I approached the kitchen door.

"Every night," Edna said, "every single night."

"Even when you were asleep?"

"I would close my eyes. Then the worst things would come out."

"Swear words?"

"Curses, defilements, abominations. I know now what they were."

"What were they?"

"A prefiguration."

I could not get past the kitchen door.

"But I wonder about one thing, Edna," Mamma said.

"What is that, Sister Gloria?"

"When you do it without wanting to have a baby, is it a sin?"

"Of course it's a sin. It says so in black and white."

I stuck my head in the door and the two women jerked around like startled birds. "Is the bread ready yet, Mamma?"

15. *His meditation on death done, he heaved a deep sigh.*

On Wednesday the weather began to change. A cold front, moving slowly in from the northwest, would bring snow by the end of the day. Interest and inflation rates moved up another half-point, and two Soviet soldiers, leading a band of guerrillas somewhere in Africa, were haggard and exhausted but smiling at the camera as they smoked cigarettes. William O. Douglas announced his retirement from the Supreme Court, and an east side manufacturer of cardboard boxes was closing its doors, moving out of state because the taxes were too high.

That morning I went to the old store, hoping to find a fire in the stove, a cup of coffee, and a good book to read for an hour or two.

From the sidewalk I could see Bruno in his place, hunched over his notes. When I saw Kate, broom in hand, I considered moving on. I had enough classifieds in a coat pocket to keep me going half a day.

"Cold out there, isn't it?" Kate said as I came in, pointing with the broom to the coffee on the stove. I picked an old book out of a box, put my cup down, and sat behind Bruno just out of view. Without lifting his head he raised a finger to say hello. The book was a history of the rise of feudal monarchies.

Kate finished sweeping at the back of the store and began carrying armloads of wood from the stack piled next to Guido's shed. The draft coming from the open door sent chills through me as Bruno sat and stared.

I looked away, tried a few paragraphs of my book. But the chill from the open door kept taking me away. I looked down every time Kate appeared with an armload of wood, feeling useless with the book in my hands.

I put it down and walked to the door. We met just as she was stumbling in, trying to balance a log in her arms. I caught the log before it fell and extended my arms to take the load. She smiled, slid the wood onto my arms, and went out for more. By the time I had stacked the wood, she met me again at the door. Again I took the wood from her and stacked it near the stove.

We brought in a full month's worth without saying a word, the open door our meeting ground. For the hell of it I rushed the last load in place, hurried back to the doorway, and feigned a look of impatience when she saw me waiting for her.

"Oh," she said from behind her load, "sorry I'm so slow."

The devil got the better of me. "You work like a man."

I waited for her to object. Instead she smiled and shut the door, closing us in together with the heat from the stove, the aroma of coffee and Bruno's music beginning to fill the room. Kate and I moved in close to watch his fingers fly, his peculiar brand of blues, dissonance, and classical making his whole body sway. Kate and I exchanged glances until he jerked the music to a stop by slamming both hands down.

"That's all for now," he said to the room.

Kate leaned in, kissed him on the neck.

"I'll put another log in."

"That was beautiful," I said. "I don't know how you do it. The way you keep at it day after day."

Bruno winced as he reached for his coffee cup. What did I know? He filled his cup and we all pulled up chairs.

"Would you like a cup?" I asked Kate.

"She doesn't drink coffee," said Bruno. "Nothing with caffeine."

"Or booze," she reminded him.

"Or soda pop."

"Only water, then?" I asked, looking for trouble again.

"If it's pure," she said, "but actually I prefer a juicy peach."

"So does he," Bruno said.

"Not that kind of peach, you sex fiends."

Bruno's eyes warned me to back off.

"Did you hear about Jefferson Park?" I asked.

Bruno reached for his notebook on the piano bench.

"It's a good thing," Kate said.

"But they're going to wreck our old park. Bruno, did you know that?"

"Yup."

Kate squared off toward me. "What does it matter as long as it puts people to work? It's just a big empty old field most of the time."

"Where we played baseball as boys," I said to Bruno, his back now half-turned to us.

"You don't play baseball any more," Kate said.

"But it's two blocks from St. Paul's."

"You don't go to church any more."

"And you won't have to work in that place," I shot back. "What if they put in a huge car dealership, or a factory for auto parts? Aren't cars the work of capitalist pigs? Do you want capitalist pigs rooting around in the peoples' playground, gobbling up the only piece of ground reminding them of their workers' paradise?"

"People need work," she said with a matter-of-fact face. "Capitalism will undo itself. It's just an opiate of the people."

"My mother still goes to St. Paul's," I said. "You say she's on drugs?"

"That's her problem," Kate said indifferently.

"You're the only one not hooked on some opiate – is that it?"

"I'm hooked on your body, Kate," Bruno said as he pushed his chair away from the piano.

"That's sick love," she shot back at him, "and you know that. Sex is nothing more than a capitalist commodity. What does capitalism have to sell? Cars, guns, sports, flashy looks – all sex, the fast life for perpetually pubescent pricks. And how does it show its stuff off? Everwhere you look these days, sex, America's daily renewable energy source, the only staple of its market economy, its chief export, the main thing on its mind."

I stopped her tirade by raising my hand. "Let's cut it out, pass a law. If we outlaw sex, only outlaws will have sex."

"And you'd be the first to be sentenced to life," she shot back.

"While you're out there enjoying land, peace, and bread. You, Bruno, what do you think?"

"Nothing," he said, lowering his eyes. "I'm all for a piano in every joint."

I leaned in close, trying to get him to look me in the eye. "Do you ever get a hard-on when you play?"

"Huh?"

"Do you get aroused? Does your dick get hard? I mean, is there semen pressure driving those goosy fingers of yours?"

"Huh?"

"Disgusting," Kate said. "Do you see what I mean about perversion, sex, the way it's taken control. There's nothing sacred any more."

"You Kate, you. He plays for you, his muse. Why else spend time in those seamy joints for twenty-five dollars a night? Well, Bruno, why?"

"I kind of like those places."

I smiled triumphantly. "See, I told you so. He likes those joints. They're full of your kind of people – divorcees, losers gazing at their dreams going up in cigarette smoke, staring at the door, waiting for someone not too ugly to walk in just once, their sweaty bodies throbbing with longing, desire, just a one-night stand, maybe a measly half-hour stand if the beer and booze don't make them fall asleep first. I kinda like those places, Kate."

She bit her lip. "I don't understand why you hate me so much."

I had to think of something quick. "Because your little brother Dylan – if that's his name these days – is trying to get into my little sister Bea's pants."

"He's giving her lessons," Kate said. "What's wrong with that?"

"Lessons?"

"On the guitar," Bruno said. "Electric guitar."

"And I suppose you approve of that. No naked strings anywhere near our little sister Bea. Nothing but big electrical sounds – industrial tunes. Metal-workers' music, penis-music plugged into a nuclear power plant."

"Sex fiend." Kate turned away.

"You mean your little hot seventeen year-old brother?"

Kate appealed to Bruno for help. "Say something, will you?"

"Hey, I've got to live with both of you. Give me a break."

"Dylan's a peoples' poet. The coming generation. That's what he is," Kate announced. "And sometimes I wonder if your little sister is good enough for him."

I held my tongue when I saw she was about to cry.

"Because a woman needs to be something more than a passive little flower," Kate shouted at us both. "Because a woman needs to believe in something bigger than herself, needs to do something for other people, people worse off than herself. Because that's the most important thing a human being can do. And I don't care what you think. That's what I believe."

She turned away from us, tears streaming down her face, and took long strides toward the door.

Bruno and I looked at each other in alarm.

"Wait!" Bruno shouted as he went after her.

I watched them make a little scene outside the store. She shouted and raised her finger to his face when he tried to calm her down. People across the street turned to watch, and a few cars slowed. Finally he reached out to draw her to himself, but she broke free, ran between two cars across the street and disappeared inside her Socialist Workers Headquarters.

"I'm sorry," I said as Bruno returned. "I don't know what it is about her. I lose it, can't control myself. I keep picking fights and don't know why."

"You don't like her ideas. Why don't you leave it at that?"

No, that wasn't it. Her ideas – what were they? Sharp-edged versions of my own. She didn't really look at me unless we were having a fight.

"You know, I don't like you coming here," Bruno said, his back turned to me. "I mean, Kate and me – we always end up fighting when you're here."

And more than anything you hate noise.

"You're my brother," Bruno struggled on.

"But this is your place. I have no right here."

"No, no, this place is family. You know that. But it's not right, the way you just hang around."

My heart fell down. Bruno also thinking I was The Bum. Bruno, little brother Bruno.

"I mean, it's time for you to do something – decide. Know what I mean?"

"I've decided."

"What's that?" he said with some expectation in his face.

"I'm on strike."

"Oh." He sagged and walked to his piano, then sat with his back to me.

"How's Nonno?"

"Fine."

"Has he been here?"

"He's in back."

"In the cold all the time?"

"He was helping Kate with the wood. Why don't you get out of here. I want to play."

Guido, his knees together, was sitting hunched on the bench outside the shed, his weight poised on his walking stick and his eyes fixed on the wooden fence. His scarecrow body was covered by a heavy overcoat that hung to his knees, his forehead lost inside a wool cap. He did not move as I approached.

"Nonno, aren't you cold out here?"

He shrugged, his face full of contempt. "I had two tomatoes out here, mostly green. The cold got 'em last night."

As I sat next to him I saw a slight quaking in his hand and knees, either the cold or the shiver of an old man flexing against the final letting go.

"You know there was a time I ate figs until the middle of October. Right over there where I had the tree." He pulled himself back and pointed with his stick.

On that spot every November he bent the tree down to the ground and covered it with an overcoat of leaves before piling on the manure and dirt and smoothing them into a burial mound.

"And now if I want a taste of figs I have to chew on my stick." He put his stick to his nose and took a deep whiff. "This is all I got left of it."

The stick curved, had given with him as over the years he stooped closer and closer to the ground.

"How's Nonna?" I asked.

"A horse. Beginning to lose her looks, but she eats like a horse."

I wrapped my jacket more tightly around myself and pulled my collar up.

"She says why don't you come over to visit us."

I had no explanation or excuse. "It's not because of you – her – I don't come."

"Don't talk to me about A*merd*ica. I know why you don't come."

I thought of presents – a little bottle of perfume, a few flowers, a china cup, the pretty hand-painted one in Danko's shop.

"You found work yet?" he asked before I could respond.

I shrugged.

"You gotta make up your mind."

"You think I don't want to work?"

"What you want to do, I mean. You gotta decide."

"There's a store I want to buy. That's what I want."

"Store? You want to buy a store?"

This place. This old place. And then when it is bought and paid for I will hand you your white apron again with the deed carefully wrapped inside. Then you will open for business again, crates filled with fruit on the sidewalk until the first snow of the year. And when you die I will bury you in back, right where the fig tree was.

"Danko's store."

"Danko's? The one with all the stuff?"

"Yep."

"But what do you know about stuff?"

"There's a cabinet-maker named Rochelle. A few blocks away. He doesn't have a job for me, but he's offered to teach me all about wood."

"Danko wants to sell to you?"

"Why not? Why wouldn't he sell?"

"Because they're trying to buy up everything – that's what I think. Tear it all down. Put something in. Something big. You wait and see. And what's Danko want? Twenty? Thirty? You got twenty thousand dollars? Where you going to get money like that?"

I buttoned my collar, tucked my hands inside my jacket and tried to move closer to him. It was then I saw a brown paper bag half-hidden at his side. As he grudgingly gave me a few more inches on the bench, he slid the paper bag behind his back.

"When does that wife of yours come home from work?" he asked.

"Around six."

We sat in his silence for a minute or two.

"You cold out here? Maybe you better go inside. I'm old. When you're old like me you ain't got too much to keep warm any more. I got skin like a snake. Here, look."

He showed me the top of his left hand, the liver-spotted skin dry and hard, stretched tight over bare bones below. "You better go inside. You'll catch a helluva cold out here."

"I want to be with you."

He stared straight ahead. "How come you ain't out looking for a job?"

I heard feet rustling in the leaves behind the fence and a small rapping from behind.

Guido shot a glance toward the fence.

"I think somebody's there."

"What?" Guido replied, straining toward me with an ear.

Another rapping on the fence.

"Someone's behind the fence."

Guido shrugged.

Feet rustling in the leaves.

"I'm sure there's somebody back there."

Bang, bang, bang. Somebody pounding on the fence with a stone.

"Oh," Guido said, starting to his feet. "I'll go see. You wait here." He moved quickly, no quiver in his steps. When he reached the fence he rapped three times. I heard a whispering back and forth, some tittering. He returned to the bench with his hat in his hand.

"What was that all about?"

"Don't you worry about it."

"Was it Sam the garbage man?"

He looked right at me and smiled, his teeth as brown as his skin.

"More ashes from Bruno's stove?"

He fidgeted without answering me, then looked at his wrist as if he were wearing a watch. "Ain't you going to go look for a job?"

146

An airplane, a silent silver speck in the sky, was slowly passing high overhead. "You're right, Nonno. I'd better get on the move."

He stood up, sweeping a glance past the fence. "I'll walk with you to the door."

My eye chanced on the brown paper bag on the bench. "What's in the bag?"

"Nothing. It's nothing. Carrots. Here, you want to see?" He opened the bag and held it under my nose. Inside, wrapped in a plastic bag, were three fat carrots.

His steps were so short and quick I had to hurry to keep up with him. When he reached the back door he opened it to usher me out of his yard.

"How about you? Aren't you coming in?"

He lifted his eyes. "I want to sit alone a few minutes more," he said in a low grave voice, "to think about death."

Just then I heard three more raps on the back fence.

"Sam again?"

"Rascal."

He closed the door on me and tottered back toward the fence. I watched from the window as he stopped to pick up the bagful of carrots on the way. Then he put his walking stick down, stepped onto an old crate, and handed the bag over. In a moment another hand appeared, this one blacksleeved, holding a thick bouquet of long parsley for Guido to take.

They talked back and forth, Guido rolling his head back in laughter, losing his footing, almost falling off the crate as he waved the parsley to regain his balance again. He kept putting his ear to the fence, nodding again and again. Then he stepped down off the crate and picked up his walking stick. Glancing back over his shoulder, he returned to his bench by the shed, wrapped his coat tightly around himself, and sat. Propped on his stick, he stared at nothing in front of him, a grin of satisfaction on his face.

At the side of the yard was a gap in the fence, a missing board. There in the gap a stooped woman in Old World widow's black paused to stick her face in the space and wave farewell with a hanky dangling from a skinny hand.

Guido, the rascal. Donna Anna, the witch.

His meditation on death done, he heaved a deep sigh.

16. *God, I said to myself as I turned away, she's beautiful beyond belief. No wonder she always pisses me off.*

Bruno got up to leave when he saw me approach.

"Where you going?"

"Across to Kate's," he said. "Everything's loose ends here. If I'm not back in an hour, it means I'm dead meat."

"I'll call the police."

Guido came in the back door. I threw another log in the stove and pulled up a chair for him. He looked tired and uncertain as he approached, and let himself go as he sat in the chair.

"Well," I said, "how's Sam the garbage man?"

The old man shrugged.

"Has he got some new deal for you?"

With a wave of his stick Guido dismissed Sam. "He's no good any more. He wants to sell me an old pair of shoes. Ugly shoes, with rubber soles. I tell him to wear them on his ears, and he tells me to go to hell. I don't want to talk about him. I want you to go outside for me. There's a couple green tomatoes I left out there. You go bring them in for me."

I found three tomatoes still hanging from frostbitten vines. One collapsed in my hand.

"That's the ones," Guido said as he reached out with both hands. "But what's the use? One little rotten spot and they don't ripen any more. What am I gonna do – leave 'em alone out there to go to hell in the cold? Where did Bruno go?"

"Across the street. He and Kate had a little fight."

"They fight like cats and dogs. They should get married and get it over with."

"You don't fight, Nonno. I've never seen you fight."

149

He stiffened. "What do you mean fight? In Italy not even the soldiers fight. Why should we fight?"

"I mean, doesn't Nonna get upset because you always come here. Because you always leave her alone."

"Alone?" He lifted his eyes to the ceiling as if to ask the heavens to quit picking on him. "Some day I'm going back to the Old Country and never coming back. What do you mean alone?"

"Well you like it here, in back."

"She's never alone. That's why I gotta get out sometimes. That Virgin of hers. Always there, talking to her. When I walk out this morning she's on her knees. When I go back she's on her knees in front of that statue again. That Virgin never smiles, never talks, never makes the bed, never gets ugly and old, and her face looks sick and pale like those skinny American girls with blond hair because they never eat enough."

"But why don't you ever bring her here?"

"Here? You don't know, do you?"

"About what?"

"Donna Anna."

"The witch?"

"Witch, what do you mean witch? She lives across the alley, in the apartment there."

"She never gets out – I never see her out."

He relaxed. "Maybe she's too old to go out."

"You're not too old."

"I'm nine years older."

"So to you she's like a girl."

His eyes searched mine, wanting to know if I knew too much.

"So why doesn't she ever get out?"

"Because nobody likes her."

"Who doesn't like her?"

"Nobody. Rosina, nobody."

"Rosina likes everybody."

"What do you know, pip-squeak? You don't know your Nonna. You don't know what she thinks. Rosina and Donna Anna go way back. They grew up in San Giovanni and they were like sisters then. I'm telling you. In 1906, when I went back to the Old Country, I go there to find a wife. Here I am,

150

twenty-three years-old, and there they are, both of them, giving me the eye when I walk down the road with my suitcase in my hand. '*Mamma mia!*' I say to myself, 'look at them.' My heart is pounding like a drum. And it's Donna Anna who smiles first – a big smile your Nonna sees and never forgets. They're both standing in the field, tying wheat in bundles, and here I am walking down the road when Donna Anna smiles."

He leaned back in his chair and put his stick across his lap.

"What do I do? I tip my hat, give a little bow, and give both of them one equal smile. Little by little I learn their names, and that's when the trouble begins. Rosina, she comes from a nice family. Her father is Giacomo, and when he's not in the fields he's cutting everybody's hair, even at night right outside Antonio's *caffé*. Her mother eats all the time, but when there's a baby being born she's the one who goes. But Anna is somebody else. They tell me I better watch out. She's got those eyes, dark as the devil, and when you look at her once you can't take your eyes from her. Watch out, everybody says to me. Why? Watch out for Donna Annunziata, her mother. They say she's a *strega*, and you know what that is."

"A witch."

"What else does she do? Donna Annunziata has a little house like a cave on the side of the mountain where Tullio's spring comes out of the ground. And goats everywhere. She says all the goats are hers, even the ones people keep in their house. When she walks by somebody's house and sees a goat she points at it and says it's mine, but you can have it for now. And if people say yes, it's okay with her. But if they say no, she gives them the Evil Eye and sooner or later the goat dies. They want to run her out of town, and the priest blocks the door of the church when she wants to come in out of the rain, but how are they going to let her go? When somebody is sick, a baby or old man, she's the one they call, and she's always there with a cure. 'You got a chicken?' she says. 'I gotta have chicken soup today.' She knows everything there is to know about roots and leaves and flower petals and weeds and mushrooms and every kind of worm. If you have the flu she mixes a plaster of mustard and worms and you have to drink a bitter soup she mixes in a bowl. If you can't have a baby she's the one everybody visits at night. To the woman a special brew made of the fresh urine of old nuns. To the man a potion made of the menstrual blood of a woman who has given birth at least three times. It drives you crazy. And in a year you have a baby in your house.

"So pretty soon all the men start saying things to me. Watch out, because Anna's mother has cast a spell on you. You better leave or you're going to have to marry Donna Annunziata's girl. Maybe they're right, I say to myself one night. Maybe it's the mother who has cast the spell, not the girl. So I'm afraid whenever I see Anna – alone balancing a jar on her head, a bundle of sticks, a stone, whatever she's carrying at the time. She knows how to turn her neck just a little so she can look straight ahead and still look me right in the eye. That Rosina, says Matteo Rossi, now she's a nice girl. Why don't you take her to America with you? I can't argue with Matteo Rossi. Anna's eyes are Anna's eyes. You can't get away from them. But Anna is her mamma's child. Her dress is dirty, smeared with mud and grass, and when I'm in Mass I smell garlic, figs, rosemary, manure, and parsley, all these odors coming in the windows of the church, and I know Anna's at the fountain in the piazza watering a goat. For months she and Rosina work side-by-side in the fields, and only God knows what they talk about when I walk by with my little smile. Then one day Anna comes out from behind a tree. She wants me to come to her house, but her house is a barn, everyone – goats, chickens, pigeons, even two wild boars – coming and going from the same door, and sleeping with Donna Annunziata in the same straw.

"Finally I meet her alone in the dark. 'Anna,' I say to her, 'do you want to come to America?' She looks at me with those eyes that make me tremble in my shoes. 'Is it good there?' she asks. I tell her my Uncle Marco has a grocery store there, all full of fruits and vegetables. No worry about food. 'How many goats?' she asks. 'Goats? No goats in America.' She looks at the sky like it's going to rain, and her eyes have a strange color in them. 'No goats?' she says, unable to believe. 'What's the matter – no grass in America?' 'Grass? Lots of grass, but not near Uncle Marco's grocery store. There's a little yard in back. Maybe you could keep a goat there.' 'One goat? Only one? How do people live? No, I don't want to go to America.'

"Do you see what I mean? Everybody lies about what I really said to her. They say I asked her to marry me, but they lie. I never asked her to marry me. I only said do you want to come to America, and she said no so that was that. Your Nonna was the first one I asked, and the only one. I went to her on my knees, my heart in my hand, and when she answered the door I had my hat off. My knees were trembling so much I had to sit. *'Madonna mia!'* I said to myself, 'just look at her!' She had skin – how shall I say – pale and smooth like dough rising under a linen, and under the hem of her dress I saw feet so small they only touched the ground when she went from here to there. Your Nonna was an angel, her face always calm, serene, like a child just waking up. Could I make words come to my own ugly mouth? Only when her mamma, who was right there all the time kneading bread, turned, pointed a spoon at me, and said, 'So now finally you come here, you animal! So come right out with it and say what you came to say.' 'Rosina,' I said, turning to the mother, 'your lovely daughter there, my Uncle Marco has a grocery store in America, all full of vegetables and fruit. No worry about food. Will you marry me?'

"You have no idea how my legs were trembling, how they wanted to collapse when Rosina's mamma looked me in the eye.

"'What good will the vegetables do?' her mother said. 'They'll rot by the time they get back to San Giovanni.' I remember the words I said next, the way they came naturally, without me sorting each one out like the spotted apples or pears, setting them aside. 'But my love for your daughter is oh so ripe. If you delay even a day, my love will burst.'

"Rosina's mother looks me up and down. 'You are Raphael's son. I know all about the blood in your veins. You'll be ripe all your life.'

"I saw your Nonna lower her head, thinking all is lost, I will never get married to anyone. But I fought for her right then and there. 'I want her,' I said, 'and America wants to see her as rich as a queen. And I will never take her completely away from you. We will come back every other year, and when it pleases you we will take you there to live with us.'

"She started nodding her head, and the very next year she died, they say from eating too much."

Guido paused. "It's been more than seventy years since I see the houses of San Giovanni. I'm going to go back – you'll see – and this time I'm never coming back. You'll see.

"'So ask her,' Rosina's mamma says to me, 'if she wants to marry you. She's the only one who really counts.'

"And there I am on my knees, my hat in my hand. 'Please Rosina, will it be in the realm of my possible happiness that you consent to give yourself to me in holy matrimony?' She said yes, two days later we go to the priest, and in three months we are in Naples trying to buy tickets for America. And the rest of the story you know – how we lived married ever after until this very day, your Nonna and me."

"Happy, Nonno?"

"Happy? What are you talking about, happy? American word! What kind of word is that? Look at us, married for seventy years or more."

"And Donna Anna, how did she get here?"

"On a broom. How else do witches go where they want? Another man came from America for her. Carlo Pazzini was his name. He brought her a new dress, told her they could live in the west where there was grass for a thousand goats, and he came here with her because he knew us. He got a job in the factory, and she got to keep a few chickens until the inspectors took everybody's chickens home with them to eat."

"What happened to him?"

"He started feeling terrible and went to church every morning and night. Then he started to drink the wine. And one morning they found him dead in bed, and they could not get his eyes to close. He had a little blood on him."

"You mean...?"

"A little blood. She couldn't have any babies and all the old nuns were afraid of her because she kept following them around with a pisspot in her hand. What was she supposed to do? She said it was his fault, because he brought her to America and she never saw one goat, not even when he took her to the zoo one day. How could she have babies in America? One night poor Carlo talked to me alone. 'Guido,' he said, 'she never leaves me in peace. She keeps after me. I'm tired all the time.' 'What do you want me to do?' I say to him. 'I don't know – but if I die don't let anything happen to her. You take care of her, my friend.'"

154

Guido tapped his stick on the floor. "I made a vow to him and he died. She's still there and there's food on her table every day. She stays on her side, I stay on mine."

I tried egging him on. "I bet she and Rosina like to talk about the Old Country every chance they get."

Guido silenced me by putting his finger to his lips. "Never," he whispered. "Enemies. Before Donna Annunziata died she laid a curse on your Nonna. I remember it: As your Nonna and I were walking out of San Giovanni as bride and groom, Donna Annunziata stood by the side of the road. Without saying one word she lifted the back of her dress with her left hand and glared at your Nonna with the Evil Eye. You would not believe the stink that followed us down the road all the way to the sea. And that was not the only thing to turn your Nonna against her. Some say Donna Anna took a lover even before her husband died. Your Nonna saw them in the doorway, the basement, in the tomato plants before the sun came up. They say she had a baby but buried it. They say he was a little devil, that man she took, not even five feet tall. And she sold her soul to him. Because Donna Anna was bragging one day to the pharmacist that when he took his pants down she saw a tail between his legs."

Guido grinned through his brown teeth. "And the pharmacist said she was always dead serious when she wanted something from him."

I got up and went to the stove. "You want coffee?"

"No, no. When I drink coffee I never sleep at night. Then day and night get all confused and I never know if I'm here or there."

"Do you still see Donna Anna now?"

"No."

"Don't you worry about her?"

"She stays on her side. I stay on mine."

"Maybe you can work something out with her."

"What's that?"

"Sam the garbage man. He likes to talk. He comes here, bothers you too much."

"So what does Sam have to do with me and her?"

"I just thought maybe you could send Sam to her. To talk to her, get word back to you."

His face brightened as he turned the thought over in his mind. "I'm not sure," he said. "I'm not sure how it would work. You know Sam's got a wife, and it's not easy for him to sneak out every day."

As Guido fell silent I saw Raphael in his face again, the same stolid but sly eyes, the same weathered brow, the jaw determined to have its own way. It had been easy for Raphael to get out every day.

"And your papa?" I asked. "Was he a rascal?"

The question caught him unprepared. His eyes withdrew from me as they gazed forward into the past in search of the man who had been absent most of his life. "To me my papa was a god."

"A god?"

"When I was a boy – over there, I mean, in the Old Country – people made a path for him when he came near."

"Because he made churches?"

Guido searched for his father and found himself looking up at an invisible shadow standing over him. "You should have seen his hands," he said. "I saw him tap a stone, listen to it, see if it had anything inside, those hands always talking about God, politics, music. The musician's hands, directing the orchestra, the men always saying yes, yes as his hands spoke to them. I remember when they danced, he and my mamma. Everyone made room for them, the circle getting smaller because they wanted to get closer to see. She was beautiful, my mamma. Tall, proud, her long beautiful hair. The men – when she looked at them their throats dried up, and her eyes were always laughing at them, saying don't be such mules. It was easy for them to get their revenge. She could read. Books in the middle of the day, right on the balcony of our house, while the other women were still carrying jars and bundles on their heads and could do nothing but lift their eyes and swallow their pride. So one day she refused to carry anything on her head, and that same night she went away and never came back."

"She left them, the whole village, San Giovanni, not him?"

"She had her reasons for leaving him."

"He wanted her to fit in?"

"No, they say he liked the women too much."

"He was unfaithful to her?",

"My mamma liked her little opera singer who made everybody spit he sang so bad. Tit for tat."

Guido laughed as his hand tightened into a fist around his stick. "I remember one of his workers coming in the middle of the night. 'Raphael,' he whispered, 'your wife – you have to keep her in.' Papa laughed. 'You want her to turn into an animal, all caged up?'"

"The workers – they loved him, didn't they?"

"Yes, but they did nothing for him, not much work for the pay they took home. And nothing for the priests who stood wrapped in their black skirts watching every move. They worked because when their work was done they would stand back from it not able to believe their eyes. Oh yes, they took their pay. They waited for it, needed it. But more than anything my papa made them love their work."

"If he was the best, why didn't he get rich?"

Guido leaned back in his chair. "Salvatore, my boy, my boy. Why are you not rich?"

The gentle wave of his blessing washed over me. But I stillI felt ashamed of my idleness, my failure to make something beautiful.

The old man leaned forward to instruct. "He was never rich because only a few wanted him. He never asked much for himself, but he demanded much of the Church – the priests and bishops who wanted the churches built. He wanted workers to go slow. He took them aside one by one, taught them the right way – while the priests looked on and complained. And when they cursed him to his face he went home and watched his tomatoes grow."

Guido suddenly pulled himself up. He looked around as if confused, then started toward the front of the store. There seemed to be urgency in his steps, an errand to run, a siren to follow, a curse to hurl after a boy running away with an apple in his hand. Then he stopped and turned precariously on his stick. For a moment he looked at me as if he had forgotten what he wanted to say. Then something clicked. "No," he said as he stared at the traffic outside, "someday I will go back. But for now I better stay here."

I pulled my chair over to Bruno's piano and searched for middle C. As I struck the note the sound, steady and standard, spread into the room. I played a one-three-five, then three notes together, surprised to hear the sound leap from the piano vibrant and strong. I played the chord again, trying to make my fingers strike the keys more evenly, my left hand useless on my lap. Placing it on the white keys, I tried a few notes, mixing them with the right hand chord. I happened upon a happy combination, a moment of strange wonderful sound, but my fingers could not find it again.

Bruno. His hands gliding, running over the keys, striding over long stretches, his sounds sad and buoyant, touching ground here and there but also wild and bizarre, and never noise.

Guido made his way back to me and fell into Bruno's chair. "How come you don't play so good? You should get your brother to teach you how."

"It's too late for me."

"For me maybe it's too late – but you, you're just a boy."

"Tell me, Nonno, was your father fired by the bishop, or did he quit?"

"He quit."

"Because they disagreed about design?"

"Ah, then you saw it for yourself?"

"I guess not. I never thought anything was too wrong."

"Nobody thinks anything is wrong."

"So does it really matter – I mean to anyone but us?"

He dismissed the comment with a wave of his hand. "If it doesn't matter, nothing matters. They called him here to do it right. If you do something, you gotta do it right."

"And they cut corners."

"They made corners. They ruined it. They change everything and in the end nobody cares what they call the place. After so many years all he can do is laugh. 'St. Paul's,' he says, and I still hear him laugh."

"What do you mean nobody cares what they call the place?"

"When you got one little important thing that goes bad, then everything goes bad. Pretty soon nobody remembers and nobody sees, and it don't matter any more that things get worse."

"Nonno, who was responsible?"

"How do I know? Somebody."

A woman walking by paused at the window and tried to see in. From where I sat all I saw of her was her dark form on the other side of the glass.

Guido caught me in the act. "What do you think?" he said with a little laugh.

"She looked pretty good."

"What are you talking about pretty good? You don't know nothing about her, not even her name. You find out her name, then you look all you want, maybe. But otherwise it's all the same and you better leave her alone."

"Tell me what's wrong with St. Paul's."

"No, you go there and see for yourself. How many years now you been going there? Open your eyes. St. Paul's. I can still hear my father laugh."

"Nonno," I said, "you should be getting back."

He pulled himself up. "You're right. All your Nonna has is that Virgin of hers, and sometimes you never know what she could do in that room all alone. She ties the rosaries together, two or three, wraps her hands in them. That's why I got tin snips under the bed. In case the beads get all tangled and she can't get in bed."

A shiver went through him. I put another log in the stove. When I returned I found him with his eyes closed, his head resting on his gnarled stick. I wanted to ask him right then and there: If I buried it in back, would it survive the cold, send out a shoot in the spring?

He slept a full half-hour before opening an eye. "Where's Bruno?" he asked in alarm, as if Bruno had been lost in a dream.

"He's okay, Nonno. He's okay. He's across the street at Kate's."

He pulled himself up. "That's all right. I don't care. But you do a little favor for me. You go there and tell him to get me tomorrow morning. You tell him I'll be waiting for him."

I buttoned his collar and let him go. He said nothing until he got to the door. Then he turned, gave me a big grin, and waved farewell.

I waited until he turned the corner at Danko's before going back inside. Across the street Kate's Socialist's Workers Headquarters looked empty and grey, one window panel still

159

nothing but a plywood board tacked up after someone smashed it with a rock. I had seen strangers come and go, unemployed losers like me, but I had never been in the place. I had no idea what went on in there, what Kate did to earn her bread and board.

I crossed the street and paused before the window. Books and pamphlets were lined in untidy rows, behind them large letters cut by hand from blue construction paper: "WORKERS UNITE." Quotation marks.

When I tried the door it opened at my touch. It seemed cold inside, as if no one had turned on the heat. There were two tables in the room and chairs along the walls, one a card table ready to collapse under the weight of the pamphlets stacked on it. The other was a large oak table, a relic from some grade school. Dust on everything and the floor unswept.

I stuck my head into a door leading to a room in back. "Hello," I called. The back room was empty and big – a mop, a few crates, old chairs, and more pamphlets stacked here and there. To my right along the wall some wooden stairs led up.

I climbed the stairs and came to a corridor, numbered doors on both sides. I walked softly up and down the corridor, stopping at each of the six doors, looking for a nameplate or clue. I was about ready to retreat down the stairs when, from one of the rooms at the end of the corridor, I heard a moaning like that of a human in pain. I held my breath and listened hard again. The moan again, heavy and deeper this time. I took a few steps and stopped. Horrible thoughts: Someone bludgeoned, left to die.

I heard the moaning again – the last door on the left. I waited to be sure.

As I crouched and leaned too close, the door, chain-locked from inside, slid open to give me a narrow view. Inside, on a steel bed bearing a grey mattress and springs, Kate lay spread-eagle on her back, her arms and legs tied with clothesline to the bed's steel posts. In a heap by the side of the bed was a confused mass of clothing, and Kate seemed to be looking at the heap, a serene smile on her face. On top of her Bruno was grunting like an old bear.

I held my breath, unable to take my eyes from Kate, her smile, her face so wanton and satisfied, and her body, sleek, hard, glistening with sweat.

God, I said to myself as I turned away, she's beautiful beyond belief. No wonder she always pisses me off.

17. *He lifted my hand to his lips and pressed it gently there, and in that moment my flesh crept.*

Late that afternoon Markels opened the door just far enough to see me standing there. Peering over bifocals hanging low on his nose, he dropped his hand from the knob and backed away. "Come in," he finally said.

He was in a T-shirt and faded jeans, the window behind him grey, the air hanging over the city heavy and cold. Clothes, newspapers, journals, and empty coffee cups littered the bed and floor. And bookshelves, leaning askew against the walls, sagged under the weight of centuries of thought.

"It's been a month."

"Not yet," I corrected him.

"You find your man?"

"Rostopov, yes."

"And your Waldman?"

"I wasn't able to find out much."

Markels lifted a brow. "No historical Waldman?"

"Just what I found in the library, a few brief notices. His personal life seems odd, but the shape of his career seems ordinary enough. He comes to America, works here and there, makes money, builds a big house, and so on."

With a shaky hand Markels poured coffee for me. It was windless outside, with soft thick snow beginning to fall. He sighed as he sank into the chair across from me, his face, tired and grey, that of a man suddenly old. "If you knew where Waldman's bones were, wouldn't you take a lantern, dig them up and look at them one by one?"

"I'm sorry," I said.

"And I'm sorry too for troubling you. I forget now and then that you are not a candidate for our doctoral program here." He spoke to faces – invisible colleagues from a dour past – to his left and right. "I must confess, Professor Teufelsdrockh and Professor Unrath, I was hoping that Salvatore here – I mean Sal – would turn out to be a jewel among the many with rocks in their heads. Hoping we maybe could come to think of him as one of us."

He addressed his colleagues as if they were sitting in silent judgment on both of us, the two professorial shades, stiff-backed, looking down like portraits of grim-faced forefathers. He suddenly got up, circled the table, then went to the window and looked out.

"I sometimes forget, you know, that I am no longer Professor Markels. When I was a boy, maybe seven or eight, my father – he sold cloth on the Lower East Side – showed me a picture of his grandfather Sol. Sol was a professor in Darmstadt, a professor of economics. I had a picture in my mind of what God looked like – a distinguished gentleman, medium build, grey hair, dark suit, small wire eyeglasses, and he sat behind a black booth pushing pedals with his feet and making everything in the world happen that way. When I saw that picture of old man Sol I saw God for the very first time. I asked my father how I could be a professor like him, and he handed me a book. 'Here,' he said, 'start figuring out how everything works.'"

"You read the whole book by candlelight in one night."

"And didn't understand much, me with that picture in my mind." He screwed his finger to his temple.

"But you've read all these," I said, taking in all the books in the room, "and you still have a typewriter, a pen. You don't need them." With a wave of my hand I dismissed the two professorial shades sitting in judgment on us.

"Oh no," he said. "I'm finished with them, Professors Teufelsdrockh, Unrath and all the rest. I never needed them, but I need a few like you. And now I'm not so sure about you."

"Sure about what?"

"Why aren't you working?"

"Because I have no job."

"Nonsense. Where's your Waldman? How come you're not figuring out how things work?" He put his finger under my nose. "Because maybe somebody's shoving so much under your nose, nothing smells bad any more. You think food comes from vending machines?" He backed off. "How goes it with the wife?"

I was thrown too suddenly off balance by his irrelevance to do anything more than nod and say she was just fine. But he had no interest in my response.

"I remember that day you brought her to class. It was an April day, wet, ugly outside – the course on the Eastern European countries. You brought her with you because we were trying to figure what happened to the Jews. You wanted her to hear that – and from me, a Jew."

Yes, I wanted to show her how smart I was, and show Markels I had something he didn't have.

He circled the table and stopped in front of the window, as if about to write something in chalk on it. "I disappointed you, didn't I? Instead of filling you with pictures of the camps, I talked about Slovakia in 1941, how people didn't have any work. Josef, for example. Did I ever tell you about him? The one with the sawmill just outside of town. And suddenly no logs to cut, no boards to make, no small endpieces to send to the man who made buttons out of them. Josef asked his cousin, who stamped tickets at the railroad station, why no more logs, and the cousin just shook his head, he didn't know. No more trains with logs in them. And if no more logs, how buttons made of wood? The cousin didn't know, and already had gone a week without a button on his uniform. Didn't the little Jewish lady have any in her shop? No, the button boxes all empty there. No buttons any more. So what does Josef do, the sawmill man? He waits, then he tries praying to God. He sees trains every day, but never the logs. Does he ask where they're going or coming from? He wants to know where the logs are. Two weeks pass and then three, a month – and he can't afford a bottle of brandy any more. He dresses himself up – suit, white shirt and tie – and waits outside the office of the magistrate. The door opens, and yes, please come in, you want to know about the logs. Everybody needs buttons, sir. My cousin at the railroad station, sir. We'll see what we can do, goodbye. And please, sir, do whatever you need to do, for my cousin's sake, please sir, yes, thank you, sir.

"And within a month a train stops in front of Josef's sawmill again. Loaded down with logs – huge hardwoods from far away. The sawmill man looks at one log and sees thousands of buttons in it – enough to fill all the boxes in the Jewish button shop. But they say no endpieces for the button man. They want railroad ties instead. And Josef says please, sir, I never cut railroad ties. They say start today. He has no heart for cutting crude ties from the fragrant logs, the saw screaming along every inch, burning the wood as it goes. And when he's done working he doesn't see or hear another train come in, this one loaded down with even bigger logs, and behind it another train and another after that. The saw screams and screams as it makes history.

"Sunday he gets three hours off. He goes to the railroad station to see if his cousin has a button yet. The station is full – all the Jews from the town are there, even the little lady who owns the button shop. 'Where are you going?' Josef asks her. 'We don't know,' she replies. 'The man hasn't told us yet.' His cousin is stamping tickets as the Jews wait in line to board the train, but no, he doesn't know where the train is going today. Nobody ever tells him anything. How is he supposed to know where the trains go these days? When it's the Jewish lady's turn to have her ticket stamped she stops and notices the button missing from the cousin's uniform. 'You need a button,' she says. 'Ah yes,' says Josef, 'but where can you find them these days? No wood, except for railroad ties.' 'No big tragedy,' says the old lady as the cousin stamps her ticket. 'I suppose now somebody will make them out of bones.'"

Markels looked out the window and uttered a little laugh. "I remember your girlfriend there that day, how she waited by the door. You, holding her hand. You didn't bring her to hear a story like that. Stories – what do they have to do with history? You wanted me to say something profound – something, perhaps, about the uniformly historical importance of buttons. But all I could think of was how beautiful her eyes were, especially when she looked down at the floor and I couldn't see them at all. I said have a nice day and I hope she would be able to visit again. Do you remember that?"

166

I remembered standing at the door watching the way Sandy smiled, how carefully she brushed past to get out without touching him.

"Certainly there have been many beautiful women. In your classes, I mean. All those years of standing in front, all those faces passing through."

He raised a finger as if I finally had said something significant. "Always one, in every class, always beautiful, and never the same one, the same face."

"You mean relatively beautiful."

"No, I mean beautiful. The prettiest one, whoever she is. Black hair, blond, round face, long face, one slim-hipped, another round, young, old – who cares, really? She is always the same. Beautiful. I would look for her, find the most beautiful one in the room, see her without looking at her."

He turned, looked out the window at the snow, and spoke in a lowered voice. "Do you remember the one – tall, auburn-haired, dark brows, deep blue eyes? Do you remember her?"

"The one you graded on the curve?"

He tossed my comment aside. "That one day she missed my class. I walk in the room, see an empty seat where she's supposed to be, and then search – crazy, everywhere in the room – for her. And when I don't find her my heart sinks. It all feels worthless – all my talk about the Weimar Republic, cabaret life in Berlin in 1929, my socio-psychological analysis of Hitler's childhood years, my account of how the bomb, piece by little piece, suddenly came together to blow centuries of science away. All suddenly lifeless – because she's not there."

"But what about everybody else? Don't they count? What about me?"

"Oh, they counted. They counted, to be sure. They got the very best I had."

"They were invisible."

"Almost yes, invisible. But they got the best I had. Because I prepared every lecture for her. All my work – words carefully picked, written down, whole passages memorized – all of them had to be just right. Don't you see?"

He rubbed his eyes with his fists, leaned away, and avoided my accusing gaze. Outside the snow continued to fall. A chill went through me as I saw myself walking home, leaving him behind, alone in the cold. I could ask him to have dinner with Sandy and me, a few hours of talk and a bottle of wine. Then we could get a pillow and blankets out, make a nice place for him on the couch in the living room. The next morning we would have breakfast together, the three of us, only he and I knowing what he was thinking that day when Sandy visited his class.

"So what do you think of my little confession?"

Sandy would be turned off. Blue jeans and teeshirt. Gawking at girls. Professor indeed. "I'm not sure what the moral of your little history is."

"We have met the enemy and he is us."

"So now I sent the Jews to the concentration camps?"

Markels smiled. "You, me, Waldman – we all did."

"I wasn't even born. I find that hard to believe."

"Saint Augustine said, 'If the thing believed is incredible, it also is incredible that the incredible should have been so believed.' Don't you believe your own good Christian saint? I do especially, a Jew."

"I know nothing about Saint Augustine."

"Of course you do. You think there's no road leading from the City of God to the United States of America, no squiggle of a path from Auschwitz and Dachau to your Waldman? You say you were not yet born when the Jews were dying in Europe, but Waldman was there all along. What if Waldman had you in mind – everything he did to please you, one of his employees? And how do you know that you are not one of his devotees right now?"

"I'm not working for anyone."

"So you think that makes you innocent? Try closing your eyes, then tell me what you see."

A little shop, Danko's down the street. I'm in there sanding away on a tabletop, getting it perfectly smooth. The place is full of old stuff, and now and then somebody interesting walks in the door, someone who wants to talk. They are a bit odd, but they all have a good eye for things old and carefully made. They all hate waste. Now and then somebody buys – a clock, a chair, an old dish – and there's always someone else with a new old thing to sell. When I'm tired of sanding the tabletop, I sit down with a good book.

"I see myself owning a little junk shop. I don't get rich but I make ends meet. I live happily ever after this way."

"Books! Why not sell my books? Here," Markels said, taking in the whole room with a wave of his hand, "they're all yours. Take them! Father to son. Put up a big sign. 'Ideas on Sale. Three for a Dollar.' You can sell the ideas by the dozen, six of one kind, a half-dozen of the other kind, depending on how good they are. Now and then have a sale – throw one in free. No charge for some of the books – no ideas, no charge. And you get to decide. There you go – you're in business now. Now you have work. Go to it, boy."

"Where am I going to find inspiration from beautiful women by selling old books?"

"Who knows? One may walk right in on you. Besides, now and then you run into an irresistible one – a thick old tome all done in leather, soft-skinned, a little wrinkled and worn. You can't help loving the feel of them, the ones you never sell."

"I had one of them once. Charles Dickens."

"See, and then you'll start keeping an eye out for buttons made of wood. Josef, the owner of the sawmill, is still looking for them. Button, button, who's got the button? The trains keep coming in, all loaded down with logs from God knows where, and he's still there cutting railroad ties for God knows who, he doesn't know and doesn't ask."

"Waldman."

Markels smiled and leaned in close. "Yes, of course, that much is obvious. Just the names change – and the dates. Waldman is a system, not a man. And we want to remember this: We keep those saws screaming because we're convinced we're innocent. We do what we do because we're all doing somebody some good. Imagine that when you see the trains straining under their load as they start up on their way to Auschwitz and Dachau."

He peered out the window again, his eyes gazing over the rooftops, past them into the alleys and streets below. "Too much snow," he said. "Can you imagine how the Jews in the camps dreaded, welcomed it – the way it comes so silently down, covers everything, makes everything clean. Winter always gives me a chill when I look at it too long." He turned to me again. "Any questions before I dismiss the class?"

"Yes. Who's your beautiful woman today? Is there one on your seating chart in the back of your mind?"

He leaned in close to my face. "You, my silly child of St. Augustine."

I quickly backed away. "St. Augustine?"

"Took pains to divide what nature joined together in holy matrimony, body and soul. He took Plato and Plato's bed and put both in his head. There the bed becomes the idea of bed. That's how it fits. So when our dear saint lies down in his bed, he feels nothing at all, not even the itch that started when he was twelve, all that pressure on his genitals induced by too many thoughts pressing on his brain. He had to get up and do something about that, build something. We end up with The City of God, concentration camp for human desires – you know, our dirty selves, teeth, hair, prick, balls. Put the squeeze on them, the boys and men. All those strings attached. You know those cheeses hanging in deli windows here and there, the way they sag in their string sacks?"

I put myself back – in the villages of Italy, boys, not yet eighteen, kissing their mothers one last time and leaving their brown villages, maybe a mule and cart waiting to carry them away one by one to a faraway hill, a monastery and tunnel corridors where prayers are murmured in the dark. For hundreds of years all those boys volunteering to spend their lives lurking inside hoods, the odors of their flesh mingling there with their prayers.

"I could go for a piece of cheese right now."

"And your woman," Markels went right on, "what about her? Is she a saint too?"

"I have a wonderful wife."

"No, not your wife – I'm talking about your mother now. St. Augustine had a mother. Monica was her name. He had to do what she said. She's my mother too, you know – and yours. The one that keeps an eye on that little worm between your legs, washes, scrubs it clean, dirty little fish. Mother Superior, you know."

"Yes, I know. She's a little rough on us."

"Yes, poor pathetic males. The women, the girls – in the convents they could marry Christ. He could come to them in visions, dreams, prayers – at night. But the men, the pathetic males, who could they marry when the heat was on? How many men do you see saying the rosary?"

"Didn't they sneak into the nunneries at night?"

"Sin. More self-hate. The men had to learn to hate what they loved – women. And they had to endure having images of a pure woman, the Virgin, everywhere in their midst."

"And had to be chaste themselves."

"Precisely. Technically precisely. Like young girls, pure brides for Christ."

"Then they could marry him."

"Then they could not marry him. Absolutely not."

"I don't get it."

Markels gave a little smile and extended his hand to mine. His felt warm and soft as he lifted mine off the table toward him. "They couldn't marry Christ because they were males, silly. No man could ever touch another man that way. It would be sin again, and more self-hate."

He lifted my hand to his lips and pressed it gently there, and in that moment my flesh crept.

18. *She seemed too eager to close the door on me, and watched from a window in the rectory as I walked toward St. Paul's.*

The next morning I reached over to pull Sandy in close. But the blanket was halfway off the bed, and the sheet felt as cold as window glass. She had dressed in the dark and was gone.

The phone persisted until I picked the receiver up. I cleared my throat, for I didn't want Papa to know I was still in bed.

"Sal," he said. "Sal?"

"Yes."

"Sal?"

"Yes, Papa."

"Sal, you still in bed? Do you think you're still a boy? You get over here right away. Bea missed all her classes and your mother is going out of her mind."

"Why? What's wrong now?"

"I'm going to my grave in this place. That's what's wrong. Your sister Bea, she's a mess, crying, and now she won't eat. And your mother's up all night praying and crying and talking to herself. You get over here right now. My leg hurts so much I can't walk no more."

"But for God's sake tell me what they're crying about."

"Some goddamn priest last night. He calls, says Bea stole a rosary."

Bea the blessed. With a pretty face but always, except when she dressed up for a party or church, too wan – a face clearly eighteen but one destined, by the time she was twenty-five, to lose her smile. Beatrice, her brown eyes Raphael's, her

173

blond hair the streak inherited from way back, Vandals and Goths. Bea the afterthought, the last of us, the girl. The little girl who took too long learning to walk, who was all screaming and noise, and always in the way. Who when she first put on makeup and high heels had to put up with jeers until Mamma told us to shut up. She who suddenly was fifteen, absent too often and too long, gone so late one Tuesday night that Papa took off his belt, waited for her at the door, and took a half-hearted swipe at her behind when she walked in. "You turning yourself into a little whore?" he growled as he chased her into the room. Later that night Sandy and I huddled with her, told her we were on her side, he was wrong. And the next year she was out late every night, Papa burning with silence when she came home, having no real heart for the strap. And I too began to wonder what she was doing, who with, and where.

Was Bea capable of theft? She whom my mother rocked in her arms; for whom a pretty new dress appeared three, four, six times a year; who always spoke last and least, finally falling silent while we gabbed on, then going her own way; who maybe kept going her own way because she never got her way. Beatrice, who never skipped church or a day of school. She would never steal a rosary.

"Who accused you?" I asked when I cornered her in the living room.

"Father Francis."

"Which one is he?"

"The one who's almost bald."

I searched my mind for a priest going bald, but suddenly they all looked alike.

Mamma leaned into our conversation. "He called here three times and told your father Bea had to get the rosary back by noon today."

Papa, who had his back to us, twisted himself halfway around. "You just go over there and tell them to go to hell, Sal."

"Why didn't you tell him yourself?" Mamma shot back. "He called here three times and I wanted him to talk to you."

"I told you to tell him my girl is no crook."

"My God, my God, the sacrilege of it." Mamma still could not believe. "Imagine stealing a rosary...from a place of God.

174

What are we coming to? How could they think of such a thing?"

I finally got Bea alone in her room. "What were you doing at the rectory on a Thursday night?"

"She made me go there," she said, her expression sullen and blank, too hard to be simply innocent.

"Mamma made you go there?"

"I didn't want to go."

"Why? Why did she make you go?"

"I was a go-between. Mom gave me a letter for the bishop. I had to put it in his hand myself. She said she was tired of calling, begging him to come here. They never let her speak to him. So she gave me a letter for him and nobody else."

"You delivered the letter?"

"No, they said he wasn't there."

"Do you have the letter?"

"Mom took it back."

"And what's in the letter?"

"She won't say, won't talk about it with me."

"What's all this rosary business about? What happened when you got to the rectory?"

Mamma was in the kitchen door, inching closer as Bea lowered her voice.

"I'll tell you what happened," Mamma broke in. "Bea went there like a good girl. At first they wouldn't let her in, but she wouldn't go away. They told her the bishop would not be back for an hour or more. Bea told them she would wait. The priest – Father Francis – took her into one of the rooms."

"No, Mom. It wasn't the priest. The housekeeper," Bea corrected her.

Sonia.

"But after a while Father Francis came out and asked what you were doing there. Isn't that right?"

"It was about an hour," Bea said. "I told him I wanted the bishop."

"Then what did he say?"

"He said it was no use – I should go home."

"Another hour," Mamma said. "Another hour and a half they made her wait."

"So you just sat?"

"No, I didn't just sit. I got bored. I walked around the room. There were pictures of old priests and stuff on the walls. There were statues and nice old rugs. There were old books – boring stuff. I just walked around looking at things."

"Was there an old Bible with a rosary closed inside?" Mamma asked.

"There were books, Bibles, I don't know what, everywhere – boring old stuff. Maybe an old Bible, but I don't remember any rosary in it."

"Are you sure?"

She paused, as if surveying all the things in the room. "Yes, I'm sure."

"This Father Francis..."

"He came in on me a second time – scared me out of my wits. I wasn't sitting down. I was just looking at stuff when he came in. I was holding an old boring book when he comes barging in on me."

"I can't listen to this any more," Mamma said, backing out the door.

"And this priest, he just stands there and looks me up and down two or three times. Doesn't say a word. He gives me the creeps."

"Did he say anything to you right then?"

"He told me the bishop had gone to bed."

"He said you had to leave?"

"But I told him I couldn't give the letter to him. I had to hand-deliver it. He didn't like that."

"He told you to get out?"

"He was really pissed."

"Who gives a damn about an old rosary?" I laughed.

Beatrice blanched. "Father Francis...he told Papa...there were jewels in it. And it was blessed by the Pope."

"What's this Father Francis' problem? Why's he got it in for you?"

Bea lowered her eyes.

"Do you know him?"

"I went to confession to him – about a month ago."

"So what?"

She lifted her eyes, her face filling with shame. "About a year ago I lifted a bottle of perfume from a downtown store.

After confession I was the only one there when he came out. He looked right at me – gave me the creeps."

Yes, he stole a long look at her body and face, caught the scent of stolen perfume. The smell of her in the room with the Persian rug, the portraits of bishops, the old boring books.

"Sal," Mamma said, sticking her head in the door again, "look at your poor sister, Sal. You've got to do something, Sal, be the man of the house this once. You go over to this Father Francis, Sal. And you've got to do it right away, because he said noon today."

An hour and twelve minutes before noon. From Darby's coffee shop to St. Paul's a walk of ten, maybe fifteen, minutes. Fifty minutes to myself, a newspaper somebody left behind, the clock in front of my nose, and maybe the blond waitress again.

I scanned the front page for something new. The price of gas was up again, inflation still on the rise. The Khmer Rouge executing anyone able to read. The dirty little Angolan war heating up. New old racial troubles all over southern Africa. Bob Hope playing golf again with President Ford, and Death Squads doing their good deeds in El Salvador.

I pushed the newspaper away. Salvatore. Savior. Why not just Tom, Harry, or Dick like everybody else? What could I do? Where could I hide?

"Can I help you with something today?"

I looked up to an unattractive face. She was in her fifties, solid and hefty, standing lopsided on one haunch, an eye half-closed.

"Yes, thank you," I said. "Two donuts and coffee black."

"Be a minute," she said as she turned, a smile on her face.

An old gentleman in a sportscoat and tie craned his neck toward me from the next booth. "She looks like a smoked ham, don't she?" he said through a smirk as she lumbered away.

She brought my coffee and donuts, wiped my table clean, and took my money with a little apologetic shake of her head. Her white dress was perfectly pressed. I emptied my pocket of change, counted it out, and slipped a grand total of thirty-seven cents under the saucer for her.

At eleven-thirty she refilled my cup and disappeared again into the kitchen through the double doors in back.

177

The gentleman in the next booth stood up to leave. "She give you the eye?" he asked, showing me a smile full of small brown teeth. "She wouldn't give me the time of day."

What would I say to Father Francis when we came face-to-face? Maybe nothing at first. We would size each other up, then step outside as men do, stand hands-on-hips facing each other while a hush fell over traffic on the street. I would let him make the first move, would want everyone to see that he started it all. He would say, Who do you think you are? And I would shoot back: Salvatore Amato. Think about that, and now who do you think you are?

He would extend a sullen hand, show the rosary to me, say there must have been a terrible mistake.

"Would you like a refill?" A waitress I had never seen before was looking down at me with big dark eyes. I tried not to notice but couldn't help seeing that her breasts were smallish but firm, her waist petite, her hair, curly and black, heaped on top of her head inside a net. Whatever happened to the blond?

"You waitresses just seem so busy all the time. You just come and go. And it seems a shame to waste that lovely hair of yours...I mean inside that hairnet."

She put a hand on her hip. "Well I do let it down now and then."

Father Francis still held the rosary up to my nose. We need to talk.

I smirked. He would tire of admitting his mistake, his hand would tire of holding it up, and then what would he do with the rosary?

I would have to be forceful and blunt. "You mean after work?"

"Maybe."

Father Francis took two steps back, his hand reaching for me the way a desperate man reaches out for help.

I didn't let him off the hook. What makes you think you can call into question our moral integrity? Accuse a teenage girl of stealing a rosary?

Should I tell her I'm a married man?

"Maybe? What am I supposed to make of an answer like that? Do you go to bed with your hair in a net?"

"Maybe."

178

"Ha, I'd like to see that with my own two eyes."

And what did Father Francis really see?

Did you see her take the rosary? How can you be sure the thing was really stolen at all? And I want you to answer me one more thing: Why should I take your word that the rosary was really there? And why should I assume the thing was made of precious jewels and blessed by the Pope?

"Ha, you'd have to stick around a long time to find that out. I work until ten tonight."

"That's ridiculous. Where's your time off? I want to see your boss."

"Ha, good luck. I never laid eyes on him."

"Who's the owner here?"

Waldman.

"Got me."

Was she supposed to kiss up to him just because? So what if the rosary was blessed by the Pope.

Waldman had her where he wanted her. He owned the place, the rosary too. And they like to say possession is nine-tenths of the law. But does a wife own a husband just because he's married to her?

"So what's your name?"

Beatrice is no ordinary name, no vulgar little teenage name. She's in Dante. The one who takes you by the hand to heaven. Did you know that – you, priest whose ear at confession time gets filled with sins, who maybe has a head so gorged with garbage he can't see anything pure. So Beatrice stole a bottle of perfume from a downtown store. Would that count against her in a court of law? What business of yours is the department store? How big a bottle of perfume? Who would have missed the perfume more, and who had the greater need – Bea or the department store? Wasn't that store full of bottles of perfume? And therefore who had the real right to the bottle of perfume?

"Maggie," she said. She turned to show me the nametag pinned to her dress. "Maggie's my name. What's yours?"

And here she was, coming right out, giving her name out to me, a stranger, as if. One of Kate's girls, a prole on the prowl.

Father Francis, did you ever have a little sister of your own? Do you know what it's like in the streets today? If you had a sister, what would you do if she stole a bottle of perfume from a department store – if she came to you, big brother and priest, and whispered something like that in your ear?

And what if she confessed another little sin to you? You know what I mean. Have you ever seen Kate's brother, that Dylan creep? Do you know what he's like with that long hair, that rock-and-roll jacket and jeans? Do you know Beatrice thinks she's in love with him? Would forgiveness as freely flow for the stolen bottle of perfume if you knew what she was doing with him? Would you hold that against her, or would you be able to step back, take a long look at the strange ways of love, and say, God bless you two kids, go ahead if you feel good about doing what you really want to do?

My name? What the hell. "Dirk."

And let us assume, Your Honor, that Bea confessed to both these little sins. That she admitted lifting the bottle of perfume, and that in an effort to clear her slate she also confessed to giving in, once, in a car, in a dark stairwell, a park.

"Nice to meet you, Dirk. Now what can I do for you?"

"Yes, get me the name of the man who owns this place. I think it's a crime you have to work that many hours in a row. Ten? What kind of slave-driver does he think he is?"

Now you, Father Francis. Have you ever commited a crime?

"Dirk, you look like somebody I know. Haven't we met somewheres before?"

No, and so I really don't see how we'll have a meeting of the minds. Take the rosary, for example. A rosary is a rosary. You say it was the bishop's special rosary. But a rosary is just a string of beads or stones having a symbolic function in acts of religious worship.

But this rosary was made of jewels.

Valuable only to the devotees of Vanity Fair. Its value outside the marketplace incidental merely, true value inherent only in the character of the worshipper and quality of worship. Thus, for the worshipper to attach spiritual value to the object itself would be to commit the sin of idolatry.

"God, maybe we have met somewhere. I know offhand I've seen your face, but I can't recall offhand just where."

But this rosary was blessed by the Pope.

An object itself cannot be self-vested with power and authority, and any vesting power or authority that itself is suspect, jaded or corrupt invalidates the investiture. In the absence of appropriate investiture, an object is a body, a thing, merely.

"Do you think? Hey man, I'd like to talk more, but I gotta keep on the move."

I understand. You must be lonely, sad, unsatisfied, tired of working long hours. "God, maybe we could get together sometime, talk, be friends."

"Really? Friends?"

Then nobody could accuse us. "We could just talk. We sure can't get to know each other this way."

"So you want to talk," Maggie said as she lifted a trayful of dirty dishes from the next booth. "So why don't you give me a call."

My dragon was swollen big inside my pants. "Sure."

Guilty! Father Francis announced to everyone in St. Paul's. She stole the rosary, and you, her own brother, know what she was doing all along and are covering up! Therefore you are as guilty as the girl herself!

Maggie left a slip of paper next to my cup. A telephone number and address. I folded it into a small wad.

"Do you have to work Friday afternoon?"

"Yep. But I get some Monday mornings off, unless I get switched around with another girl."

Yes, switched around with another girl. Waldman had plenty of girls working for him, a long lineup of girls waiting for his call. If he couldn't get one from the neighborhood to come in right away, he'd call one further out, suburban girls, country girls, girls from towns in other states further west. And they'd be satisfied with sweeping the tips into their pockets with one hand, loose change with scraps of food, money that had passed through hundreds of hands, dirty fingers full of germs from God knows where. Was there any clean money anywhere in the world?

"Sure," I said. "Maybe we can work it out."

My heart leaped when I looked at the clock. Quarter past twelve. "Oops, gotta run," I said, tucking the thirty-seven cent tip under the saucer again.

When Sonia saw me she only half-opened the door, frisking me with her eyes.

"Father Francis is in St. Paul's," she said, "and I don't know when he'll be back."

"What about the Bishop?"

"He isn't here, and I don't know when he'll be back."

"What do you know about this rosary business?"

"What I know doesn't count here. I was instructed to return the rosary to its place if one was brought back."

She seemed too eager to close the door on me, and watched from a window in the rectory as I walked toward St. Paul's.

19. *He gave me a smile that made me blush and turn away, and without saying a word lay down in Maggie's open arms.*

The doors of St. Paul's open like the cover of a leather-bound book. I watched from the curb until a priest stepped aside, then began making my way against the stream of people on their way out of a late-afternoon Mass. Eyes ignored me as I approached the doors, but one stooped woman, taking tentative steps, paused and stood in my way as if trying to remember where she had seen me before. I brushed by, wary that she was still watching as I went in.

Behind me the doors closed softly, sealing me off from the traffic outside. Just inside the vestibule doors the vast space of the nave opened into view. For a moment I was transfixed the way I always had been when I entered here, suddenly singular in a vacancy greater than any I had experienced in the streets, my eyes searching for the source of a faint eerie hum circling in the silence that enveloped me as I took a few steps down the center aisle. I stopped again and took a deep breath. From an invisible vantage point high overhead, I saw myself look to my left, my eye taken by a familiar stained-glass window depicting St. Francis preaching to doves, donkeys and goats.

The poor saint's gaze took in the pews running in straight rows on both sides of the aisle, a few souls left over from Mass hunched in prayer here and there. In side-altars other saints in shadowed niches slowly turned as I approached, their eyes unmoved as they followed me. To my right a woman with a shawl over her head was crying quietly into her hands, and toward the front two nuns sat in silence staring at the cross looming in the distance high beyond the altar rail.

The clack of my shoes was too loud on the tile. At a side-altar the Virgin, her gown spread wide, stood open-palmed, her view of me obstructed as I passed by a confessional booth made of dark wood. The words ran through my mind: Forgive me Father, for I have sinned. It has been how long? – I can't remember – since I have been here.

I sat in a pew. How many times had I stared into the silences here waiting for voices, guilty and innocent, all of them mine, to whisper about evil and good, all words finally indistinguishable in the familiar grey of the stones? Here I made a First Communion, and here, again in my best suit and tie, I was married with familiar faces smiling me down the aisle. And here I now was, twenty-eight years old, man and boy resonating in the same flesh.

I got up and walked forward again. In the stained glass to my left Gabriel was pointing his sword at Eve, while Adam, also clad in animal skins, followed her along the path leading away from The Tree. On my right Jesus was hanging painlessly on a cross adorned with clusters of grapes more brilliantly purple than Guido's figs, the inscription "I Am the Vine" bled into the glass at His feet. High overhead the cathedral's white dome, skull-capped and crowned by a gold mosaic fringe, slowly opened into view. My eyes took flight and circled the inside of the dome, then slid to the floor again. Faith without Works – what good was Faith without Works? Ahead of me, at the end of a long well-polished corridor in my mind – in some square glass building full of desks and filing cabinets – I saw a small door. Knock, and the door shall be opened to a decent job. As I approached the door it receded from me, all belief narrowing to pointlessness.

It was cold. As I pulled my coat tighter around myself I saw a youth in the transcept to my left staring at me. He was blond and pale, his collar pulled up high, his face vaguely reminding me of Beatrice. As I turned to get a better view, he ducked behind a column and disappeared.

Who was he, this form? Had I confused him with one of the saints in a niche, or was he some idler too? Here! Of all places why here? If behind some pillar we met face-to-face, what would I say to him? Words – remembered from a book: The cathedral teaches that work of any kind demands respect. Another lesson she would teach men is to expect neither riches from manual labor nor fame from learning. A boy's words these, dreamy and idealistic – or a man's, words as weighty as the pillars of Chartres? Words like the stones of St. Paul's, each in its place, inherited, believed by a few. And who were they, the men, horses, mules who built this place, workers who dragged tons of stones across the prairie from some nameless mountain in the west, all of the men tied to the stones by thick hemp, holding their breath to concentrate their strength, waiting for the cue, the conductor's baton, then pulling together to move the mountain here? How many of the workers paused to wonder at their work after crossing the bridge at the foot of the hill beneath which the river, steady and calm, wound its way out of sight? And how many doubted when they saw that dragging the stones uphill the last hundred yards would require one last insane effort of will. Enough of them gathered themselves, summoned the strength, and pulled as one, the stones not magically flying up the hill, each haul weighing them down with weariness and age, leaving them with nothing to look forward to but the sun going down and the moment when they could drop their ropes in the dust, go to the women and children waiting for them, and walk home to their wooden shacks.

And what did Raphael's intransigence represent? A stubbornness in the blood, ego insistent on showing itself off and determined to make a last stand in the stones of St. Paul's? Or a dream – original, studied, and deeply felt – crying out to be planted in new soil?

As I went forward toward the altar the saints kept telling their stained-glass stories overhead – those in the east going about their daily rounds indifferent to the statues below, those in the west alive with the allure of the autumn sun. Halfway to the altar I passed an old woman who fixed me with an accusing eye, while on my right, Peter, brilliant in the sunset glow of the western window, held up a finger to instruct. I turned away from him toward Joachim in the east, stranger alone with his sheep, his story one more I never learned. I became aware of the muffled din of traffic outside, the five o'clock rush of cars impatient to get away from the grey silence of St. Paul's, from Guido and his old store, Donna Anna his witch, the old house, old neighborhood – everything emptying into the freeways leading out and away, the cars, once past suburbs and farms, letting themselves go on the prairie and desert lands, turning their chrome smiles toward a sunset destiny beyond there while Peter, his finger still raised, still offered advice from behind: Go west, young man. The future is bright, the past old and dark. Look forward to that future out west, because in this country you can do anything. The sky's the limit, your whole future in front of you. There, on a California beach, is a beautiful setting sun and a vast parking lot.

I looked up, straining backward to see into the dome again. St. Paul's had gone wrong – that's what Guido said. But how? *"Walls?"* Those were Guido's words. "My boy, my boy, in the best cathedral you have supports, not walls!" *Walls.* Four walls here too – like any ordinary house, warehouse, factory, or prison cell.

Suddenly I saw it for myself: The four central beams crossing the nave where it met the trancepts, the curve of the arches beginning there, resting on them, the central shell two crossed rectangles on which were heaped vaults, ceilings, spires, and dome. Not a set of arcs rising out of the ground itself, each stone balanced, perfectly cut, leaning on the next, the whole, growing from each stone, converging on itself, releasing its centrifugal weight into the sky. It was instead a set of piles, stones heaped on stones, all of them pressing down.

Yes, all wrong. The men who had lugged the stone had to be impressed by the way their work amounted to something big. St. Paul's was huge and would not cave in soon. It was monumental, spectacular, grand, a mighty fortress for a beleaguered God. But from the moment Raphael was betrayed the workers began getting less than their money's worth when they stepped forward in line to receive their wages at the end of the week.

My eyes went up again, circled the dome, again finding the beams crossing the right trancept over my head. I could not take my eyes from the beams, the way they crossed from column to column under the dome. Too much weight there, too much for these legs of stone to bear without sinking away some distant day and bringing the whole heap down. I thought of Raphael, heard him damn the plan to go ahead, his words: We're not building a warehouse here. We're building hope and

186

faith and charity. The burden should flow from an imagined center, each stone weighed, shaped, brought to balance toward the center, all the stones pulling their weight, leaning in on each other, their gravity flowing like water into the earth even as they rise and converge to the mystical point.

I shifted uneasily, knocking my shoe against a pew. The sound leaped off the wood and reverberated through the nave. To my left the nuns were still there, and the woman in the shawl was glaring at me as if everything, everything was my fault.

She rose and made her way toward the side aisle. I saw the pain and cold in her bones as she genuflected, turned and hobbled away. Rosina? Someone like her. I wanted to raise my hand, whisper to her, but was paralyzed when she stopped, looked at me one last time, and shook her head no. Too bad, too bad, her eyes said, everything is too incomprehensibly bad. Above the altar the emaciated Christ hovered, his arms spread like shorn wings. He looked down at the altar with his changeless grief, his eyes sad, apologetic, his face bearded but his features delicate as a girl's.

Yes, He was for them, one of them, the women who streamed out the door at the end of Mass, the men covering their frailty in the formality of the dark suits they wore, the boy resembling Beatrice who lurked with intent. This place was for women especially – the nuns staring in silence at him, the one weeping in her hands, the one hiding under her shawl: Mothers, midwives, teachers of ABC's, scrubbers of pots and pans and floors, harvesters of turnips and cabbages, bakers of bread, and waitresses all.

God was love, and they deserved all his love. Mamma, Sandy, and Kate, and why not Maggie too?

I discovered my hands in my pockets, my right hand fondling the slip of paper with Maggie's phone number and address. Where was Maggie now? There – on the altar before my eyes, her waitress dress white as the altar stones. She lifted her head and offered a weak smile. With one hand she slipped her hairnet off, and then her hair, thick and black, fell over her shoulders and face. She smiled as she kicked one shoe off and then the next, and in a moment her dress fell to her knees, her naked form cold against the stone. She reclined on the top altar step and signaled for me to come to her, my heart beating wildly as I approached, the Christ looming larger and larger on his cross above us both.

I stopped when I was next to her. He looked down at me with sad longing eyes, then drew his arms in from the crosspiece and silently slid off the cross. The stones were cold on his bare feet, and he had long lovely hair. He gave me a smile that made me blush and turn away, and without saying a word lay down in Maggie's open arms.

20. *"There's something about that look in his eye. If God's there, I think you can see Him in the way a man looks at you. Don't you think, Glo?"*

In bed that night I curled my leg over Sandy's thigh and she suddenly opened up. As we made love in the dark I closed my eyes and saw Maggie's face. "God," she said as she turned away and pulled the blanket under her chin, "I can't seem to get enough. It was unreal."

I spent the next day in the library lost in books about cathedrals, scanning every index for a sign of Raphael or Pierre Vente's names. Nothing in any of the books, so many of them big and beautiful, full of color plates and scholarly discourses on the symbolic significance of details. I took incoherent notes, not knowing what use they would have, and when I looked up it was already past five. "God," I said to myself, "is this Maggie's day off work, or did she say Mondays?" I looked again at the clock. What the hell was I thinking? I'm a married man.

I called Sandy at work. Why did I always call when the place was packed? She had people waiting at four tables for their food and they always blamed her. The new cook was sloppy and slow, and no, she wouldn't be home until after ten tonight. I told her I wanted to go wild again tonight as soon as she got home, that I would pick up a bottle of champagne. But she cut me short. Yes, she was working late. Why not? "And I forgot to tell you that your mother called," she said. "She wants you to call back. If you're looking for something to do on a Friday night, why don't you go see her?"

I got there about eight and knocked. Inside I heard a shuffle of steps as if someone were listening next to the door. I knocked again and the door opened only a crack. "Praise Jesus," I heard a voice say. "He's come home again."

Edna Conklin, wearing a maroon houserobe that stopped just short of her ankles, opened the door. She pulled the sash of her robe tight, her breasts, big and firm, an obstacle I sidled past.

"I thought you were a robber," she said, "but you're just a dear."

The heap of curlers on her head reminded me of a mattress run over on a highway, but I couldn't help noticing that her face, though pale, was pretty indeed.

"What are you doing here?" I asked.

As she put her hands on her hips I again noticed her very small waist.

"Where's my mom?"

"Oh she's out. I'm here taking care of things."

"What's Mamma doing?"

"Buying a new coat."

She had bought a new coat less than a year ago.

"She saw this new coat. On sale downtown. I gave her a little talking to and she made up her mind to get it after all." Edna gave me a big tolerant smile. "I bet you'll both be happy with it."

"And where's my dad?"

"Oh, he's with her."

"What do you mean with her?"

"Oh the Lord. The Lord can do wonderful things. You don't have to worry about his leg. He's been getting up and around on it since I came over to help. He's been standing up by himself and wanting to try it out."

"So he went out with my mom?"

"I told him I thought it was okay."

"But the sidewalks are slippery."

"You mean, what if he falls?"

"That's exactly what I mean."

She smiled, her teeth perfect and white, gold-filled in back. "If he falls, he'll pull himself up by the bootstraps again. Don't you see? We pray for him day and night. The Lord says we've got nothing to worry about."

190

I walked past her as if I owned the place, searched the living room and then poked my head into the bedroom as if someone might be hiding there. While Edna watched from the door, I sat in Papa's chair and loosened my shoes.

She walked over and sat across from me. "You gonna wait here for them?"

"No," I said with a smile as much like hers as I could manage. "I have come here to turn back the invading barbarian hoards – the Vandals and Goths."

"Oh my," she said as her face shrank in perplexity. "Do you think the Negroes are moving in?"

"I saw one," I said big-eyed. "Walking down the street just a while ago. So now I'm here to say hi to my folks."

"You never know," she said as her smile returned. "But I feel safe and secure from all alarm now that you're here. And your mom has been so happy these past few days. Did you know there's a special sale on coats?"

"Really? Sale? Do you know the Italian word for salt?"

"Oh dear me, no."

"When they came here off the boats from Italy they couldn't believe how much salt there was in the stores."

"I didn't know that," Edna said.

"Yes, but they learned. The early bird gets the worm, and a penny saved is a penny earned."

"Yes, and your mother's such a dear. She's been saving up all her life, one penny at a time. That's her little secret, you know." Edna let her fingers drop three invisible pennies into an invisible piggy bank in her lap, then lifted her eyes. "You know," she said, "when I think of your mother's new coat I think of Joseph."

"Joseph?"

"His coat of many colors."

"Ah yes, why didn't I think of that?"

"Don't you think it was really nice that our Lord let the father of the little baby Jesus have a coat like that?"

Christmas was only a month away. Was there something really pretty, fine, well-made in Danko's store, something Sandy would rave about? "I have no idea what I'm going to get my dad for Christmas this year. Got any ideas?"

"Oh yes," she said, lifting her eyes again. "You should give him love. That's all he really wants. That's all the Lord really wants us to do to be saved."

"Saved?"

She looked at me with pitying eyes that suddenly seemed bottomlessly blue. "You aren't saved, are you?"

"No," I growled.

"Do you want to be saved? Do you want to kneel with me and ask Jesus to come into your life? I will, you know. All you have to do is say yes."

She was saved by the pounding of feet on the mat outside the door.

"Edna, Edna," Mamma called from outside. "Would you open the door? My arms are full."

I stood behind Edna while she opened the door for Mamma, loaded down with a big package and bag of groceries. Papa, standing as tall as I had seen him in days, looked past her with a face full of his ordinary contempt. While Mamma lumbered in and put her things down, he stood motionless staring straight in. For a moment I thought he was looking at me, but when he became aware of my presence he jerked his eyes to attention. I had caught him staring at Edna Conklin, her smile again wide as she stood next to Papa's chair.

Mamma smiled. "Like you say, Edna, praise Jesus. I got a nice surprise."

"Did you eat?" Mamma asked me as she and Edna were putting the groceries away.

"Yes."

"When?"

"A while ago."

"Did you eat good? Do you want a glass of milk?"

"Milk?" She knew I didn't drink milk. "Why don't we put a little coffee on?"

"Oh, we don't drink coffee any more, except in the morning for your papa and maybe one more time after that."

"What do you mean we don't drink coffee any more?"

"Because it keeps you awake all night," Mamma said, her voice defiant. "It's no good for you."

Edna, the big smile fixed on her face, appeared before me in the living room, glass of milk in hand. I let her stand until she tired and put the milk down.

"She's one of them," Papa said after Edna left the room.

"What do you mean?"

"She's one of them. Your mother. Now she's going to their church." He gave me a shrug of helplessness and turned away.

One of them! She goes to their church! Edna's church? I could imagine only endless fields swept by drifting snow, the prairie broken here and there by white farmhouses, square and plain, sad eyes inside looking out blankly from bigbrowed windows at cars hopelessly speeding by. And every five miles down the road ahead a small squarish white building with a steeple on top.

"What kind of church is it?"

He shrugged. "How do I know? Protestant."

"Protestant?" The word was big, misshapen, full of sharp edges. "What kind of Protestant?"

"How do I know? The kind that says praise Jesus all the time, halleluiah, praise the Lord and all that."

"But what's the name of the church?"

"They don't have a real church. They got a place that used to be a movie house – down near Fifth. They call it a church. A pentacostly church. That's what they call themselves."

I saw once more the grief on Mamma's face, she too one of the women in St. Paul's, all alone in that big place, beads hanging from her fingers, her face in her hands. She turned and pleaded for help, and I turned away from her. Then she stood and walked out of the place without throwing even a backward glance at St. Paul's, its stones grey in the late afternoon light, its towers those of a castle standing solid against the traffic all around. Outside Edna Conklin took her by the hand, led her to a waiting cab, and drove her to the movie theater on Fifth, a destitute house of vanity brought to its knees, its carpets, woodwork, and windows scrubbed inside and out, converted to Christ. Saved.

"It's a shame to waste your milk," Mamma said. "Drink it down. It's so good for you." She got in my way. "Here. How do you like my new coat?" She stood before me holding her head high, chest thrust out. Then slowly she turned to model the coat, a long green woolen with a white fur collar.

"Gloria, it's all you," Edna said.

My father turned away. "Seventy-four dollars, plus tax."

"No tax on clothes," Mamma corrected him, "and I saved the money myself."

"A penny saved is a penny earned," Edna chimed.

"I like it, Mamma. I like it a lot. On sale?"

"On sale, yes. It was a big sale."

"And the coat isn't the only thing your mother found," Edna said. "Is it, Sister Glo?"

"Oh no. I've found something much more rich and beautiful, Sal. You won't believe it, Sal, but I'm saved."

I shriveled the way spiders do when touched by a pointed thing.

"Praise Jesus."

My father stared at the floor.

"It was Tuesday night. Sister Edna here took me to her church and the priest there asked me to get on my knees. Then Jesus my Lord and Savior came into my life." She began buttoning the coat and put the collar up.

"Never before has she felt such a love of Christ come into her," Edna said to Papa. "It was about eight-thirty when He entered her life."

"So you want to go to hell," Papa said, still staring at the floor. "If you want to go to hell, it's your business. Just leave me out of it."

"No one asked you to come to church. I'm not going to force you, are we, Edna?"

"Oh no. The Lord wants your free will."

"I don't force you," Mamma said. "I just pray. The Lord knows your heart – every secret of yours." She unbuttoned her coat and took it off. "And the Lord knows every secret in your heart too, Sal." She handed the coat to Edna, who turned toward the front closet. Then together they went to the kitchen, where they fell to whispering.

"It's that goddamned rosary," my father said. "That's what got her going on this new thing of hers. She cried the whole goddamned night when the priest called and accused Bea of stealing that goddamned thing. Can you believe any more what's going on?"

"We have to be patient, Dad. She'll come to her senses again."

"Come to her senses? Does it look like she's come to her senses yet? The priest calls. Your mother goes over to the church to find out, but they don't let her in. We send you, but we don't hear no word. I call the priest to come over here because of my leg, but he says she's got to go there. Edna takes her to that Jesus show of hers, and now she won't go to the priest. And we got a mess."

Edna's rear end appeared in the kitchen doorway as she bent down to sweep a pile of debris into a dustpan. She stood as she turned toward us, broom in hand, and smiled equally at both of us.

"What's with her?" I whispered.

"You mean her?"

"She's causing a lot of trouble around here."

"She's not so bad – it's the rosary. Edna cleans up, does a few things."

"But don't you think she's a bad influence?"

"Got me. I don't know what she is," Papa said with a bewildered shake of his head. "She's one of them bitches, I think."

"There's no such thing as a witch, Papa."

"I said bitch. Bitch is what I said."

"Do you think Mamma believes everything Edna says?"

"Bah! I hope you're right. Maybe she'll get over it. As soon as they get the rosary mess cleared up. As soon as a priest gets hold of her. Your mother's no damn fool. She's not going to throw her soul into hell after all these years going to church. No priest will let her do that, and I don't blame them."

I had never heard my father care so much about souls. He hadn't been to church in years, yet had never been out of The Church. "But still, don't you think we should keep an eye on Edna?"

"You looked in the cupboards?"

"No."

"You look in there. Your mother – you know she ain't what she used to be. I don't know what's wrong any more. She don't work like she did. She's tired all the time. You look in there. Edna's got all the dishes piled up nice. This house is okay now for a change."

"So Edna really helps out."

"You betcha. You look here at my leg."

He pulled his pantleg up and showed me a clean square patch of gauze. "She changes it every four hours – used to be a nurse aide."

"But still I think we should keep Mamma away from her."

"How we going to do that?"

"Tell her. Tell her not to come over so much. You said she was a bitch."

"How we going to do that? She's not that much of a bitch. She's got a right."

"What right?"

"I can put up with it," he said. "Her ex-husband was a dirty bum and she needs a place. So we make a little deal with her."

"What do you mean a deal?"

"She's got your room."

Edna had made little cakes and brought them out on a plate.

"Your milk's getting warm," Mamma warned again. "You don't want to waste food. It's a sin to waste."

"We should say a word of grace," Edna cautioned before anyone got a chance to lift a fork.

"Gloria, get me a glass of wine. There's a half-gallon next to the back door. This goddamned leg of mine, all swollen up again. Hurts like hell since I went out with it."

"You shouldn't drink so much wine," Mamma said as she turned to go. "I get tired of running up and down the steps all the time."

We held ourselves back from the cakes until he had his glass of wine, but it was to Edna we all looked for permission to begin. "Every head bowed, and every eye closed," she said, lifting her hands over her head. She stretched out a closed-eyed silence until we obeyed. "Praise the Lord. We come to you, sweet Jesus, again once more as we come closer to the month you let your only begotten Son be born on that Christmas Day in a manger only about a month away now. And we ask you, sweet Jesus, to consecrate this food to the use of our bodies and for it to fulfill us our physical needs and You feed our soul. For He who dwells in the secret place of the Most High shall abide under the shadow of the Almighty. I will say of the Lord, He is my refuge and my fortress, my Master and King.

Therefore, I pray, forgive us our daily sins, lead us not into Satan's snares, and bless these cakes in sweet Jesus' name, Amen."

We opened our eyes to my father, his jaws working on a mouthful of cake. Mamma gave him an evil eye. "You should wait for us. Edna wasn't done with her prayer."

"This wine tastes like a horse's ass," he said as he coughed up some phlegm. "You don't eat cake and drink wine. I should've learned that from your Nonno, Sal."

"You should say I'm sorry to Edna, Paul."

I had seen him lift his leg and fart through his lips when he was a little drunk, if there was someone special in the house.

"I'm sorry, Edna."

Edna, cold-shouldering him as he ate, turned to face him after Mamma spoke. "The Savior has heard your words, and He loves you a whole lot." She beamed as she began gathering napkins on the coffee table in front of me, then turned suddenly my way. "For God so loved the world that He gave his only begotten Son that whoso liveth shall not perish but live happily ever after."

I let her smile. Then a devilish whim came over me. "Why was God so worldly?" I asked with the most innocent face I could put on. "Why should he so love the world, this vale of tears?"

Edna took my hand. "God was no worldly man. His kingdom was in heaven."

I took my hand back. "But why did he so love the world that he gave his only begotten son?"

She had to stop to think. "That wasn't our world He loved."

"Who in the hell's world was it then?" Papa wondered out loud.

"It was the other world," Edna said, a little unsure of herself.

"You mean heaven?" Papa offered.

"Heaven."

"Oh," I said, admitting defeat.

"God loves his heavenly mansion," she instructed me. "He so loved it he gave his only begotten son to the world."

"But," I protested in my gentlest voice, "how do you think God went about begetting a son?"

"The Virgin Mary," Mamma said. "She's the Holy Mother of God, Sal."

I scratched my head conspicuously. "If God is the King of heaven, then Mary is the Queen?"

"Sure, Sal, sure."

"But if she's God's queen, how can she also be the mother of God?"

Edna shook her finger at Mamma. "I tried to tell you, Glo, about that Virgin Mary of yours. You put too much belief in her."

I turned to Edna. "But if she didn't do it, who did? I can't see God having a baby. Can't imagine it."

Edna gave a sad long smile. "You see, it was a spiritual birth."

"You mean it just took place in God's head?"

"No, no, no," Papa broke in. "She was a virgin. That's what made it what it was."

"The Immaculate Conception," Mamma said.

"No," Edna said. "She was a virgin but that wasn't the important thing, because God didn't actually – if you know what I mean. He just thought it and Jesus was born."

"That's what I think," Papa said. "I think Edna's right."

Mamma gave a weary sigh. "I don't know. I'm always tired these days. There's some things I just don't understand. And I wish," she said turning to me, "I wish you'd drink your milk before it gets too warm."

"I think he doesn't really believe in God," Edna said as she opened into her most tolerant smile.

"Oh Sal believes in God. You believe in God, don't you Sal?"

I took a long drink from the glass of milk. It was warm and sent a wave of nausea through me, but I managed to lick my lips clean like a cat. "Not to believe in God would be like believing that Beatrice stole a rosary from a bunch of old priests."

Mamma liked my words, but Edna gave me a crooked stare. "Then do you believe in God?" she asked, her eyes narrowing.

"Let me put it another way," I said as I leaned in closer to keep her from missing a word. "Believing in God is like believing in little green men from Mars."

198

"God will not be mocked," Edna proclaimed. "Answer me yes or no."

"Do you believe in little green men from Mars?"

Edna paused long enough to wonder. "I don't know."

"Answer me yes or no."

"I just know," Mamma broke in, "that Beatrice would never steal."

I lowered my eyes and lied. "I also believe she didn't steal the rosary."

"See, I told you he believes," Mamma said, turning to Edna. "I'm not bragging, but my kids are good kids."

I left Edna in the kitchen with Mamma and found myself standing outside of my old room, a light under the door. I looked in and saw the same old place – the old oak dresser in the corner, the top of its mirror still cracked; the roundbacked chair next to the bed, its black paint streaked and dull; the wallpaper, the faded flower print, Mamma's choice two decades ago, and the wood floors still covered by three small rugs.

And the bed – a steel-poster sagging in the center, the very place I had dreamed all my dreams, my childhood horse, airplane and raft, my teenage backseat of some forgotten friend's Chevy or Ford. I saw myself there asleep, still a boy, still dreaming, hearing my voices. I had an impulse to enter the room, close the door behind me, and lie down in my own bed again.

"But maybe he really believes," I heard Edna say to Mamma in the other room. "There's something about that look in his eye. If God's there, I think you can see Him in the way a man looks at you. Don't you think, Glo?"

21. *"That goddamned Waldman," I muttered through my teeth. "Over my dead body will he get away with it."*

Papa didn't chase me down as I was preparing to leave. He was content to let me have it from his chair.

"Think a little about us – your mother, Sal, maybe now and then, all she did for you, how she's tired all the time. It's a damn good thing somebody's here. At least Edna knows how to lift a finger now and then."

And I did not.

"And sometimes I think you forget we got Italian blood. We made America what it is. Don't you forget that."

"And Sal," Mamma said, standing on her tiptoes to make herself heard, "don't forget it was an Italian who discovered America."

The next morning I awoke to the presence of a newspaper next to me and the aroma of coffee in the room. Sandy had left a little note next to the coffee cup. "Today will be your lucky day, and maybe tonight I'll get lucky too. Should we make it a date?"

I spent too much time reading the newspaper. Every day the same old bad news from Cambodia, so many dead, thousands missing, whole pages missing too, the words there lost chips from bullet-riddled walls. Generalissimo Franco was on his deathbed in Spain, but there was no photograph of anything significant, no clear picture of stout Latin American colonels reviewing their marching bands, Franco's smirk alive on their faces. What did empty doorways and beds, barrios, slums, huts, children squatting in dust, licking fingers, their faces wide-eyed for sisters, fathers, brothers disappeared, matter to men in command? The price of gas was up another three unholy cents, and there was not much Hope visible anywhere, for this week he was not playing golf with a president. And yes, help was wanted everywhere: Did I want to sell vacuum cleaners door-to-door or coupons by phone, and there was one opening at the car wash on the corner of Madison and Third.

I walked by the old store and found the door unlocked but nobody home. In back everything was covered with the snow that had fallen a few days before. No footprints anywhere on the sparkling blanket covering the yard, and only near the back fence where the fig tree once stood did any stubble or stalk show through. The snow made a thick soft cap over the eaves of the shack, had drifted in a swirl around the crate on which Guido so often sat.

I resented Bruno being across the street in Kate's place. I wanted him here, with me in Guido's old store. What drew me to him? His unpremeditated commitment to an art so irrelevant to politics, economics and guerrilla activities, the commitment of a child gazing with thoughtless intensity at apes in a zoo. Reading the newspapers made my gut twist and turn, but Bruno and I were alike: We both wanted to find a habitable hiding place away from a world growing too ugly for words. Bruno, we're brothers, I whispered as I closed the door and walked down the street.

Slugging through dirty snow the cars seemed tired, as if they had lost their way. To my right three blacks, sharing a bottle one of them concealed in his coat, stood together outside the laundromat. I had seen them wander by one-by-one before, but never together like this in our neighborhood. Sporting a wide-brimmed hat, another one across the street stood next to a fire hydrant. He seemed to be enjoying his smoke, waiting for something to happen on the street.

Then, in front of Danko's place, just to the left of his door, a grey figure in a dirty woolen coat faltered as he took a step toward the curb. Suddenly he collapsed like an empty burlap sack. Another old man – this one short, stoop-shouldered and outfitted in a black fedora and topcoat – backed out of Danko's shop, his arm supported by a younger, taller man in a dark business suit. The old man in the fedora paused for a closer look at the heap on the ground. Backing off, he put his shoe under the fallen man's arm, lifted the arm off the sidewalk with his foot, and let it fall again. Then he and his assistant hurried into the back seat of a blue sedan parked at the curb, and in a moment the sedan turned the corner and was gone.

Danko appeared at his door, lifting an arm to wave at the blue sedan, and saw the fallen man. He bent down to him, then disappeared inside his shop. I heard a shout from across the street and saw a form darting between two cars.

"Here, quick!" Kate shouted, "give me your jacket!"

The fallen man was still breathing, his fist tight around the throat of an empty bottle of wine.

"He's just drunk," I said as I helped Kate slip my jacket under his head.

"How do you know he's just drunk? How do you know he hasn't had a heart attack?"

Danko looked down on us both. "Charlie," he said. "He's never been this bad before. I already called an ambulance."

By the time the ambulance arrived, the three men sharing the bottle at the other end of the block had disappeared. Kate's brother Dylan, in a denim jacket and jeans, joined the group gathered to watch. The black leaning against the signpost had come close. He stood looking down, his face full of contempt, asking us why we were making such a fuss. In the grey apartments above the stores I saw a few parted curtains, but I couldn't make out the face of any one person watching the scene below.

I followed Danko in and waited while he answered the phone in back. The shop seemed cluttered but clean. A few big items were gone – a tall cupboard that had stood for years against the back wall, a curved glass case full of china figurines, and an elegant walnut secretary, the first thing to catch the eye of anyone entering the shop.

My wallet was safe, a lump in my back pocket, and so was my loose change. Was this Friday or Saturday? My heart skipped a beat as my fingers found the slip of paper with Maggie's address on it.

I wandered to the table on which Danko had arranged the figurines from the curved glass case. The figurines were peasant folk, German or Swiss, all of them smiling through painted faces. I lifted one and saw the price: Twenty-seven dollars.

Other nice things – an old mirror, its frame solid oak, and a sewing case big enough to be a baby's crib. On a table a pile of china plates, blue Oriental scenes all around. A wall clock, hand-carved, showing twelve minutes after ten. Sandy would love the clock.

Danko reappeared. "What's with Charlie?" I asked.

"Charlie." Danko sighed, the name sliding down, not able to get up. "He's been coming here for years. The first time – way back I don't remember when – he said he'd sweep my floor for a dime. So I let him sweep the floor."

"For a dime?"

Danko gave me a cynical look. "Charlie did a lousy job. He pushed the broom up and down two, maybe three times. Then he took his hat off and stood at the front door with the broom in his hand. 'You done already?' I ask him. 'You got a ten-cent sweep,' he says back to me."

"You gave him his dime?"

"I give him a dollar and a month later there he is again. He says he'll sweep – for a dollar this time. I want to kick the bum out, but he looks lousy, tired, so I give him the broom."

"And he gave you a helluva sweep?"

"He gives me another lousy sweep. I ask him what's wrong with corners. 'What do you expect?' he says, 'This ain't my floor.'"

"So you kicked him out?"

"No, I want to, but the wife – you know that little stove in back – she had some soup, and the next thing I see is Charlie saying the soup, Missus, is so good."

Danko moved over to a carved Victorian chair upholstered in a thick maroon, and motioned for me to sit in the matching loveseat across from him. He leaned forward as he talked.

"And then Charlie, he falls for my wife. He didn't have nobody, nothing. So he goes away two, three weeks, then comes nosing like a dog. I hand him a broom and the wife fixes him sandwiches and soup. He sweeps around a little here and there, then goes in back with her. For her he does little things – wipes the table off, the dishes, whatever she wants."

Danko gave out a big laugh. "Then he's gone again – two, three weeks, and just as you say I'm rid of him now, there he is at the window looking in. Now maybe this time, you say, he's going to sweep the floor right."

The old wall clock – Sandra's clock – struck three times. The smaller one just to its left showed fifteen minutes after six.

"Charlie," Danko went on, "he got better at sweeping, but he always missed one spot. Always one corner with a little mess. You know, the more he hung around with the Missus, the smaller the corner got. But he always left a little mess."

"Then what happened?"

"She had to go to the hospital. You remember the cancer, don't you? And Charlie went away until two years ago. When he came back he looked real bad, real bad. Never said nothing to nobody, just sat in a chair. I couldn't get him to sweep, do anything. So I just give him a couple bucks and he's gone – a day or two, a week, a month – I never know how long. And all the time the drinking gets worse."

"And then this happened – today."

Danko stood up. "Everything happens today. When I don't want to sell something too nice I jack the price up pretty good."

The chair and loveseat would be better than the clock. Sandra would come home one day and be totally surprised. "What are you asking?"

"Two hundred. One-fifty for you. Be cheaper if you bought everything. Then I say goodbye to everything just once, and go."

"I can't right away."

"Sal," Danko began with some reluctance in his voice, "you still thinking about this place? I got an offer today."

My heart sank.

"And I was wondering – you still interested?"

I turned away from him, ashamed. "You know what my problem is."

"I know you ain't got much money now. But maybe you can get help from the family. You know – down payment. Your father maybe, or an uncle. You got any rich uncles who are crooks?"

Only one, an insurance agent who lived on the north side. He came to weddings and funerals, eyes following him wherever he went.

"And then," Danko went on, his eyes still apologetic, "I have to wonder about another thing."

"What's that?"

"I mean, you really want to get into this line of work?"

I spoke before I was sure of myself. "It would be very nice."

"But you never done it."

Raphael's portrait, the one in our living room, would end up in a store like this. People would stop to stare, wonder who he was.

"I like nice old things."

"You got to know a lot about antiques to make a go of it."

I shrugged.

"So how you gonna make a go of it?"

I had an urge to defend myself, but the words wouldn't come. Did I have seventy-five cents in my pocket today?

"I thought maybe you want to start coming here so I could show you some things."

"I've had an offer to learn the properties of wood – from a man named Rochelle. A cabinet-maker not far from here."

"Rochelle? Wonderful! He knows everything. He does what I can't do myself." Danko leaned away from me. "I got to be in Florida in nine months. You got to get a down payment pretty soon."

"I'll try."

"And if you don't, Sal, I have to sell. You understand my situation?"

"Who's my competition?"

"The one who was just here."

Charlie lying in a heap on the sidewalk outside.

"The old man in the coat. With the hat. You see him go out?"

"Yes. And what, if I may ask, was his name?"

"Some name – he gave me a card." Danko pulled a business card from his shirt pocket. "Southwest General Corporation. That's who he is, I guess."

Waldman. How disillusioning to see him in the actual flesh, merely a man, shrunken, too old to walk on concrete without someone holding onto his arm. But still hanging on, swinging another little deal. Why didn't Waldman leave us alone?

Because he was bored in his mansion on The Hill. Because he was a bachelor.

Like God in his heaven when all was wrong with the world.

Rochelle was not surprised to see me enter his shop. "Where you been?" he asked like a father who had waited up late for his son.

I gave him a fake broad smile. "Just out."

He returned to sanding the edge of a cabinet door. "I thought you wanted to learn something. I thought you were going to come back right away. You got a job?"

"No job. I still want to learn about wood."

"How do I know you're not going to fool around, waste your time?"

"Where's the new boy you hired?"

"He's going to leave."

"For a better job?"

"A different job."

"Better pay?"

"That's right."

I ran my hand over the sanded edge, and it slid easily over the front of the cabinet door. The grain of the wood was clear and smooth, the air fragrant with the sawdust that had drifted down on everything. "It's nice," I said.

"I do quality work."

I ran my hand over the other side of the cabinet door.

"Needs a little shaving, if you know what I mean. I gotta do this now."

He threw himself into his work again as I wandered the shop. Next to the windows he had lined up his power tools – four different saws, a drill press, and the sanding machines. Here and there in the room piles of lumber smooth on both sides, fine to the touch. And right in the center a big wooden box full of scraps. It was there I stopped longest to rummage and touch.

I called across to him. "What do you do when this box gets full?"

"We use it."

To my left in a corner stood a small parlor stove.

"Different people come from time to time – people who carve, make small things, fool with wood in their basements. I give the scraps to them, whatever they want. And I burn a little too."

I picked up a dark red board and instinctively put my nose to it. It smelled pungent and sweet. "What's this?"

He had to look twice from where he was bent over his cabinet door. "That's not a domestic wood. That's French cherrywood."

"All the way from France?"

"Lots of good wood in that box."

"Where'd you get French cherrywood?"

"France."

I rummaged some more, tried a few more pieces with my nose. Then I became aware of Rochelle, wiping his hands on his apron, standing over me.

"The cherry," he began, "it's for a beautiful thing. Some man – lots of money – he came in here, told me he wanted a special thing. His daughter was getting married and he wanted a bed. He had a sketch, a beautiful thing. Then a list of woods. Twenty-two kinds of wood on the list, fifteen from overseas. You ever hear of a Lydian apple tree? I saved a little piece of that. Red elm, dogwood, rosewoods, all kinds of nut trees – pecan, chestnut, hickory, butternut. And wood from a lemon tree. Special instructions for that. Had to be cut from a tree in full flower. That's what his note said and that's what I had to find. It took five months."

"A wedding present?"

Rochelle smiled. "And the headboard had to have two pieces of yew. From the English cemeteries. So when it was done I could smell lemon in the room, and when I put the oil on all the colors came out."

He savored the memory of the bed before speaking again. "So you want a job?" He took my arm. "Come in back."

Over his workbench he still had his three unfinished violins. How did he make wood curve the way it did, and how did he get the grain on the backs of the violin to match?

"Are you on strike?" he asked.

"I don't have a job."

"You know I don't mean that. I mean are you on strike in your own way?"

"Yes, usually."

"Either you're on strike or you're not."

"You tell me."

"You're on strike if you know what's pissing you off. Is someone screwing you?"

Waldman.

"How are things at home – your family life, your wife?"

"Generally okay."

"Not good enough."

"My father's always after me to get a job. He wants me to work the way he did – like a dog."

"And your mother?"

"You know – how mothers are when they love their kids. She's always there for me."

"And your wife?"

"Generally okay. There's nothing wrong with her."

"Not good enough. You fooling around with somebody else?"

"No."

"You really want to learn about wood?"

I could see it. I would spend mornings saving old chairs and tables from certain doom. Across the window in letters not too big or small I would paint "SALVATORE," my own name, and a few would understand. In summer Danko would return to his old place, smile, approve of how I was carrying on, forgive me for not naming the shop after him. And in the afternoons, when I had moments to spare, I would piece together a bed for Sandy made from a hundred and twenty-two different kinds of wood.

"Yes."

"My boy's leaving in another week. I pay minimum wage. See you Monday after next. Eight a.m."

As I stood on the street outside his door, I took another look at his place. It was not pretty to behold – a long flat warehouse made of old brick. And yet Rochelle had made a life in it.

When I became his faithful son he would will it to me someday.

Unless someone took it away from him.

"That goddamned Waldman," I muttered through my teeth. "Over my dead body will he get away with it."

22. *She threw the morning paper on the bed and blew me a kiss. "No, I'm perfectly satisfied, thank you."*

The room was cold. Sandy, curled around her pillow, was not awake to see the first streak of sun fall across the bed. My trousers were thrown carelessly over the chair. In a corner of the top drawer of my dresser, hidden under the jumble of socks and underwear, was the wad of paper with Maggie's address and phone number penciled on it.

The phone rang as I was sliding my arm around Sandy to pull myself closer to her. I recognized its voice without lifting the receiver. Sandy threw my arm off and propped herself on an elbow, her face saying oh no.

"Sal? Is that you, Sal?"

Suddenly my dream – the one that only minutes before had played itself out – returned: Mamma was walking away from St. Paul's, tears streaming down her face, and I was running home to hide. My father was part of a terrorist group. They were going to blow up some important place. When I ran home to see if he was okay, I found him sitting bent over in his chair, his eyes hollow, his face wrinkled with age. No words came as I stared at him, and then my legs, aching and limp, caved in under me.

Was that me? Who else would be in bed with my wife? "Yes, Mamma. It's me."

"Sal, we haven't heard from you in so long. You ever going to come to see us before we die of old age?"

I searched my mind. Today was Monday. Wasn't it just yesterday that I had stood at their door trying to get out, Edna blocking the way? No, no, last Friday night.

"Sal, you haven't been here in a month."

"I was there just a day ago."

"No, I mean a visit. You never stay when you come. Is your Sandy up from that bed?"

"Not yet."

"Why not?"

"It's early yet."

"Doesn't she have to work?"

"She's awake now."

"Is she going to have time to get your breakfast on?"

"Probably not."

She gave me one of those long deep sighs that lets everyone for miles around know she's given up all hope. "I don't know. I don't know about anything any more. How you two can keep going on like this."

I moved the phone away from my ear. "Like what?"

"I don't know. She works – and you do *what?*"

I play. Sandy put her head back down, and I began stroking her hair. "I work around the house."

"I don't know, I don't know any more."

"What don't you know, Mamma?"

"I don't know how you can keep on this way."

"I don't know what you mean."

"I mean you stay home and she works." Behind her my father's voice egging her on: "Ask him if he'll do something for a change."

"I'll kill a dragon, Mamma."

"Don't try to be funny, Sal. You don't even want to start a family."

We said nothing for a very long time.

"Is anything wrong?"

"What do you mean?"

"I mean, between you...with Sandy?"

"Not that I know."

She lowered her voice. "Maybe you should go to the doctor. Who knows? It might be something wrong."

The devil got the best of me. "Oh no. We do it every day – before breakfast normally."

Sandy's eyelids fluttered. She was somewhere else, nervously acting out a drama with somebody else. She looked beautiful as I gazed at her in the silence created by my mother's speechlessness, and in that moment, for no good or bad reason at all, my penis decided to rear its ugly head.

"I don't want to know about your personal life," Mamma said. "What you do is your business, not mine."

Sandy lifted her face, eyes heavy with sleep. "What is she doing calling in the middle of the night?"

"It's not night," I said. "It's morning."

"I said I don't care what you do in the morning, Sal." Her voice suddenly had new conviction in it. "I told you it's none of my business."

"Is the coffee on, Sal?" Sandy groaned.

I signaled a no with my head as Sandy, with another show of disgust, let her head fall to the pillow again. "I remember you saying it's something you would always do for me."

"And your father wants me to ask you if you got a job yet." I could hear him carrying on an angry stream of talk behind her.

"I've got an interview."

"Praise Jesus. Halleluiah, praise the Lord." She turned away from the phone and told my father the news.

"What's the job in?" she asked.

"Computers."

Sandy opened a suspicious eye and saw my penis staring at her.

"Computers." I heard the silent amazement of my father as she delivered the word to him. Computers. Now that was something worthwhile, something to be proud of.

"Do you have a chance for it?"

"There's a catch. I may need more math than I have."

"Oh Sal, don't let that stop you, Sal. Take the job if they give it to you – and then go to night school."

"How can I go to night school?"

Sandy started up. "Hey bud, I'm the one who's going back to school. Don't you forget. I'm not going to be a waitress all my life."

"You got Sandy who can help you out. And if you get really stuck, well, I got a few dollars saved up."

"Shut up," my father said in Italian.

"We'll see, we'll see. I've got to interview yet."

"Why do you lie so much to them?" Sandy, wide awake, hissed at me.

213

My little dragon was still rearing its ugly head.

"Sal, will you come over right after the interview?"

"I don't know if I'll have time. It's in the afternoon."

Papa was listening in, telling her what to say. "Where, Sal, where is the interview?"

"I don't know the exact address. I've got it on a piece of paper in my wallet. And I don't have my pants on now."

"Caught with your pants down," Sandy sneered, "by your mommy." She muffled her laughter in the pillow.

"I'll make you bread, Sal. I was going to make bread today, and if you come over I'll make bread for you."

"I don't know, Mamma. I was going to take Sandy out to dinner tonight."

"You are? How nice," Sandy said out loud. Then she moved in close to my ear. "Why don't we stay here. You can eat me instead. If you really loved me, you'd eat me right now."

"Don't be crazy, Sal. You can go out to dinner free right here in my house."

"Oh no, it wouldn't be right. You going to all that trouble again. Too much work, Mamma. You look tired enough these days."

"I'm tired, it's true, Sal. But I got Edna to help."

"The one woman I really can't stand," I whispered down to Sandy.

"Your mommy?" Sandy laughed.

"No, Edna, the one my father's hot for."

"Sal, you dickhead. You think everybody's hot for everybody."

"How's Edna, Mamma?"

"Oh, she's good, really nice. She does dishes now. She's okay. She teaches me about the Bible, Sal."

"What about the Bible?"

"About the Golden Calf."

"The Golden Calf?"

"How mankind worshipped it until Jesus came. Did you know the priests had women living with them in the churches then?"

"Better to marry than to burn?"

"What Sal? What did you say, Sal?"

"I said did she tell you about the bull that laid the golden calf?"

"No Sal, I don't think so Sal. But Sal, did you know that the women in those churches then, the ones the priests had – they weren't married, Sal. And that's why Jesus came. Did you know that?"

"Sal, it's your turn to put the coffee on," Sandy mumbled into her pillow. "I did it yesterday again."

"Hold your horses," I snapped.

"What did you say, Sal?" Mamma asked as Sandy slid her hand under my balls and gave them a gentle squeeze.

"I told Sandy not to scramble the eggs."

"You get a good breakfast, Sal, and then you'll get that job."

"You don't need to worry about me, Mom."

"Don't call me Mom. And you be sure to come over tonight. Praise Jesus, your father listens now when Edna tells about the Bible, Sal, and today I'm going to make bread just for you. You be sure to come, Sal."

After she hung up Sandy did not take her hand away. On the street below a big truck groaned as it started up in low gear. Sandy looked up at me with a wry smile "Your balls are hard, like little olive pits."

As her hand warmed, I felt a yeasty swell.

"After you get the coffee, Sal."

"Yes, then what?"

"I want you to hop back in here before I go to work."

"What brings this sudden surge of passion on?"

She took her hand away and spoke to the ceiling. "Your Mom, I think, and God knows what else. And I'm thinking of quitting my job and going back to school."

She pulled me down and within a half-hour left me limp on the bed.

"Do you want your coffee now?" I asked.

She threw the morning paper on the bed and blew me a kiss. "No, I'm perfectly satisfied, thank you."

23. *I would have to make it up to her, have to make something up to everybody.*

Franco was still breathing, and Kissinger was still calling shots everywhere in the world. Papa, fighting off the Monday morning blues that inevitably set in after the Sunday NFL games, had a Redskins-Vikings game coming his way on Monday night TV. And I really had a job, with a week ahead of me with nothing to do. Waldman. Why not go after my man?

As I rummaged in my dresser for a pair of clean socks, my fingers found the little wad with Maggie's address and phone number on it.

Maggie. Pretty waitress in white. Why not a little chat to start the day right?

My dragon began rearing his ugly head again. Why? Didn't he ever get enough? Wasn't Sandy almost too much just an hour ago? Why then this new swelling triggered by a frayed wad of paper with a few pencil marks on it? My penis was beyond me – had a mind of its own, and no mind at all. What was its connection to me, my morals and thoughts? Hidden away, stuffed inside my pants in a damp nest full of ambiguous odors, we shared a common base no more than an inch and a half in diameter. Attached to me in this tenuous way he lurked out of sight, most of the time curled up like an old sleeping cat, only now and then allowed out into the light of day over some toilet or urinal, and then to perform work unrelated to his real interests in life. His real interests in life: A while ago Sandy, now Maggie, and later today who knows, some new face and form on the street. Different and all the same, his nose, or eye, or whatever it was that he groped with in the dark, always zeroing in on the one most momentarily beautiful.

I showered, brushed my teeth and hair, my dragon standing straighter as I put a dash of deodorant under my arms.

Finally, I pulled my trousers up and wrestled it back into its nest. Now stay put, I said out loud, you damned ignorant fool.

At the corner of Franklin and Fifth my fingers found the wad of paper again. Maggie lived two blocks away, and there was a telephone in the laundromat across the street.

We could talk, get to know each other, be friends. Besides, I had promised her a call. Why not?

Because my motive wasn't pure. Because my penis was swollen again at the thought of her. I should retreat, go back to Bruno's, talk to him, or hole myself up in a cozy corner of the library.

Maggie. I had a headache, needed caffeine. Why not a little chat over a cup of coffee with her? Because I was a married man, and a married penis was not allowed to swell in the presence of a woman who was not the wife. No little chats or cups of coffee with anyone else who caused a swell. Dammit! Why not?

I crossed the street to the laundromat, my fingers trembling as I dialed.

"Hello?" she said, suppressing a yawn.

"This is Dirk – from Darby's. You remember me? I'm in the neighborhood."

"Oh," she said. "Where you been? You said you'd call."

"Do you want to talk – like we said?"

"Oh Dirk, I'm a mess right now."

"I could give you a little while to freshen up."

"Okay, but I work at noon, and you can't come over too soon."

"Sure, sure. But do me a little favor, okay? Would you put a little coffee on? I'm dying for a cup."

"I'm trying to think. Are you the one who likes it black?"

I found a drugstore with a magazine rack. Cars, boats, crossword puzzles, wrestling, *Playboy*, *Writer's Digest*, *National Inquirer*. *Cosmopolitan* and *Vogue*. Unreal faces and forms, contemptuous smiles. Sandy? Yes and no. Maggie? No.

I dawdled until the owner finally asked if I could be helped. Maggie's time was up. "Just looking," I said as I backed toward the door.

Dirk. I rather liked the American sound of the name.

Maggie's place was an upstairs flat, a lonely house, white and plain, crowded between apartment buildings made of brick. The curtain in the downstairs window parted slightly when I came up the walk. I paused at the doorbell trying to recall Maggie's face, just as a stout woman loaded down under a bagful of groceries at the bus stop across the street began looking at me. No, none of your business today. Maggie was slender, good-looking enough, even if her skin wasn't perfect. And she knew how to stand – there in her white dress with a coffee pot in her hand. Her breasts? I couldn't be sure. And did she wear white shoes? Yes, maybe white shoes. And no apron. I was sure of that.

The woman at the bus stop shifted the grocery bag into the other arm. She looked my way and we exchanged a mutual stare. I rang the bell.

"Do you want to watch TV?" Maggie asked before two minutes were up. "We could just watch a morning show."

Her dress, a cotton print, slipped down slightly to one side, and she kept hunching her shoulder to keep the dress in place.

"You have a wife, don't you?" she asked as she turned the TV on. It was an old movie with Spencer Tracy and we were in the middle of things. "Do you want to talk about it a little with me?"

I'd come empty-handed. A bottle of wine, maybe a burgundy. Me standing at her door with a flower in my hand. No, a flower wouldn't be right. And the woman across the street at the bus stop would have seen.

"Yes, I'm married, but I don't have a job."

"Is your wife fooling around at work with her boss?"

"Probably."

"I had a boyfriend like that once. He was a rat."

"She's not a rat," I objected. What would Rochelle say if he knew I was fooling around on my wife?

"Oh I see," Maggie said. "You two just weren't meant for each other." I saw now that her hair, dark brown near the roots, was too curly and thick. I didn't want to run my hands through it. "Maybe it went wrong from the start."

"I sure don't know what went wrong."

"Maybe you both just fell out of love. That happens, you know. After I found out Karl was fooling around on me, I just knew we weren't meant for each other any more."

"Isn't it hard to know?"

"Do you want some milk in your coffee? How silly of me. I almost forgot to ask."

"No thanks."

"I believe love has to be true." Maggie's voice softened when she returned with a coffee mug. "It has to be a total thing – you know, body and soul. That's the only way for me. Excuse me for asking, but do you and your wife do it?"

I took her hand, small and cold, and gave it a soft squeeze. "Usually before breakfast."

"Do you do it a lot?"

"Sometimes I think I'm oversexed."

"See, then maybe you don't love her. You just love her body, not her for who she is."

"I'm not sure I know who she is."

"See – have you tried loving her for who she is? Not her body, just her."

In the movie a tall man in a grey suit had just put a black bag of jewels in a safe, but a private eye knew the jewels were false.

"I'm very much concerned about who she is. I'm trying to figure out who I am too."

"Do you go to church?"

"Yes."

"Good," she said, as if relieved to settle something big. With my free hand I began running my fingers over the underpart of her forearm. As smooth as the finish of the cabinet door I had stroked in Rochelle's place. I would go home in a minute or two, rummage in a drawer for the finest sandpaper I could find, and sand some board or stick as smooth as it would come.

"Do you think I should leave?"

"Oh no. We're just talking, don't you think? I don't mind at all, if it's okay with you. You know what I mean?"

Her waist was very small, and I could see that her ass, small but nicely round, was firm beneath her dress. From where I sat I could see into her bedroom. Her bed, neatly made and covered in a white cotton spread, had steel posts painted dark brown.

"What's your father like?" I asked.

She looked startled, confused. "What do you mean?"

"I mean, what's the nicest present you ever got from him?"

She gave it some thought, then flashed her wrist at me. "I got this watchband about two years ago."

"Oh, that's very nice."

"You know what I think? I think you're very intelligent." She gave me her other arm to stroke.

"Why do you say that?"

"Because you want to talk, get to know who I am. A lot of men just don't want to talk."

What was I doing here? She was cute, she was nice – decent, nice enough. My dragon was aroused again, pushing with all his might against the walls of his dank underpants cell, but I wanted out.

"I'm not easy to get to know," she sighed.

"Oh yes, it's always hard. I don't think I know myself yet."

She drew closer to me. "Don't be silly. I think you're a really nice guy."

If I took the job working for Rochelle, Maggie's place would be on the way. "Do you always work the same hours?"

"I work most mornings and afternoons...weekdays. On weekends my hours are all mixed up."

"Does he give you time off for lunch?"

"We get an hour."

It would give us a half-hour, no more. That would be just right – three days a week, maybe two. No more than that. I would want to be rid of her after that.

But she would want more than that. And she would deserve more, then begin requiring it.

"Because there's a chance," I said, "for me to get a job just a few blocks from here. I thought maybe, maybe we could get together at lunchtime now and then, maybe arrange our schedules, or something like that."

"Maybe we could meet here," she said, her eyes lighting up.

It would be easy enough. All I would have to do is reach over and pull her close. She would relax under my kiss, would twist herself around, let me press down on her. In the movie the rich old woman who owned the real jewels thought the private eye was after them. Though she couldn't get out of bed, she hid a gun under her pillow, was going to surprise him with it when he walked into her room.

"That would be nice," I said.

And maybe it would be nice. I would be able to tell her about work. She would ask me to build a cabinet for her, and I would surprise her by making a very special one, a little chest for necklaces and rings, one sanded smooth, hand-carved on the top and sides, lined with cedar or some other special wood.

Then she would wait for me behind the door, grab me by the belt, and lead me to the bedroom while unbuttoning my shirt with her other hand. Downstairs the landlord, standing as tall as he could, would stare at the ceiling, strain to hear the sound of the old steel bed bouncing above. When we were done, she would lie back smiling and satisfied, and I would leave without saying a word.

"Yes, it would be nice," she said, "because we could get to know each other better that way."

She slid down to her knees. "Does anyone ever rub your feet?"

"No, not really."

"Here, then." She untied my shoes, slipped them off, and turned me so I would put my feet up on the sofa.

"Now you just put your head back," she said as she began kneading the bottoms of my feet. "Now close your eyes. What do you see?"

"Jesus," I said, "that feels really good."

No, I told myself as she began peeling off my socks, don't you dare begin unbuttoning her dress. Let her do what she wants, but don't lift a finger to do anything you'll regret.

"I just love doing this," she said as she began kneading my feet with her palms. She closed her eyes and tossed her hair away from her face, her breasts, suddenly tight against her dress, pointing their big-eyed nipples at me. "Don't you just love it too?"

Ah, yes.

And why should I care about what anyone would think? No, she wasn't a cover girl. She was a waitress simple and pure – lonely, pretty, nice, not into books, a working girl. But she was something else too. Yes, Kate was right: Working people were not just a proletarian lump. They were caring and giving and worthy and generous.

"Am I making you feel good?" Maggie asked, her eyes still closed.

"Ah, you are indeed an *artiste*."

Papa would scream: What the hell are you talking about? You think we go around loving everybody, just like that? What if I did that? What if everybody did that? You want to break your mother's heart? How would you like it if some stranger off the streets started rubbing her feet? Use your head a little bit. Here I put in half a century's worth of full eight-hour days in the factory, and some good-looking lady walks by. I see her face a few seconds and you want me to leave off what I'm doing and follow her down the street, call her some name to make her turn around? And what do I say to her? You want to see what I do? See here – I make the side part for carburators. See how nice it is, this work I do? I make three hundred a day. You impressed? So she says she wishes she had a car, wants to rub my feet, says put your head back, relax, you worked too hard all your life. I'm going to let her do that to me? Get out of here!

"Quit squirming," Maggie said. "Just relax and let me finish with you."

Finally she stood, threw her hair back again, and walked to the bathroom. I heard the faucet run, and I thought no, yes, she's washing herself. I heard the toilet flush, and when I opened my eyes again she was kneeling at my feet, a steaming towel in each hand.

"There," she said, "now you just let me put these towels on your feet and work them in a little bit. Why don't you close your eyes again?"

"And how can I ever pay you back?" I said as she was slipping my socks on again.

"Oh don't worry about that. This is free. Don't you always leave me a tip at the coffee shop?"

When I had my shoelaces tied, I slipped down on the sofa, lazy and satisfied, the television still blinking in the room.

"I know it isn't love," Maggie said as she backed away. "I know all you want is my body. That's right, isn't it? You just wanted to fuck."

The news was on. I never found out how the movie ended, and I had missed the beginning, the title, too. "Maybe you're right," I said, "I probably just wanted to fuck."

"Men," she said in resignation and defeat. "You're all alike. You're all rats!" She retreated into her bedroom, her shoes in her hand, and slammed the door.

My dragon was dead, limp, defunct in his cell. As if he did not exist, had no claim, no grip on me. I picked myself up and worried as I walked toward the door. Would she ever rat on me, make trouble? I would have to call Mamma and tell her I wasn't coming over for dinner tonight. I would prepare a fabulous meal and take Sandy to a movie afterward. I would have to make it up to her, had to make something up to everybody.

24. *I pressed the rosary tight in my hand as I hurried away from St. Paul's.*

Silence sealed the lies in.

"Tell me," Sandy said. "I don't get it. I don't see why anyone would end a movie that way."

Maggie's sad face lingered before my eyes.

"I think the tennis ball was all in his mind," she went on, "and I think he was going crazy at the end."

Yes, yes, the tennis ball was all in his mind. "But he still seemed to be enjoying the game. After a while he could even hear the tennis ball."

"It still doesn't make sense, didn't end the way a movie should. He goes to the park and takes pictures of the girl – blows the pictures up and discovers a murder's taken place. Then he finds a body but can't prove it's really there. Then those two teeny-boppers drop in on him and he drops everything."

"Just to screw them," I said.

"For nothing really – he just screws them right in the middle of things. Here he's got a murder on his hands, and what does he do? He buys a propeller, sticks it in a corner, screws the girls, and forgets the whole thing."

"The propeller's a decoration, maybe."

"That's art? I'd throw it in the trash. I think the movie was sick. I think the man who made it was sick. What's his name?"

"An Italian name – Antonioni."

"I got cold in there. Were you cold?"

"It's supposed to freeze again tonight."

I moved my pillow closer to her and put my hand on her bare leg.

"Brrr...." she said.

"Here, take a sip of my wine. It'll warm you up." I propped her head up and helped her take a sip. She leaned her head back against my chest as I pulled the covers up and tucked them in under her. Her breath always seemed fresh. "Wanna do it?"

"Didn't we do it this morning?"

"No, I think we just told my mother we did."

"No wonder it was so good. Did we leave the phone off the hook so she could hear?"

"No, don't you remember? You wanted me to hang up."

She sidled up closer. "I don't remember anything. I was still asleep."

"How did your day go?"

"Nothing to report. And you?"

"I know I've got that job with Rochelle, but I checked out a couple other leads, just in case. Got the usual runaround – fill out the application forms, wait to hear from us."

She looked up at me. "I know it must be boring, frustrating, humiliating for you."

"This one guy, he wanted somebody to take inventory for him. As soon as he heard my name I knew I'd never get the job. 'You're Italian,' he said. 'I was in Italy during the war.' He told me I would hear from him."

"What's he got against Italians?"

"You never know. Maybe because we're smart enough to surrender right away to the side that wins."

"Surrender? You'd never do anything like that."

"I surrender only to you. I am your slave, will do anything you want. Here I am – yours. Just you and me. And let's never go out again, not take a chance on the streets. Things are getting worse and worse out there. An old man was mugged just a block from the old store, and there was arson half a mile away."

"I think it's best if you stay away now and then. Or you'll get bored with me. Me? I'm just a waitress, Sal."

I lifted her chin and gave her a long Hollywood kiss. "Enough said?"

Wrapped around each other we began drifting toward sleep, my heart more full of love for her than ever before. Just before I fell asleep I lifted my head. "The propeller – that's the part I still can't figure out. It's got to connect somehow. Do you think it's got anything to do with the protest demonstrators – the ones who wanted to ban the bomb?"

"Huh? Probably more with the teeny-boppers," Sandy said without opening her eyes.

The next morning the phone screamed at me in a voice I knew by heart.

"Sal," Mamma said, "you gotta come over right away."

I went over right away.

"Look at her," she said, "look at what they've done to your little sister Bea."

Edna, not sure she could see anything wrong, leaned in close to have another look. Beatrice, her face hanging down, sobbed softly into a white handkerchief.

"Do you see that letter in her lap?" Mamma asked.

"Goddamn bastards!" said Papa.

"The letter says they could excommunicate her if she doesn't return the rosary."

"That's absurd," I said. "Nobody does that. They're just trying to scare her into taking it back."

Beatrice suddenly sat upright and turned to me. "I'm not scared. They can go fuck themselves. I didn't steal their fucking rosary. Dylan says..."

"I don't give a goddamn about what Dylan, that bum, says," Papa shot back at her. "And if I ever hear you say that word again, I'll kick your ass from here all around the room."

Edna's eyes, horrified, opened wide.

"You gotta go right now," Mamma said to me. "Your father's been too sick and I'm tired all the time. You're the oldest son, the one with a college degree. You know how to talk to them nice. So you gotta go right now to St. Paul's. Do it for me, please, Sal."

Sonia suppressed a smile when she opened the rectory door. "I suppose it's the rosary again," she said as she stepped aside to let me in.

"Hail Sonia. I don't suppose anyone's here – Father Francis, or maybe the Bishop himself in the flesh?"

"Nobody," she said.

"Can I come in?"

227

"Sure. Wait as long as you want."

She led me to the same chair in the waiting room and looked me over before disappearing through a door to the left. It was not yet ten but the eyes of the old bishops were up and about, all of them watching me from their places on the wall where some clever hand had framed and hung them for good. The books, their bindings cracked like old skin, hadn't moved since I saw them last, and a bonewhite Virgin, solid on a long oak table, kept staring at the floor. On another table across from me stood a big open Bible, no doubt the one in whose fat embrace the missing rosary once had lain.

I heard no sounds, no noise even from outside, and the snow beginning to fall was greyed by city sky. Carelessly I walked to the big old Bible, open to the Book of Hosea, and began rummaging through its pages, turning handfuls at a time. Surely a rosary could get lost in this book, fall into it and disappear, overwhelmed by the screed of words wailing like desert winds too distant and ancient to make any sense.

"Are you looking for something?" Sonia asked from somewhere behind me.

"The rosary," I said as I slowly turned.

"You won't find it here."

"You know my sister didn't steal anything."

"They think she did."

"They have no proof."

"They need no proof."

"It may not matter to my sister what they think."

"Then why should it matter to you?"

She moved closer, then stopped when we were face to face. "Am I wasting my time?" I asked.

"Maybe. I told you there's nobody home."

"Nobody? You're here."

She smiled. "Of course I'm here. I'm always here. They wouldn't eat without me."

"So you're the cook?"

"The best."

"Do they appreciate you?"

"Do any of you appreciate any of us?" she said blandly.

"So you live here?"

"Excuse me. I have things to do."

She left me standing in the middle of the room. I looked around, ran my eyes down the row of bishops on the wall, and meandered to a bookcase. Next to it, cut so that its lines matched the panelling on the wall, was a slim doorway. I gave the doorknob a twist and the door clicked open. For a moment I stood still, listening for any slight sound. Before me stood a narrow spiral staircase made of stone, the steps corkscrewing toward a dim light below. I looked around and started down, noticing that the stones lining the walls were more and more massive as I descended. At the bottom of the steps I faced another wooden door, open just a crack.

I saw an unmade bed in the middle of the floor, and as my eyes adjusted to the light the foliage came into view – a tangle of leaves and vines emerging from planters and pots surrounding the bed.

"You have no business here," she said. She had followed me down, was glaring at me.

I smiled as I looked into her eyes. "Lovely plants, but how does anything grow down here in the dark?"

"I have my ways."

I turned away toward the open door. "What's in there?"

She kept glaring as I stood in the doorway looking at a room lined with books. I walked to a small desk in the room, turned on the light, and quickly scanned some of the titles on the shelves. There was a long set entitled *Scriptures and Sermons,* another called *Church Histories,* and a row of tall thin volumes called *Ledgers of St. Paul's.*

She followed me in but suddenly froze, lifting her head to listen carefully. "He's back. Nobody's supposed to be down here."

She backed away. "You stay here until I tell you it's all clear." She smoothed her hands down over her skirt, took a deep breath and ran her fingers like a comb through her hair. Then she bounded up the stairs.

For a long minute I stood as still as a stone, straining to hear voices, feeling an occasional footfall on the thick carpeting above. There was a small window over the desk. If worse came to worse, I could break the window to get out.

Minutes passed. I looked around, trying to breathe quietly. It was clear: I was in the church archives, catacomb where church fathers laid to rest their useless hoard of words. I began scanning the shelves again, pulled a volume out and began reading a sermon that made no sense. I returned to the *Church Histories*, found nothing interesting but a full-page photograph of St. Paul's under construction, and a few useless paragraphs outlining the reigns of the bishops who held sway until the end of the Second World War. *Ledgers of St. Paul's* had lists of names, page after page recording dates of birth and death. I found my name, then Bruno's. Then I worked back – Gloria, Paul, Guido, Rosina, and in the first volume, right where it should be, Raphael, the year of his death underlined in blue.

I scanned the shelves again, lifting my head now and then to any small noise above. Then my eyes fell on a three-volume set entitled *Transactions*. I flipped through the first volume and found lists of dates, collection totals and bills paid. I was about to turn to the other side of the room when my eye caught a volume that seemed out of place. Squat and thick and bound between brittle boards, it was entitled simply *Diary*, the word scripted in thin white paint on its black leather spine. I opened to its front page. The name "Adolph Waldman," written carelessly in black, greeted me.

It began in the middle of things.

June 19, 1923. Must write a diary before it's too late. On this day, twenty-one years ago, my mother died.

Then a gap of almost three weeks.

July 2. Rostopov I'll never forget how interesting. Didn't believe in luck. I got lucky today – earned $100 in one day. Should have told him so.

July 12: There's no way to tell which way things will go now. Who knows, maybe the unions will get in.

Aug. 6: Moved out of the hotel room into my own flat. Bedroom and bath. Nowhere to put my steel box but next to me when I sleep.

Aug. 7: A man cheated me today. I counted the change right in front of his nose, as you're supposed to do. But he lied right to my face.

Aug. 8: They treat all of us like dirt. I'm no nigger or Jew. They have no idea about me. Someday they'll find out, when the revolution comes.

Sept. 27: Nothing today. Work, wash the clothes, read the newspaper. Study tonight on my own.

Dec. 3: They laughed at me when I told them I would be the savior of America. I will work my way up one step at a time. Then who will laugh?

Dec. 9: I bought a savings bond today. Keep it in the box with the rest just to be sure. I thought about telling Sylvio but changed my mind.

And that was all for the first year. I heard footfalls above, voices, and a door slam. Terror rose like a wave in me. Quickly I closed the diary, hid it under my coat, and crouched behind the desk.

For long minutes I heard nothing but the beating of my own heart, and I dared not move. My hands started to sweat. Finally, when my pulse slowed and I didn't hear any more from upstairs, I settled back against the side of the desk and opened the diary again.

I turned immediately to the last page, my spirits falling as I saw myself cut short.

Feb. 19, 1939: Must try it again. Too cold here, maybe should go west again. Not sure if politics is my cup of tea.

America? Disconnected bits. Some information yes, but knowledge no. And what had he become since 1939?

I skimmed the pages hoping to chance on a revealing line or two.

June 7, 1926: Too hot today. Can't stand the heat. Sylvio distrusts me with his talk. Meeting at the bank tomorrow at one.

No entry for June 8. No entry for more than a month.

July 26, 1926: The Bible says beware of false prophets. That woman who cleans my house tried to make my bed again. I should hire a nigger and be done with it.

September 3, 1930: They came around again today and I told them never mind. I need a new place away from here. The priest – he knows.

Sept. 4, 1930: Jews – I can smell them a mile away. Lumber is slow. Everything is slow. No need to push things now.

March 12, 1936: What is going on over there? This Hitler is trying to save Germany. I don't know if I should go there before a war breaks out. But there won't be a war.

Random, I thought as I skimmed. Random thoughts, impressions, beliefs, prejudices – disconnected, discontinuous, separated by large vacuoles that must have been filled by the stuff of his life, daily detail, business, travel, some hate and maybe – Sylvio? – a love. I looked for Sylvio after 1926 but found nothing more of him, and no more of any one name, male or female, but one:

August 27, 1924: Gertrude. How could a woman so pure, so full of the spirit, give herself to such a beast?

And more vaguely:

May 30, 1932: I went to hear what Pantera had to say. She claims Mary kissed Him on the lips. You have no proof. That's what I yelled at her right in front of everyone. She said she had proof – maybe there was a scroll in a cave. I laughed in her face. Have you ever seen it? And she said no. Then you're a liar, I said.

And in the next entry a strange *non sequitur:*

May 31, 1932. I got it. Hard to believe I got it without offering one cent more. I put the deed in the box. Bad dreams. All those acres of trees finally mine. What a mess in the bed. God forgive me for that.

June 1, 1932: Went to see the Bishop about what Pantera said.

June 13, 1932: Told the Bishop what my offer was. He told me to wait.

I was ready to skim on, turn ahead a dozen pages to see how his deal with the Bishop turned out. Then one word, standing tall at the bottom of the page, arrested me on the spot: "Raphael."

June 16, 1932: The Bishop told me to come back again.

June 17, 1932: She kept me waiting for more than an hour, but I got to him this time. Said he liked my idea, would think about it, but didn't know how he could pull off the change. He said people get used to things, don't want to change. I said right is right and wrong is wrong – not tradition. He said he could see I wasn't Catholic, and inside myself I said Thank God. He said the cathedral's name had been decided long ago. He didn't like the name but what could he do, there were laws. I said what law is there but the Law of God? He said there were two men who built the cathedral, Italian and French. The Italian wouldn't sign unless they used that name. I said, Who knows about the contract? He said it's in the books. I said we both know God's Law is highest law. He said yes, so I asked him if Raphael is still alive. He said gone, dead. I said what's the difference then? I told him they should make me a saint for that kind of dough.

And two days later an entry out of nowhere:

June 19, 1932: Gertrude. Now there was a saint.

Gertude. Who in the world was she?

June 22, 1932: The Bishop called again. Didn't keep me waiting this time. Said he knew the way. Said he found out Raphael did not live up to his part of the deal. Said Raphael built the cathedral wrong – went against the Bishop's orders, wanted to build the walls his way. So he quit, walked out on the job. I asked the Bishop if the contract was no good. In his opinion it was a breach. He thought the name change would be OK after all, and I said good.

Aug. 27, 1932: Got a letter from the Bishop. They'll go slow on the altar. So I sent him the check. Even if he was Catholic, I said, he knew how much I hated whores.

I didn't get it. Waldman and the Bishop worried about Raphael's contract even while his bones lay in some graveyard in Italy. The name change? What was that all about?

I heard a click above me and slammed the diary shut. "Hurry," Sonia whispered down at me. I kicked the diary under the desk and scrambled to my feet. As she met me halfway on the stone steps she paused, looking me up and down. "Hurry," she said again as she stepped to one side to let me go. "He's upstairs in his room." She put something in my hand. "Here's the rosary. Get out of here, but you be sure to come back with it in a couple days and tell them you got it from her."

I pressed the rosary tight in my hand as I hurried away from St. Paul's.

25. *"She said she would never go to Mass again. She said the new altar was the Devil's work."*

When I was in the bedroom alone I took the rosary out of my pocket and laid it on the bed. It was beautiful, pure gold, the beads all intricately cut precious stones. How much could it be worth – a thousand, two, maybe ten thousand? I put it in an old sock and hid it in the corner of my underwear drawer.

I found Rosina in her apartment alone. *"Finalmente,"* she said without looking up.

Finally. Finally I had come to her door. She stepped aside to let me in. "Sit, sit down," she said as she led me to a small table next to the stove. "A little wine?" She wiped a glass clean with her apron and poured. On a separate dish she placed a brown cookie with an almond on top. The cookie was dry and hard, but I broke off a small piece and waited for it to dissolve in my mouth.

"I feel so guilty, Nonna, for not visiting you."

"Ah, it is ugly to be old," she said, dismissing herself with a wave of her hand. "When you're old nobody wants to look at you any more."

The lines on her face were deep, curving like the ridges of a worn windswept plain, and the skin on the back of her hands, liverspotted and taut, seemed like a membrane stretched over birdlike bones. Her shoulders, covered by a woolen shawl, were stooped, and she inched her way around the kitchen tentatively, as if reluctant to go on. But behind thick brows her eyes were focused and bright. Someone was home inside, alert, sharp, intense.

"How's Nonno?"

"Eh," she dismissed him with a wave of her hand. "He never stays still. Him – he is at the old store again today. Running around all the time."

And he leaves you here alone.

"He's a little off," she said, circling her finger around her ear. "It is no picnic to be old." She nodded toward her Virgin on a table next to the window and made the Sign of the Cross.

I pulled out a chair for her but she refused. She had to work – a dish to put away, a table and counter to wipe clean again – rituals memorized by hands.

"He goes to the store – that is his day. Then Bruno brings him back. He eats a little, but I can't force him any more. If he wants to die, what can I do?"

"Maybe you should go with him, Nonna, spend some time with him there."

She slowly shook her head. "No, no. He doesn't want me there. I am old now. He waits for the women to come back there to buy oranges and apples from him. He just sits there half asleep until Bruno brings him home."

She chose a dish from the cupboard and began polishing it with a towel. "I put my years in there. I swept enough floors. Enough is enough."

"Enough is too much."

"What?" she said, straining to hear. "Now he will never have enough. I don't know what he will do now."

"What do you mean not enough?"

"Donna Anna – she died last night." She leaned down close. "The widow and the witch. *Dio mio,*" she said crossing herself again. "She lived in the ditch. Crazy in the head, like her mother in Italy. There she was, old like me, talking like a little whore with him through a hole in the fence."

"And now God took her to himself."

"Eh," was all Rosina said in reply, speeding Donna Anna on her way with another wave of her hand. She circled the table to get the bottle of wine. "And now they got the store too."

"What do you mean?"

"Nobody told Guido yet."

"Told him what?"

236

"Bruno got a notice three days ago. Not even two more weeks and we're out. He paid the rent, but they told him December first, two weeks."

Waldman.

She sat in an old chair and stared at her little shrine, a statue of Mary surrounded by candles on a small table covered with a white cloth.

"Nonna, did they say why we have to move out? And can you remember back? Can you tell me something about when you were young?"

"Ah Salvatore, what can I tell you? I don't know anything any more. What do you want to know from me now?"

I took the chair next to her shrine. "Everything, Nonna. About when you were a girl, when you came here. About St. Paul's, when they were building it."

"What do I know? When I was a little girl I always stood on the balcony of the old house in San Giovanni. 'What are you always staring at?' my mamma asked. 'I want to go to the sea,' I said. 'But the sea is too far away.' 'But I think I can see it,' I told her, 'there in the sky.' There, in the Old Country, the sky was always blue, full of space, open and clean. I wanted to see a boat with white sails. But the boat Guido and I got on in Naples had no sails. Rusty, with rings like a bathtub nobody every washed. They made us go downstairs like cattle, and we had to take turns looking through a little window to get a breath of air. No more standing on the balcony looking for white sails. That's the way it is, The Life."

"You always wanted to go back to the Old Country?"

"Eh, what can you do?" she said as she ran her hand down her wrinkled sleeve. "When the boat started to move I waved goodbye to the girl, the one on the balcony. We try to see out the little window of the boat, and I see her standing there like it is today. No, here we got everything we need."

"You mean memories?"

"No, no, no. I can't remember nothing no more. Everything is confused."

"Not even about Raphael, St. Paul's, what it was like when the church was new?"

"Ah, you mean when Donna Anna was young like me? You should see her then, the way she walked in front of the men, showing off her behind and long hair. Just like when she was a girl in Italy. We all wanted to be like her. We saw all the men turning their eyes. Guido was the first. Oh, we had it in for her."

"And St. Paul's. Tell me about that."

She pushed herself up from her chair and began looking about the room. On the table with the shrine she spotted a green little dish. She picked it up and wiped it with her apron, then began looking around the room for something else. She spotted the half-eaten cookie I had left on the table and picked it up. "Eat," she said, holding it in front of me, "you have to eat."

"I'm full, Nonna. I can't eat any more."

"Dio mio, what can I give you then? He says he's full. Over there everybody wanted to eat."

"You can give me something else."

"You want a sandwich? Let me fix you a little sandwich and soup."

I had to take her hand to sit her down again. "No, please. Some other time. Today I just want words."

"Words? You going to eat words? Over there we always had plenty of words."

"Nonna," I said, "why did they change the name of St. Paul's?"

"I don't know," she said with a little shake of her head. "But I know we were all happy then. All of us – we were young women then – we were happy when they changed the name. All of us but Donna Anna. Miserable one. She never said a word, but we all knew she was against the change." She leaned up close to me and whispered. "Do you know what I think? I think that's when she sold her soul."

She hardened her conclusion by drawing stiffly back from me.

"But why – why were you happy with the change?"

"Who knows? We were young women. We all had men who worked, and in those times they worked all day and night. We had no bathtubs then. What could we do for them? We always had enough to eat, but sometimes they walked right past the table without looking at the food. Imagine, too tired to eat. All they wanted was to soak their feet and go to bed. Who knows why they changed the name? We all liked the new name, that's all."

238

She looked around the room for something to wipe clean.

She turned to the Virgin, crossed herself, and stood a long moment looking at her Queen. The Queen was unmoved, her eyes looking dumbly at the floor, only her hands visible beneath her outspread robe.

"But Nonna, what was the original name? Was it Mary?"

She gave me a puzzled look.

"The cathedral. Did it used to be called St. Mary's?"

She said no with a shrug.

"Cathedral of the Sacred Heart?"

No.

"Notre Dame?"

"No, it was The Magdalene."

Magdalene? Waldman's horror, the one he wanted to erase from memory. "Nonna, are you sure?"

"What do you mean am I sure? I remember when they took the side altar out, the one across from the Virgin's altar. Someone gave the money to build a better one there, an altar to St. Paul."

"But what did the people think about the change? Did they go along with it?"

"What do we know about such things? They took the Magdalene out, and the new altar was nice. And in a few years the men don't care about anything any more. One by one they stop going to Mass."

"What about Guido – what did he say?"

"What do you think? He was like his father. Nothing could make him happy. Only your papa was happy. He was handsome and his name was Paul. When they changed the name, he said it was for him. He thought he was a king."

Rosina crossed herself.

"There was only one who raised her voice, and such a voice. You know who I mean. Donna Anna. She said she would never go to Mass again. She said the new altar was the Devil's work."

26. *I had never touched a gun before.*

"So what are you going to do about it?" Markels eventually asked.

I had hurried to his place, but had to pound on the door to get in. I found him in bed, his face turned toward the wall, his eyes alert.

"Seymour," I said, uneasy using his first name. "Seymour, it's Sal. Are you ill?"

He stirred, turned over on his back, and stared at the ceiling. His breathing was regular and slow, and I saw nothing wrong except the look of defeat on his face.

"Seymour, Waldman took the store away from us."

Nothing from him.

"And I found out something else."

Only his lips moved to form the words. "I've found out enough in the last year alone to make me sick for the rest of my life."

On the small sink across the room dirty dishes were heaped high, and the floor was littered with newspapers, empty cans, dirty clothes. Books everywhere as usual, his small writing desk surrounded by sheets of paper crumpled into balls.

I raised my voice. "What the hell is happening here?"

Slowly and clearly the word escaped him like a breath. "Nothing."

"Nothing? What do you mean nothing? Look at this mess. How can you stand living in this mess?"

"I'm learning how to become an American. I make a mess and when I don't like it anymore I go somewhere else."

It had caught up with him – the solitude gone stale into loneliness, the waste of his talent and energy piling up around him until there was no more escape from it.

"So what are you going to do about it?" I asked quietly, gently. "This mess."

A small smile came to his face as he turned his head toward me. "I think nothing would be best."

"Bullshit. You'd be better off dead."

His smile broadened.

"So you'll just lie here until you starve to death? Come on," I nudged him, "get up."

Nothing.

"Come on. I want you to come home with me. You've got to eat something."

He gave me a crooked look.

"So I'm supposed to just leave and leave you in the middle of this garbage heap?"

"Things are taking care of themselves."

"You're killing yourself. That's what you're doing. You're letting yourself go."

He smirked. "I've been drafted to serve in the natural selection process. Anything wrong with that?"

"Waste – that's what's wrong with that. I don't like to see anything well-made thrown away."

"I'm a Jew. I know about waste."

"They didn't throw themselves away."

He turned toward me, propped on an elbow. "I die, you die, we all die. What's the difference when?"

"You sound like an idiot undergrad. Now get out of bed."

"But I've thought of everything," he said with a jeer. "I leave a note behind. In the note I say there is no hope. A long note – a doctoral dissertation note, full of reasons that come straight from the testes."

He gestured with his hand to his balls and with a sad little shake of his head saluted them.

"Get out of bed."

"No need. My note will do its work. Everyone will pity me and from that will emerge a renaissance of love. And I'll add a clause to the end, bequeathing all my books to you."

"Get out of bed."

242

He let himself slip back down, his eyes fixed on the ceiling again. "I don't know if I ought."

"Come on, get up. I've got some news."

"You're divorcing that nice woman of yours?"

"No."

"You've inherited the fortune you so richly deserve?"

He tilted his head slyly toward me. "You've read a book?"

"I found out about Waldman."

He slowly pulled himself up. "You mean you finally got off your ass?"

"So what are you going to do about it?"

While he washed his face and hands and I cleared the dishes off the table, I explained everything, beginning with the rosary.

"Waldman fits the type," Markels said as we sat with our coffee, "the poor boy who made it big in America. But there's also something peculiar, odd."

"The religious drifts, the obsession with God."

"An obsession with justification, the need for control. He has to be in control. Why else have the name of the church changed? Everything had to be his way."

"And as he takes more and more in, everything becomes more untidy for him, more out of control."

"And the racism – the hatred of blacks and Jews."

"If they're building a heaven they've got to have devils for their hell."

Markels threw his head back. "So what do we do? Line them all up in front of a wall and let the chips fall where they may? Or maybe ship them to a country club with a high barbed-wire fence. Allow trucks in to bring them fresh meat, alcohol, golf balls, hymnals, and young pretty boys and girls."

"I say shoot them one by one – up close. Make it a personal thing."

"You surprise me with such talk, Mr. Sal."

"Wouldn't you have killed Hitler if you had the chance?"

"The Hitler question is another thing."

"No, he's not. Don't you see? Waldman is Hitler. Hitler would have been nothing without all the Waldmans out there who add up to him. Waldman gives people dirty little jobs, and Hitler threatens to take them away if the people don't do what they're told. They work perfectly together, Waldman and Hitler, because they're one and the same, inside each other."

Markels grinned. "Inside each other. So now you think everybody is somebody else. That idea would make our job interesting, wouldn't it? Think of all the new books for people like us to write. By your logic, then, if we kill Waldman we kill Hitler too, and six million Jews, give or take one or two, would still be alive?"

"We didn't kill Hitler, and the Second World War is still going on. And he's still alive, still putting the squeeze on people who get in his way – blacks, Jews, homosexuals, anybody odd, you and me."

"So now you want me to kill him too?"

"Would you have killed Hitler if you knew then?"

Markels stared at the floor. "I would have killed him, yes."

"There."

I tried to back off, let him be the professor again. "But there's something I still don't understand, old man."

He lifted his cup, empty except for a few dregs.

"Why make a thing of changing the name of the church?"

Markels smiled. "Names. So you say we're all inside each other. Isn't Magdalene one of your Christian bad girls, woman they called whore? Waldman was just a money whore, not the other kind. How could he have one of his churches named after someone like her? He paid big money trying to get her out of himself.

"So what are you going to do about it?" Markels asked.

"I just got a job," I said. "It isn't much – helping a man make kitchen cabinets, a trade, maybe a craft."

Markels looked into his coffee cup and tried not to smirk. We both had to laugh at how messy the room was.

"How about dinner at my mother's on Thanksgiving afternoon? I want you there too. We can't really say no when she wants us to eat."

"That would be nice," Markels said. "But do me a favor on your way out."

He walked to his bed, threw back the sheets, and reached under the mattress. With his head he motioned for me to come closer to him.

"Take this thing out of here," he said as he stood up and handed me a heavy object wrapped in an old teeshirt. "It scares the hell out of me."

Inside the teeshirt was a small black pistol, bullets visible in its chamber.

I held the thing carefully away from myself. "Christ! What were you planning to do with this thing?"

"Do? A Nazi thing," he said with a wry smile on his face. "So maybe you better put it under your coat when you leave. Get rid of it. Throw it in the sewer."

"I will, I will. But you have to promise me. Promise you'll clean up this mess."

When I left he was already busy clearing the trash around his bed. Inside my coat pocket I kept one hand on the gun, careful to keep it pointed away from myself. I had never touched a gun before.

27. *In my room Edna was crying again. I got up and backed away from Mamma's bed.*

Mamma prepared a great feast for everyone.

"The Jew?" she asked when I told her about Markels. "You want him to come to Thanksgiving dinner here with us? How nice."

Edna, who listened carefully to everything, turned away. A Jew would not be necessary.

At one o'clock everyone began to appear. Rosina knew enough to come first. "Guido will come – in good time," she said. Sandy and I were next, for we knew it would be proper to be present early enough to help. Then Markels, confused by Edna's stare at the door, arrived. And Dylan appeared, packing Beatrice under his arm like a guitar, but letting go of her as soon as he saw Papa. And then Guido, silent and slow, climbed the stairs and stood like a beggar at the door. At last came Kate and Bruno, their faces on guard, both of them dressed in their Sunday best.

I saw their secret immediately – the swell under Kate's dress that could no longer be draped or bound in, the unmistakable ripening of new life.

"Praise Jesus," Mamma said, "the whole family is here."

Raphael stared down at us from his place on the wall.

"Sal, how many of us?" Mamma asked. "How many places should we set?"

I tried counting them in my head but had to start over again. "I think it's twelve, Mamma."

The aroma of fresh-baked bread filled the house, making even the three inches of new snow covering everything outside seem warm. In the dining room Papa and Bruno tried to figure out how to add a leaf to the old table, while Edna, holding the leaf, waited for them to do it her way. In one corner Kate had introduced herself to Professor Markels, while in the other Bea gazed speechlessly into Dylan's eyes. Guido, leaning forward on his cane, looked like his small tree with its leaves all gone, and in the kitchen Rosina and Mamma, both white-aproned, stood over big pots stirring with wooden spoons.

"Is there anything I can do to help?" I asked as I stuck my head into the kitchen. I made sure that Sandy heard me ask.

"So now he wants to do woman's work," my father said loudly enough for everyone to hear.

"Go, go," Mamma said, "this isn't work for you."

"Oh let me help," Sandy popped up, acknowledging, as she passed me in the kitchen doorway, that I at least had tried.

"Oh God, Dylan!" Bea suddenly shouted in the other room, with Guido, sitting just four feet away, not moving an eye. "Do you really think the Beatles will ever get together again?"

Mamma appeared in the kitchen door and beat a spoon on an empty pan. "Quiet everyone! Sandy says Sal's got an important announcement to make today. Isn't that right, Sal?"

Bruno tied Kate up and made her big with child, but Bea is safely on the pill, thank God. "Not now, Mamma, not now. I'll make the announcement when we're all at the table sitting down." I smiled big and flashed Mamma the "V" for Victory and Peace.

In the living room, just to the left of Raphael's eyes, Kate had already discovered that Markels was merely another liberal.

"Is the table ready yet?" Mamma asked.

"They're trying to get it in the slot," Edna said as my father and Bruno pounded on the table leaf with the palms of their hands.

"Sandy," Mamma said, "I'll let you set the table the way you like."

"I don't think it'll really happen," Beatrice said to Dylan.

"I keep thinking of Humpty Dumpty," Markels professed to Kate. "Do you remember when he says it's not whether a word can mean so many things? It's who is to be master. That is all."

"Goddamn," said my father, rubbing his leg. "I'm sick and tired of this thing."

248

"Do you know what I think?" Mamma said from the kitchen door, pointing at Markels with her spoon. "I think you, Edna, and you...."

"Seymour," I said. "That's his first name." Yes, the Jew.

Mamma turned toward me with one of her big smiles. "I think Mr. Seymour and Edna should sit together and get to know each other good. Maybe those two could have a date. Don't you think?"

Guido's head was nervously shaking back and forth, trembling as if the cold outside was too much for him.

When finally we were all seated Mamma stood over us, holding her spoon high like a conductor's baton.

"Praise Jesus," she announced, throwing a glance toward Edna. "Now Paul, will you give thanks to Jesus for bringing us all here together, family and friends, as one in the spirit of Christ?"

Guido did not stir.

My father, who had drunk half his glass of wine, was reaching for the broccoli. Bea nudged him on the arm.

"Will you give thanks for this our daily bread?" Mamma smiled.

"Eh?"

"I mean pray."

Papa's eyes, accusing her of betraying him in front of a crowd, swore revenge on her.

"Praise God," Edna mumbled.

"Hail Mary..." he began.

"Bless us, O Lord..." Mamma reminded him.

"Bless this food which we are about to receive through thy bounty in Christ almighty amen. In the name of Father, Son, Holy Ghost, amen."

Some of us made the Sign of the Cross. Markels, nodding slowly as if he understood, was tugging at a few long hairs on his beard.

"Will you lead us now, Edna?" Mamma said.

"Now we always got to pray twice before we eat?" Papa asked.

A silence descended as Edna slowly panned the faces at the table, her eyes suddenly sad and weary of the world. When she was sure that everyone was perfectly still, she spoke: "Every head bowed and every eye closed."

249

She extended a hand over the table and looked us over just to be sure.

"My dear Jesus, Lord and Savior of the world, we pray that you will look down on us from your throne in the palace of God and have mercy on us, sinners that we are. See us all here sitting before this wonderful supper that you have made for us on this Thanksgiving Day, and make us worthy to receive it by reminding us that you have a hand in everything. Keep constantly before us all the prefigurations, great and small, so that we, souls in the dark, may read your handwriting on the wall."

My father opened his eyes, and, with his hands folded in prayer, stared at his glass of wine. I noticed a crack on the ceiling over his head.

"And thank you Jesus for allowing us all to assemble together here irregardless of race, nationality, color or creed – so that those who are lost in the night of atheism, sins of the world, the flesh, and the Devil may see the light written in your holy writ."

I wondered if Kate's baby would be a boy or girl.

"Bless all sinners who love you with all their heart, bless my uncle Phillip who is in a hospital bed, and all starving children everywhere in the world hungry for your Word, and bless the President of these United States of America."

"Amen," my father said.

"And most of all," Edna said, pausing to be sure we all would hear, "bless us, O Lord, this bread, noodles and meat which we are about to partake as the body of our Lord and Savior. And everyone," she concluded, "says..."

"Amen."

"Wait a minute!" Mamma held a glass up and hit it with her spoon. "Sal has an announcement to make – a surprise for all of us."

Kate squirmed in her seat and crossed her arms over her lap.

Guido, his face barely visible over the pasta heaped high on his plate, suddenly broke out of his trance. "Gimme some cheese."

I handed it across to him as I stood. "Ladies and gentlemen," I said as I tapped my fork on my glass, "I wish to

250

inform you that at eight o'clock last Monday I began regular employment with the Rochelle Woodsmith Company."

"He got a job!" Mamma said, still surprised.

"Finally," Papa said, disappointed.

"Let's drink to that," Markels said, raising his glass.

"Sandy, if you drink milk on top of wine your stomach will go bad," my father warned.

We drank to my new job. Guido, who had a mouthful of bread and cheese, waited to swallow before he drank, and Edna, who had water in her glass, felt left out.

And I could see that Dylan was getting used to the taste of home-made wine.

For the next five minutes words, passed around the table like slices of bread, were swallowed whole. As always, Papa led the race to the second plateful of pasta. "Lord," Edna said with wide eyes, "how big you eat." To show her how, he rolled an extra big mouthful on his tablespoon.

"God bless," Rosina said. "Look how we eat here. God bless America."

Papa sat back, let out an exhausted breath, and loosened his belt. "Those two kids should be shot!" he announced.

Dylan and Beatrice darted glances back and forth, and Bruno lowered his eyes.

"You read the damnedest things in the papers these days. Those two kids – one's only thirteen – they make a bomb in their basement and try to blow their teacher up. Can you imagine such a thing?"

Dylan's eyebrows arched involuntarily.

"You gotta ask what kind of people these are."

"I don't know," Rosina said, shaking her head and crossing herself.

"Shouldn't we ask what lies behind their act?" Markels, anxious to blend in, asked as politely as his face would allow.

No one was surprised when Kate leaped right in. "Maybe we should ask if the teacher had it coming. Maybe he had it coming. Did anyone think of that?"

"It was a she," Bea said. "I saw it on TV last night."

"Was she blown up?" Dylan asked.

"Naw, just her front porch," Bea replied. "And the thirteen-year old lost a finger."

"Serves him right," Sandy said.

Guido poured himself another glassful of wine. He winced after he swallowed, and I saw the chill run a crooked path up and down his back.

"The question is," Kate went on, "who is really to blame? Just because the boys did it doesn't mean they're to blame."

Dylan knew what she was talking about. "Yeh, maybe Society is to blame."

"Bullshit!" my father roared.

"What I mean is they had to have a good reason for doing what they did. That teacher must not be all pure. She must have done something wrong too." Kate scored her point with Guido, who swallowed it with another swig of wine.

My father looked at me. "Maybe she asked them to do their work."

Markels tried to get Kate off the hook. "The point is that maybe we're treating the symptom, not the root cause."

"That's the point. We have to get to the root. Maybe the teacher did something wrong. And maybe somebody wronged her too. Maybe there's something wrong with the school – with the principal, the educational set-up, the curriculum, the whole environment."

Beatrice cut Kate off. "That's all Dylan was trying to say. He was trying to say it's all Society's fault. That's all he was trying to say." She sat back and folded her arms.

"Maybe we've got blame and responsiblity confused," Markels offered.

"No," Kate said, "the root cause is economic."

"The little bastards were rich kids," my father said.

Markels' eyes lit up. "Then it's transference."

"No, inversion," Kate said, addressing Markels.

Guido looked around, confused.

"Those little bastards are perverts!" Papa shouted.

"Paul!" Mamma yelled, "watch how you talk!"

Kate, her neck reddening, raised a finger to silence everyone. "The point is that we're making scapegoats of the apparent perpetrators of the deed. Here we have a complicated situation, two boys who do something wrong – I don't question that – but two boys who are part of something bigger than themselves, this something bigger also wrong and therefore very wrong. What if, for example, the teacher abused the boys' rights? What if her principal encouraged her to do that? What if it were part of a pattern?"

Dylan knew what the real trouble was. "What if they hated English?"

Kate's glare told him to shut up. "And consider what might have been happening in the boys' home life. What if the parents drank too much?"

"They didn't." Bea said. "They were members of a church. Their moms were really shocked when they heard what their boys did. I saw the whole thing on TV."

"That's not the point," Kate said.

"I think we're still confusing the concept of blame and responsibility," Markels chimed.

"Why should the boys be the only ones punished? Why shouldn't there be a reform school for the teacher?" I watched Kate build it in her mind – no walls, no bars on the windows, a nice lawn, everyone learning a trade.

Rosina put her hands up to her ears. Bruno, stuck in the middle of some part for the left hand, was toying with his butter knife. When Kate elbowed him, he turned away.

"I agree with Kate," Sandy said. "Maybe some teachers need to go back to school – and maybe some principals too."

"But how can anyone prove anything?" Bea asked. "How do you know who to believe?"

Dylan knew. "It's all up to the individual. I'm not going to say something's right or wrong. It's all up to the individual. You can't argue with that."

My father's lip curled down.

"Oh my sweet Jesus," Edna whispered to herself.

Within a half-hour the pasta was almost gone. Hands reached across for an olive or two, one more slice of bread, another spoonful of meatballs and sauce.

"Sandy dear, would you give me a hand with the turkey," Mamma asked from the kitchen.

Rosina appeared with two more hot loaves of bread, and the wine went around again before the turkey appeared on a large platter made of stainless steel. Rosina began to cut it up as plates went around.

"Bruno, do you think what Dylan says is true?" Bea, craning her neck to get around Guido, needed to know.

"Huh?"

"That the Beatles maybe will get back together someday. Do you think it's really true?"

"How should I know?"

"Well, you should know," she accused.

"Why should he know?" my father stepped in. "Bruno plays music, not noise. "

"The turkey looks wonderful," someone said.

"Noise?" The word hung meaninglessly above Dylan's brow. "What do you mean noise?"

"You know what I mean. Screaming, junkyards, factories – noise." My father hissed the word across the table at him.

Guido's head was nodding, perhaps toward sleep.

"Wait a minute!" Kate barged in. "I don't think it's fair to call Beatles stuff noise. What they did was historically significant."

Markels' eyes widened.

"And to demean their accomplishment is to demean all the accomplishments of the post-Liverpool generation."

"Accomplishments?" Sandy asked.

"A whole revolution, that's what."

"What kind of revolution?" I asked, skeptical.

I felt Bruno kick Kate.

Sexual revolution.

"Lifestyles," Kate said.

"Long hair, loud noise, dope." My father glared at Beatrice. "Dirty clothes, dirty everything."

Dylan protested. "That's a generalization. You can't make a generalization. It's up to the individual."

"It's music of the people," Kate said.

Dylan appealed to Bruno. "But music-wise, what do you think of the Beatles? Don't you think they're great?"

"I think they're great!" Bea said.

Bruno tried to escape by stiffening into a long silence. All eyes except Edna's, lifted above the idle babblings of this world, waited for his words. "They were innovative, they were popular, but they were not great."

"You're discriminating against them," Kate shot back, "because they're popular artists."

Bruno turned slowly toward her. "You don't know anything about art."

"And you don't know anything about historical dialectics."

"What's wrong with the Beatles' music?" Bea asked, on the verge of tears.

"There's too much noise in it," Bruno said calmly. "Just listen."

Mamma smiled, proud of her second son, and my father drank to him.

"There's good turkey and there's bad turkey," Markels said, a piece of it stuck in his beard, "and this, Missus, is good turkey!"

"You gotta know how to make it," Mamma winked as she left for the kitchen again.

On Edna's plate was a pile of bones already picked clean.

"And I made this especially for you," Mamma said as she stood over me holding a platter with a roast on it. "I know how you like leg of lamb."

"Lamb too? Isn't the turkey enough?"

Edna set the platter down, sliced a couple thick pieces off, then handed the platter to Papa. "Would you pass the bread, please?"

At the other end of the table Bea and Dylan were quietly in concert. "Elvis was great, better than the Beach Boys probably. So why doesn't Bruno think the Beatles are great?"

Guido was not listening, so he had nothing to say. He perked up with the arrival of the lamb, and was busy probing with his finger for a strand of turkey stuck between his teeth. Rosina was going back and forth with dishes.

"Should I clear the table?" Sandy, smiling at me, asked Mamma.

"There's no need. You just sit and eat."

"There's no respect for authority these days," my father was saying to Markels. "No one cares about the Old Way."

Markels was careful to be seen listening attentively.

"You're a teacher. You see what they're doing. You see the kids these days – they don't respect their elders or anything else. And no one believes in God. And everywhere you look people make fun of President Gerald Ford. And," he leaned close to Markels, "why don't some of them people work like everybody else? They want everything handed to them."

Edna, sitting between my father and Markels, was working on her lamb. "Praise the Lord," she mumbled as she swallowed.

"Isn't that right, Edna?" my father asked.

"Oh yes," she said. "The Bible likes work. Only good works will get you to heaven. It is easier for a man to pass through the eye of a needle than it is for a man who doesn't want to work to inherit a room in Jesus' heavenly house."

Kate watched them all, waiting for anyone to go too far.

"What I would do with those boys who tried to blow up their teacher is put them in jail and make them work."

"Teach them how to work," Edna agreed with Papa.

Sandy got up, turned away from the table, and disappeared into the kitchen. In a moment she returned and began clearing the plates.

"In principle," Kate said, "labor has a redemptive quality, but under the circumstances, in this case punitive, the experience would be counter-productive."

"What did she say?" Mamma asked me.

"She means," Markels said loudly enough for everyone to hear, "that the boys would only grow up hating work if they were punished with it. It wouldn't work."

"Who ever said you were supposed to like work?" my father said. "We all hate to work. That's life."

"Dylan," Bea coolly corrected him, "plays guitar. That's his work."

"You make me sick," Papa shot back. "I told you – work is not play. If he plays that thing he doesn't have a job."

"Maybe," Kate began again, "maybe the boys are really innocent."

"Oh, now I know what you're going to say next. Dylan's too young to get a real job," my father said with a cynical smile.

"No, I mean the boys who made the bombs. Maybe, maybe it was the parents' fault."

Guido, finally succeeding at pulling the strand of turkey out from between his teeth, looked about before slipping it under the rim of his plate.

"Right now we send the boys to reform school. Why not send the parents to reform school?"

Papa pushed his chair back from the table, got up without saying a word, and headed for the bathroom.

"What do the parents have to do with it?" Mamma asked.

"They have plenty to do with it," Kate said. "Aren't parents the ones who are supposed to raise their children right? Were these two boys raised right? The answer is obviously no. Therefore, did these parents succeed or fail? Don't they need reforming too? Therefore, why not send them to reform school?"

Papa left the bathroom door open, as usual. When Kate finished talking he began pissing in the toilet, a strong steady stream. We waited respectfully for him to finish, then passed what was left of the leg of lamb.

"Original sin," Edna reminded us, covering everyone at the table with a sweep of her extended hand. "It all goes back to Adam and Eve and that's why there's only one way we can be saved, God's grace."

"Amen, Sister Edna," Mamma said.

Papa returned to the table. "Why not send the boys' grandparents to reform school?" he sneered as he sat down. "They did a bad job too. And then let's send the great-grandparents away too – if there are any left."

"That's absurd," Sandy complained across the table to Kate. "Where would it end?"

Raphael was still staring at us from his place on the wall.

"The question is why begin with the boys," Kate shot back.

Rosina, balancing dishes in both hands, slowly backed out of view into the kitchen.

"The question," Sandy said, "is who's responsible."

Markels raised his finger to make a point. "And maybe that means finding out who was in the best position to be able to respond."

I raised my hand. "Can I say something? Let's look at it this way. Let's assume we have a neighborhood that's going downhill, a neighborhood like ours. Let's assume there was once a group of individual shopowners – like Nonno here, and Danko on the corner – who did good work. And then slowly it all began to go downhill because someone with big money was squeezing the small guys out, buying them out, closing them out, ruining them. And then when the neighborhood began to go downhill the poorer people started moving in – let's say the blacks. And let's say there was violence in the neighborhood in a way there never was before – muggings on the sidewalks, holdups, murders. Who would be most responsible?"

"The capitalists," Kate said.

"The niggers," my father said. "Why don't they work their way up like us?"

Bruno, weary, rolled his eyes.

"The curse of Ham," Edna was explaining as Mamma cut the chocolate cake. "It all goes back to the curse of Ham. You remember him? Ham was the African who lied to God and then God got even with him by blackening his face. Now they're all black over there."

"Wasn't he originally Semitic?" Markels asked.

"Semitic?" Edna asked.

"It's like semantics," I said.

"What's this semantics?" Papa asked Markels.

"Jewish philosophy."

Edna's eyes widened with understanding. "So Semitic means Jew?"

"Was Ham a Jew?" Mamma asked.

"How can you compare Jews and niggers?" Papa roared. "Jews are white."

Dylan was quick to connect. "And is that why Jews can't eat ham?"

"The two can't mix," Edna agreed.

Kate, smirking at Markels, got up from the table, muttering something to herself about the post-Liverpool generation as she brushed past. When she returned she ran her hands down over the front of her dress as if to smooth some wrinkles out. I caught my father watching as her hands paused to caress the slight bulge beginning to show itself around her stomach, and I could see that he was vaguely aware of something different, something wrong.

"I guess I'm old-fashioned," my father said as if to resolve all arguments at the table for good. "I guess I believe in telling the truth. That's the way I was raised." He sent a thank you toward Guido with a nod of his head, and Guido blinked both eyes once in return. "And that's the way our people were raised."

"Ham lied to God and we know what happened to his race," Edna said. "That has not happened to us, but it will if we stray from the simple old-fashioned truth."

Raphael kept staring down on all of us.

"Take the way things are today." Papa paused too long. "Do you know what I mean?"

Even Edna knew what he meant.

"Kids, I mean. The way they fool around these days."

Dylan and Bea froze.

"No honest girl would fool around before marriage."

"Dad!" Bea's face flushed before the word was out. "Do you think everyone's an animal?" She got up and stormed out of the room.

Mamma, suddenly sad and tired, saw me watch Bea rush past.

"And I drink to the fact that my father, all his life, was an honest man." Papa lifted his glass to toast Guido.

Guido, suddenly close to tears, blinked again.

"I drink to an honest man," my father said, and we all lifted our glasses high.

Rosina lowered her head.

And Mamma was still looking at me, her eyes sad, longing, full of love.

Beatrice returned to the table, her face recomposed. As she brushed past Guido's chair I saw my father's eyes, caught by the sway of her delicate young form, follow her. And from the corner of his eye he saw me watching him. The wine was beginning to get to him.

"And next I drink to you, my oldest son, and his lovely wife. For six years now married."

Sandy lowered her eyes.

I froze, unable to lift the glass to my lips. Maggie. What if she calls in the middle of the night? What if she causes trouble for everyone?

Sandy's eyes were as lovely as the wine. Maggie was bad news, a terrible mistake. My glass met Sandy's and we sipped while everyone watched.

My father next turned to Kate. "You, Bruno, have a woman who speaks her mind. She doesn't always agree with me – that I admit. But she says what she thinks." He lifted his glass to them. "May you two live happily ever after – when you decide to get married someday. And then – I want you to get busy making a son. By then maybe Sal will own a car." He finished his wine in one gulp, twisting his face as he forced it down.

259

Dylan reached for Bea's hand, but she stiffened at his touch and yanked it away. Mamma, her eyes lonely and full of pity, kept looking at me until I could not stand it any more. To escape I eased my chair back so that Sandy's head came between Mamma's eyes and me.

"But for sure," my father went on, pointing at Sandy and me, "these two are set now, so they'll have one of their own pretty soon."

Art.

"Now that I have a job I'll be too tired, Papa."

Sandy blushed and turned away.

"It is a sin not to have kids when God gives you the ability." Rosina, speaking from the kitchen door, was firm on this point.

"Ah," said Edna, "there are many sins in the world. Hell is full of sinners."

Markels' jaw stiffened. "Does the stench of burning flesh down there smell slightly sweet?"

Mamma's eyes quickly abandoned me. "Professor Markels," she said gently, "please do not mock the Word of the Lord."

He turned away, appealing to me to help him escape.

"You and Edna should love one another," Mamma said to her.

"Oh I do love him," Edna pleaded with us. "I love him in the Lord."

Mamma perked up. "See? And you're single, aren't you, Professor Markels? Maybe you and Edna could go out on a date, don't you think?" She laughed and tugged at Papa's sleeve.

Papa pulled away, and Markels dared Edna with a tooth-filled smile.

Mamma grabbed at the sleeve again. "Then maybe they could get married too."

"I'd love to have two more babies," Markels said, still challenging Edna with his eyes.

"Enough is enough!" Papa roared as he put his glass down. "Leave them alone! Sometimes, Gloria, you go too far. Sometimes you act like a child, like Bea over there."

"Children always go too far," I said. "It's natural."

All eyes turned toward me.

"What do you mean?" he said.

"Sometimes children do things their fathers never dared."

"In my day, young man, we kept it in our pants."

Rosina disappeared into the kitchen again.

I couldn't keep my trap shut. "Do you really think that if boys keep it in their pants, girls will keep their panties on?"

Bea looked horrified. How could I talk like this in front of everyone? And Bruno reached for Kate's hand.

"If there were one stain on my daughter's wedding dress and she dared to wear it at the altar, I would make her pay."

"What makes you think you could see the stain?"

"Stop!" Mamma said. Guido, his eyes widening, was suddenly alert.

"If she were pregnant I would throw her out of the house."

Instantly Papa's suspicion about Kate became a fact. He turned abruptly away from her.

"Your own daughter?" I said. "You'd throw her out?"

"Do we have to talk like this now?" Bea said, breaking down.

I could not stop. "But what if she were not pregnant?"

"Stop!"

"Then I would beat her," Papa said, "until she was black and blue."

Rosina appeared in the kitchen door again. "Coffee? Who wants sugar and cream?"

Markels thanked and thanked, bowing and backing his way out of the house.

"What a nice man," Mamma said. "Didn't I tell you I always liked Jews?"

Bea and Dylan excused themselves while Sandy and Rosina poured the coffee around. I had exposed their hot young love, talked about sex. Now Bea would hate me for years, not forgive a brother who had crossed her this way. In five years, ten, maybe twenty, after she had endured a crisis or divorce, we would meet somewhere for lunch, and we would talk and talk. And I had crossed Bruno and Kate again, given their secret away, released the flood of shame in which we all had to swim. Was I honest or fair? No. Maggie was never a friend. If I were honest, I never would have lied about wanting

261

to be her friend. If I were fair, I would have told everyone at the table my secrets too, yes, how Maggie rubbed my feet. Then everybody could have been inside everybody else.

A silence fell. Bruno and Kate had their heads together as Sandy joined me at the table, her face stiff and serious. Sandy had kept her place all day, kept her peace. But there was too much she had to eat. I owed her more than one. She had tried hard to fit in, so hard she seemed absent most of the time, the only stranger in the house. I wondered why she put up with us, me.

Guido left the table and took Papa's chair, and Rosina in silence joined him in the living room. Raphael, no longer amused by the table talk, and no longer marveling at how Beatrice resembled the wife who had abandoned him, looked stoically down on his son and daughter-in-law.

I overcame an urge to smash things – tear every plate and cup off the table with a sweep of my arm, smash everything to bits on the floor as Mamma once did, nameless years ago when I was still a boy, while my father sat in silence grinding his teeth.

"Enough is enough," Mamma said wearily, sinking into a chair.

"Enough is too much," I said to Sandy, covering my cup with my hand as she offered me more cream.

Papa, turning his glass in his hand, sat with Edna next to him, his face full of scorn. He regretted his words, regretted his life, and wanted to take everything back.

"Tell us, Sal, about your job," Mamma said. "What do you do?"

"I'm the assistant to a man named Rochelle. Minimum wage. I'm making cabinetry and learning about wood." I will take notes while he pieces together a violin from maple two centuries old, and a bed made of exotic trees from every part of the world. And together my boss and I will dream of the girl about to lose her maidenhood on the bed we made.

"Where do you think it will lead, Sal, this job of yours?"

"In a few years maybe a partnership. Maybe profit sharing." He has no son.

Papa shook his head no. "You need a college degree to make kitchen cabinets? What did we send you to college for? Sometimes I just want to know what's eating you. Why don't you just come out with it, say what's wrong, and maybe just once just say what you want." Everybody waited for me. "Well, don't just sit there. Tell us what you want. What is your dream, what you really want to do?"

I want to make enough to get by without feeling useless and criminal, preserve well-made things without adding to the mess all around. Maybe now and then look up at the sky, let the moon and stars and bottomless black remind me of how small and insignificant I am in this here and now moment of space, how vital it is that at least, on balance, I do no major harm.

"Not much. Someday, I suppose, I'd like to own a small shop – maybe like Danko's place, the one on the corner near Nonno's store." And the street, crowded with little shops, would overflow with people who called each other's children by name. "That would be enough for me. That would be worth working for."

"Lot of good that will do you now," he said. And these words were the closest we came to mentioning Bruno's eviction from Guido's old store.

Papa quickly distanced all of us. "And I wouldn't count on getting money from me when I die."

Mamma pulled herself out of the chair at the end of the table and left the room.

"Gloria! Bring me a cup of coffee."

Mamma appeared behind him, her unsteady hand already holding a cup.

"This is a good woman. No man," Papa said, turning to Edna, "could ask for a better wife."

Mamma handed him the coffee. "You see if you want more sugar. I put in two."

Suddenly Edna dissolved. She began sobbing and hid her face in her hands.

"Sister Edna! What's wrong?" Mamma said, leaning in close to her.

She choked like a car trying to start. "I don't know, I don't know. Sometimes I just want to die. I don't know. Sometimes I just want to die."

My father pushed his chair back. "Oh Gloria! Do something for her. Make her happy somehow."

"Oh, oh," Edna cried.

"Here, here," Mamma said as she helped Edna up and led her to my room.

Kate and Bruno left with a hasty goodbye.

"What's the matter with you?" Papa hissed at Mamma. "She's still crying in there. Can't you do anything to make her stop? It makes me sick."

Mamma sank down again in a chair. "I'm tired," she breathed to herself. "I've been cooking all day. If you're so smart, you go in yourself."

Sandy was busy clearing the table.

"What can I do, Mamma?" I asked.

My father left the table and went to Edna's room. Mamma, saying nothing, shook her head, her eyes tired and hollow.

Sandy came to Mamma. "Do you feel all right? Is there something I can do?"

Mamma sank further into the chair, her head swaying back and forth. Too bad, too bad.

"Dylan and I are going out for a walk," Bea announced from the other room. And in a moment they had escaped down the stairs.

I required Rosina to stay put, then helped Sandy clear the table. My father was still in Edna's room. The door was open about six inches, and I could hear no more sobbing inside. As I went back and forth from table to kitchen sink, I saw Mamma become more and more alert, as if trying to hear what was going on in the other room.

"Sal," she said as I came near, "help me to the bedroom. Will you, please?"

She leaned heavily on me and took slow, dizzy steps. "Good night," she waved at Guido and Rosina as we passed by.

"Too early for bed," Rosina said.

"She's really beat," I explained.

Then I was alone with her in the room, she pulling a blue wool blanket over herself on the bed.

"What is he doing in there? Tell him I want to say something to him."

I went to Edna's room, rapped softly on the door, and told him that Mamma wanted him to come to her. "Okay, okay. Just a minute, okay. What does she want now?"

Mamma was staring at the door when I returned. "Is there anything else I can do?"

I saw her eyes come to life with a new idea. "Yes. Come here and take my hand."

Her hands were warm.

"Now would you kneel – right here at the bed? Would you let me pray for you?"

Oh God, anything but this.

"Please."

I kneeled down next to her. She did not release my hand.

"Oh God," she began, addressing her closed-eyed prayer to the ceiling, "sweet wonderful Jesus, son of Mary and God. You, who are goodness and love and God's grace and purity forever, hear a mother's prayer for her son. Take hold of my son's soul. Teach him the good way, the right way. More than anything, my God, I want my son safe in your holy bosom. I want his soul to be yours forever and ever."

She propped herself up and looked down at me.

"Now you pray a little, Sal. Don't be afraid. Ask God to do something. Ask God and he'll do it. All your dreams. All you have to do is ask."

The door flew open. "What do you want?" Papa said.

"I want you to pray with us too. Shut the door, and pray with us."

He looked around, confused. "What the hell you talking about?"

In my room Edna was crying again. I got up and backed away from Mamma's bed.

28, *No reason at all.*

Sandy, tight as a fist, said nothing all the way home, and I, unable to take her hand, had to go it alone. At the front door I managed an apologetic smile as she waited for me to find the key.

"That was some carnival, wasn't it?" I said as I let her in.

"That's the last time." She had made up her mind hours ago.

I threw my coat on a chair and sat down. The twilight sky was full of heavy damp clouds, so maybe it would snow again. Maybe the sky would gently descend on the earth, silently lay a blanket on her. Maybe tonight we would sleep a deep soft sleep, and tomorrow, tomorrow lift our heads from our pillows, look out at the clean white snow and smile at each other again.

"Would you mind hanging your coat up when you come in the house?" She snatched it up before I had a chance. I let her go, looking for somewhere to escape.

She was standing at the front closet door, my coat over her arm, when the phone rang. We looked at each other, waiting to see who would move first. It rang again and again. Finally she threw the coat down on the floor and took long strides to the phone.

"Hello?"

She looked with confusion at the receiver and hung up.

"Nobody there?"

She walked back toward my coat.

Again the phone rang – once, twice impatiently – and this time she turned directly to it.

"Hello."

267

She waited for answer. "Hello? Hello?" Slowly she put the receiver down.

"Wrong number?"

"I don't know" she said. "Some crank, some jerk."

Maggie. Causing trouble. "Say anything?"

"No."

I turned to the window and stared out until a sense of indifference began settling in. Then over my left shoulder I felt Sandy's shadow again.

"What's this?" she said. "What in the hell is this thing?"

Her eyes were terrified. She held Markels' pistol as if it were about to explode in her hands.

"Oh that," I said, taking it from her. "Don't worry about that. It doesn't belong to me."

"What's it doing here?"

"It belongs to Markels."

"Put it down! Get it away from me!"

I put it on the table near the door. "He wants me to get rid of it for him."

"What do you mean?"

"He had it. He's been very down, depressed. He's afraid to have it around."

"What in the world could be going through his mind?"

"The neighborhood's going downhill. And he's been very down, afraid."

"You're going to kill somebody with that thing."

"Markels has been depressed. God only knows what's been running through his mind. I spent a long time with him one afternoon this past week. Had a helluva time trying to get him out of bed. Finally he gave me the gun – to get rid of. That's what I was doing all last week."

"Well get rid of it," she said. "Get rid of it right now. Take it out of here. Throw it in a dumpster and make sure nobody sees."

"Okay," I said, "okay, okay. Where in the hell is my coat?"

I put the gun into the inside pocket of my coat.

"Where you going?"

"Out. Just out, somewhere. To get rid of this thing."

"How long will you be gone?"

I grabbed some change from the jelly jar. "I don't know. Not long. How long does it take to get rid of a gun?"

268

She was almost in tears. "Please don't be gone long."

"What's wrong with you?"

"What do you mean what's wrong? Don't I have a right to have something wrong? What about me? All day at work I have to look pretty and smile, and with your folks it's the same thing. Don't I have a right to a life of my own?"

I tried pulling her close but she broke away. "Sandy, please, sit down with me."

"With that thing in your coat? No. Please, hurry up and get rid of it."

The gun seemed cold next to my leg, heavy, too big for my hand. Night had fallen and the streets were empty except for an occasional sedan doing a bump and grind from one stop to the next. The shops along Grand were all closed, a few of the storefronts fenced in by padlocked gates. Yellow windows looked down on the street below, shadows now and then visible behind curtains and shades.

Ahead of me someone disappeared inside a doorway. I wrapped my hand around the gun and crossed the street.

How to get rid of a gun? Just throw it in a sewer or leave it in a garbage can? And in a city like this one now, why get rid of it at all? If someone were suddenly to jump out, a man would have a chance.

I found myself in front of Danko's place, no light on inside, but in the window something new, a loveseat, Victorian era, upholstered in green and blue. In my right pocket three quarters, a few pennies, nickels, and dimes.

I could see a light ahead of me in the window of Guido's old store. Bruno awake, doing his thing. If I stopped maybe he would want to talk, help me make sense of things.

I put my face to the window but saw no one inside. Across the street Kate's building was dark, all but one bulb burning in a window above.

I tried the door but found it locked. A cold wind swirling down into the street sent a chill through me. I pulled my coat closer and rapped on the door. Inside I could see papers scattered here and there, a light on in back, but no glow in the wood stove. And behind the stove, at the back of the store, the door leading to the yard was open wide.

I walked to the corner and around Danko's place until I came to the alley I still knew by heart. At the end of the alley a lamp on a wooden pole threw a shadow down from the eaves of an old garage. Beyond the shadow in a past daylight I saw boys playing kick-the-can, and Sam the Garbage Man inching by in his old pickup truck, and Donna Anna stooping down to pick young dandelions every spring.

I tightened my grip on the gun.

I found the latch to the wooden gate and walked into the yard. To my right the old crate that Guido sat on next to the shed, and a few old vines above patches of hardened snow. The light glowed through the open back door.

I approached and rapped twice. "Bruno," I called in a hush. "Bruno. Anybody home?"

The wind chilled me again.

"Bruno." I called more loudly this time, hearing nothing but a car horn blare twice at the corner of Grand and Second Street.

I called one more time, then entered, my hand still on the gun. The wood, piled high next to the door, blocked my view, so I walked forward cautiously, leaving the door open behind. Hanging over the room was the stale odor of a fire going out.

"Bruno!"

I saw his hand first, groping as if trying to crawl. He was on the floor next to the piano.

Oh no! Oh God no!

There, his left arm lost under his hip, Bruno lay in a pool of blood.

I bent over him, afraid to touch. His face, beaten and bloody, had no trace of my brother on it. Oh God, Oh God! I lifted his head in my lap and looked for a sign. As I leaned in he groaned and turned away. Oh God! He would not die right here, right now, my coat, hands, shirt still warm from his blood. I saw the sign, the slow rise and fall of his chest, and laid his head gently down.

"Quick!" I screamed into the phone. "Send an ambulance as fast as you can! My brother! He's dying! My brother!"

And moments after the siren screamed to a halt in the street Kate appeared in the door.

"No!" she screamed as she ran toward us, "No! Who did this? Who would do this to you!"

Her screams rushed out the door and circled wildly in the streets. In windows faces appeared, and cars went out of their way to have a look.

Just before they lifted him onto a stretcher he returned to consciousness, mumbling incoherently while he turned his head to and fro.

"Bruno," I whispered down at him, "there, there, you'll be okay now. We're here. They'll take care of you. We're here with you. It's Sal."

At the sound of my name he tried to open his eyes. "Don't," he stammered. "Don't."

"Shhh."

"Don't. Don't tell Mamma."

"Shhh. Shhh. Try not to talk."

"Who did it, Bruno?" Kate hissed. "Who did this to you?"

He tightened his hold on my hand.

"Shhh, don't worry about it now."

"Who?" Kate said, her face next to his.

"Them."

Them?

"Two black guys. They came in from the back."

"But why? Why?"

He tried to open an eye. "No reason at all."

29. *Why? Why did he keep asking why?*

There was a reason, because people don't turn bloody black and blue by themselves.

I left Papa behind to calm Mamma down and follow the ambulance to the hospital. Kate was the first to notice me striding away. "Where are you going?" she yelled after me. I was too insane to explain that there is a reason for everything, for Bruno's being so suddenly black and blue – that I needed to confront the cause face-to-face. "Maybe you'll be happy now," I shouted over my shoulder at her. "I'm going to do something for a change."

I kept walking without turning back, my hand, unable to free itself of the dead weight of the gun concealed in my coat, burning to set things right. My feet knew the way. Within minutes I was in the south side, standing on the corner of Twelfth and Wayne. This is where they lived. *Loro,* Guido called them, a look of mystification on his face whenever he used the word. *Them.* Blacks.

Lazy. Papa's word summing them up. Why don't they want to work? His answer looping back: Because they're lazy, that's why.

To my left three tall ones on the curb, one of them leaning down to talk to faces in an idling Oldsmobile. Looking in the window of the liquor store across the street an old man in a ragged tweed overcoat. Shoes and used clothes piled in the darkened window of the shop next door, and then a storefront church, curtain drawn behind a handpainted sign – PAN-AFRICAN FREE GOSPEL CHURCH. Across from it a grocery store, its window fronted by an iron grate; a small light inside dimly showing off rows of cigarettes, soda pop,

273

chips. A woman's laughter coming from the open doorway of the poolhall next door. A neon sign throwing a dull red hue on the snow piled on the curb. A woman alone at the far end of the street, her coat too short, her face lost inside a collar pulled high, two teenagers throwing words at her as they passed.

I began walking south on Twelfth as a police car slowed to check me out. Up ahead three youths were standing in a doorway, one of them gesturing wildly with his hands. Three youths, not two. I was looking for two. Sulking just inside the doorway was another one, his eyes fixed on me. *Them,* I thought, maybe *Them?*

Two, not one. The two I wanted here, somewhere in this neighborhood. Two bars on this block, another storefront gospel church, a joint for doing hair and nails, and cars with two, three, four faces in them, slowly cruising by. Hey, what's happening, man?

Then I saw them – both of them looking in the window of the liquor store. The taller one, seeing me stare at him, elbowed his partner. Then they turned and walked away from the liquor store, disappearing around the corner. I ran a few steps, slowing when I saw a woman staring from across the street. As I got to the corner I saw the two again, looking in the gated window of a jewelry store halfway down the block. They saw me and took off, running this time.

"Hey!" I yelled as I ran after them.

They ducked into an alley just as I caught up.

"Freeze, you motherfuckers," I said, pointing the barrel of the gun through the coat.

They stopped and turned to face me, their eyes looking for a way out.

"What the fuck you want, man?" said the taller one.

"I want the motherfuckers who beat my brother up."

"What the fuck you talking about?"

"You know what I'm talking about. My brother Bruno, that's who."

"You be motherfucking crazy, man, with that thing. We be the only brothers we know. You dig?"

My voice trembled. "Where were you an hour ago?"

They looked at each other before the shorter one spoke. "I be home with my mamma."

"And I be there too," said the other one.

"This motherfucker be my brother. We all be brothers, man. You dig?"

Liars. Both of them liars. They were the ones. *Loro.*

"Why you pointing that motherfucking thing at us?"

Then we all looked up. Above, from a yellow window on the third floor, a baby began to wail, its cry persistent and shrill, full of anger and hopelessness. Suddenly there was nothing else.

"Okay, okay, you sonofabitches, both of you. So get going now, get the fuck out of here. But never again," I hissed as I lowered the gun and backed away. "I'm warning you, motherfuckers. Don't you ever show your faces in my neighborhood again."

I found myself on the freeway overpass, looking down through the fence at the traffic streaming by. On all sides, beyond my ability to see, the city stretched on and on, its lights suffusing a misty haze into the sky. Out there people sat in their living rooms watching TV, others in corner bars sipping a beer while a jukebox wailed out tunes full of heartbreak and love. In neighborhood joints here or there black musicians sat at pianos playing their blues away into the night. And now Bruno would have his own blue tune to play.

There were reasons for everything, but what was there to see in the incoherent city below? Once grass and trees grew wild here, deer, gophers, rabbits, buffalo, wild boar, snakes. No more snakes. One by one the trucks came, pouring concrete over their holes. Then trees were planted in rows, and grass became crewcut lawns. Mother Nature's wildness scraped bare, framed, charted, sold. How many gardens would never grow here, how many acres of tomatoes, peppers, corn, everything locked indoors now? Where was She to go, this fertile Mother of us all, to escape the physical abuse being heaped on Her? Were we destroying each other, ourselves, because our art was crude, made of concrete and steel rather than the stuff of life? Was the violence in our streets Her way of getting revenge?

Who do we blame? Should we descend, stalk the city streets again, this time more carefully, studying strangers' eyes to find some trace of a memory of their having beat my Bruno bloody and blue? Or should we try for something more scientific, fingerprints, set up a streetcorner stand and require everyone passing by to prove they didn't have a hand in the affair? No, that would be too slow, too full of holes. Better to stand where I was standing now, take the gun out and empty it on traffic below. Then at least we could walk away feeling as if we had done something real.

Who was to blame for a system going – perhaps hopelessly gone – bad? Edna knew beyond doubt: The Architect of Lies. And I, looking at the city all around, its fiendish glow churning in smoke and haze, could see why Edna was so sure. The city, like the insane demons that sometimes got the best of us, was a bizarre and terrifying engine too powerful for any one person to control, modulate or fix. And Edna knew what to do: Shrink, turn away from it all, curl up in some house and hope to get by until the Final Trumpet sounds and the Great Architect puts the Architect of Lies in chains, destroys his City of Destruction and sets up his turnstile outside the walls of his Celestial City so that his Ednas, all smiles, one fine day could file in one by one.

And what did I, Salvatore, have to do to be saved: Be like Edna, more or less. Because indeed there was Hope. The Vietnam war was a tragedy but Hope was a success. He had teamed with Sinatra to take their show on the road, and they both returned from their mission smiling, Hope's Texaco stocks up another two and a half points.

To my left St. Paul's rose out of the shadows of the buildings surrounding it, its twin spires and campanile visible against the background of night sky. It seemed unmoved by the traffic surrounding it, inert like a massive rock rune. From here, the vantage point of the freeway overpass, I looked down at it, not required to see it brooding over me. And for the first time I saw it in relation to The Hill curving up away from it. The Hill was higher than St. Paul's, the mansions on top looking down. From there Waldman, architect, would be able to keep an eye on his construction projects.

And I had a gun in my pocket, my hand, no longer terrified and no longer free of it, burning to set things right. I could shoot a few blacks who maybe had bloodied Bruno's face, but no black was more guilty for Bruno's bloody face than a man named Waldman.

I wound my way up The Hill toward Waldman's house, my heart racing when I stood at his front gate. It was imposing and high, impossible to scale, but I quickly noticed that Waldman too had made an innocent mistake. No lock on his gate. It gave way to my touch, far enough for me to pass through. I followed a cobblestone walk leading to the porch, waiting for dogs to go wild or an alarm to sound. I heard nothing but an airplane passing high in the sky. I checked my watch: 10:32. Above me the brow of the house looked down, and in the window the same light shone.

So this was the house that Waldman built. This the first front porch step paid for by the pennies and dimes saved in a steel box from work done maybe sweeping floors. These the next twelve steps that came from the sale of bathtubs to men who stood in line waiting their turn to carry a tub away on their backs, and these the pillars holding up the porch, each erected from the soaring interest on bonds bought on a whim in some solitary broker's office in the middle of a downtown. The rafters of the porch cut from the interest on the bonds, interest leading to the stock that kept multiplying even after the market crashed in '29. And inside were the oak beams for this house salvaged from a wilderness of timber that paid the debt on the company that made switches – for everything. And these were the walls built out of stone by hands not smooth enough to buy whole neighborhoods at a time, not black enough to seek out an irrelevant vengeance by bludgeoning Bruno almost to death. This was the house that Waldman built.

My hand was furious when it found the pistol again.

At the door I stood in silence looking at the iron knocker to my left. It fell on metal too thick to carry sound to the heart of the house. I heard nothing inside, my hand already on the doorknob when the door suddenly opened just enough for me to make out a face inside.

An old man, bent over and in nightclothes, searched for my face with tired eyes. "What do you want?" He turned on a light over my head.

"I'm here to see Mr. Waldman."

"You crazy?" His eyes still had not found me.

"It's very important."

"Huh? What's your name?"

"Dirk. Brother Dirk. Don't you remember me? Bishop James sent me here."

He stepped back for a better look. His confused eyes, still searching for my face, saw only the darkness outside.

"You can't come in. You better go away."

"Don't trouble yourself. I'll go up. Your master called, is expecting me right away."

He gave way, let me get between him and the stairs.

"I know the way."

I climbed a dozen steps before I looked back and saw him at the bottom of the steps, small and bent, straining upward to get a glimpse of me.

I hurried up more stairs. When I came to the first landing the old man seemed dwarfed below. The staircase, broad and bannistered in heavy oak, turned up and away out of sight, two, maybe three more levels up. Corridors led away from the staircase, and off the corridors rooms, their doors all closed.

In the empty silence I saw Guido in his store, every morning restocking the cans and boxes on his shelves and piling the oranges into careful pyramids, then walking his broom through the narrow aisles before opening the doors, always free and easy around the precarious stacks, just as in back he moved with certain mastery around his vegetables, planting each foot carefully on a bare piece of ground.

Waldman had fifty rooms to wander, lose himself in, digressions, diversions, convolutions of some grand scheme or dream. At one time in his life he no doubt devoted himself to perfecting them all, papering each wall and hanging each tapestry just right, then moving on to the next, bewildered by the opportunities still ahead, the work yet to be done. Keep out, he said whenever a project was done, don't spoil it now, go somewhere else out there. He kept one room and one small light to himself, one bed, one view from a window, one chair old now and smelling of dust and age, and maybe somewhere too, in a memory too dim to be seen but still visible enough to be believed, one dream and one love poisoned by envy, resentment and regret and by a bitter need to even some old forgotten score.

Bruno's face returned to me – swollen, bloody, no music there. And I saw a big-faced boy in a business suit, one of Waldman's boys, ushering Guido out of Danko's store.

I started up the stairs, not looking back.

At the top of the second landing I opened myself into a room crowded with furniture enshrouded in white sheets. Nothing. I walked softly to the third level and tried the corridor to my right. Nothing again – no light, no sound.

Then I saw it, the last room on the left, a thin slice of light visible on the floor beneath the door. Waldman in there, scheming, counting his dollars as if they were words with meanings that would never change.

And his Gertrude – where was she now?

I felt for the gun, then knocked on the door.

A shuffling of feet behind the door. A voice, strong and clear. "What is it you want?"

"Our father," I whispered.

"What?"

"Our father who art in heaven."

I knew he stood within inches of me, for I could feel a heat, a pressure coming through the door. He waited to hear more, then fumbled for the latch.

His eyes, glazed and confused, missed me entirely, looking over my right shoulder. I nudged the door open and stepped into the room.

Then his eyes found me. "I don't know you," he said, suddenly afraid. "Who are you?"

He seemed too short, shrunken, only a few strands of hair left on his head. His blue robe was open in front, its sash trailing behind him on the floor.

"Who are you?" he asked again.

I looked him up and down once more. "Don't you know me? I am the savior of America."

His eyes turned in, as if searching for a familiar face on a crowded city street. "Huh?" he said.

"You don't know your own son?"

"Son? There must be some mistake."

"There is no mistake, father."

"Father? You've got me confused." He leaned in close enough to read the lines on my face. "I'm not married to anyone. Never have. What are you talking about son?"

"Magdalene's my mother's name. Don't you remember? Don't you know you've been married to her all these years?"

"This is some joke."

He stiffened, drew back, his voice full of the habit of command. "What do you want here?"

"My inheritance. I came here to pick up the deed for a little shop on Second Street."

"I don't know what you're talking about. There's only niggers living there."

"I'm a nigger too. Can't you see?"

He made a move to get a closer look.

"I don't want you here. Get out or I call the police."

I closed the door behind me. "Kick out your own son?"

"What do you want? What are you talking about?"

"I'm talking about every shop on every Main Street in the world, Mr. Waldman. Do you think your will will always be done?"

"I don't know what you're talking about."

"I'm talking about old grocery stores."

"I don't know anything about grocery stores."

"Old family grocery stores. The ones, Mr. Waldman, that give us our daily bread. You ever eaten daily bread? Come with me and I'll give you a taste."

"I don't want to go anywhere with you."

"Then you'll end up in hell."

He made a move toward the door. "Karl! Karl! Call the police right away!"

I stepped in front of him. "Haven't you heard? Karl's on strike for a living wage."

He finally understood. He was alone, the enemy in his house. "What do you want?" he whispered.

"The grocery store."

He straightened himself, wrapping his robe around himself tight. "Good. I'll have my lawyer here first thing in the morning."

"No lawyer, Mr. Waldman."

"What do you mean, no lawyer?"

"I want you to forgive us our debts."

"What do you mean?"

"You promised to sell it back to us. So I'll give you a dollar for the store."

"A dollar? You want a handout. In my day we worked for what we got."

I took the gun out. "Did you build all this yourself?" I said, taking in the house with a sweep of the gun in my hand. "Did you lift one stone?"

He tottered back, falling into a chair to the left of his desk. "What are you going to do?"

"I'm here to make you a lifetime deal. For a grocery store."

"Grocery store? I don't understand."

I fumbled in my pocket, scattered my change on the desk, and carefully counted it out. "One dollar."

He turned it over in his head. "But then you have to go away."

I walked to his chair and stood over him. His robe was open, leaving him half-naked and shivering. His penis, visible under a fold of flesh overlapping his belly, lay dead next to his right thigh. Poor pathetic wrinkled thing. Here he was, The Capitalist, with no child named Art, an old man on his last legs unable to pull himself up any more.

He was trembling as I tore a blank sheet from a note pad on the desk and scribbled the words with his own pen:

> *I hereby sell to Guido Amato for the total sum of one dollar the old grocery store on Second Street which is now under lease to him.*

He looked up weakly, squinting as he tried to make sense of my face, and signed his name in an illegible scrawl.

I was standing with one foot on the sash of his robe. I picked it up and tried its strength between my hands.

In a coarse whisper he said, "There, I signed."

"It's a worthless piece of paper. You know that well enough."

"Fifty-five thousand – I've got it in the safe. It's yours, but you have to go away."

No. My heart said no to him, and my hands, disconnected from reason or sense, tightened into fists that would not let loose of the sash. You squeezed us, I cried through my hands, you squeezed us and now we will squeeze back, let you know what it is like to strangle for fifty years. I sent the cry through my trembling hands as I pulled the sash taut and held it in front of his face.

Waldman let out a sob, then opened his eyes wide.

"Why?"

"Why? Because you're a destroyer of dreams."

His eyes, bulging with fear, did not understand. "But *why?*" he said again, his voice quavering with bottomless innocence.

My hands let the sash fall. Then he caved in, collapsed in a heap like an old rag.

I snatched the piece of paper before I ran out of the room. "He's dead," I whispered to myself, hearing as I ran the wail of sirens coming my way. "My God, what have I done? I've killed a man."

Walking wildly through city streets I found a sewer grate and threw the gun in. *Why?* Why did he keep asking *why?*

30. *But I could not stop my tears, and could not lift my face from my hands.*

My hands trembled all day at work, and I had to sit as I read the afternoon newspaper. **Elderly Millionaire Assaulted.** The old man was frightened and confused but resting comfortably in General Hospital. Police were looking for clues, but had few leads.

I walked home with my face turned away from passing cars, afraid to betray myself by throwing nervous glances behind. Sandy was late as usual. I decided to wait until ten to give her a call, relieved to be left alone with the newscasts on TV. Still few details about the Waldman assault, and when I finally fell asleep the police still had few leads.

The next morning Sandy was asleep next to me, her clothes on the chair smelling of cigarettes. She had thrown a blanket over me and taken off my shoes.

"You look sick," she said as I tried to open my eyes.

"I am."

"Flu?"

"Probably. I feel pretty awful."

She got up and walked to the bathroom. "Why don't you stay in bed."

"Why don't you come back to bed?"

She looked in the mirror and smiled. "Not right now. I have this urge to shop. Should I pick up something for your flu?"

Within a half-hour she showered and was on her way out the door. I stayed in bed waiting for her, dreaming of how I would pull her in next to me, make love, then, as we were face to face on the same pillow, confess about my night in Waldman's house.

She shopped all day, and the next morning she left early for work. That evening I went to the restaurant where she worked, hoping to take a table and flirt with her. I had it all planned. Just as she was done with her shift, I would order a bottle of wine and beg her to sit for a little cheese and bread. But she was long gone when I arrived, and by the time I got home she did not want to wake up for me.

There was no sleeping as waves of anger and fear kept passing through me all night. Tomorrow morning, Monday December 1, Bruno had to be out of the old store. I wanted to be there, but he said no, stay away, and keep Nonno away. We were finished there – we had to get used to the idea. I saw myself holding the sash in front of Waldman's face, my mind on fire, my knuckles white from pulling on it.

Terror gripped me when the phone began to ring. I had my story, my alibi prepared. But as I picked up the phone I was ready to surrender myself, tell the whole truth.

Bea's voice, quiet and clear: "Sal, Mom died last night. In her sleep. Papa called for her to get up, put the coffee on, but she never opened her eyes. They say it was a heart attack, Sal, but I think it was what they did to Bruno."

Her voice became brittle, thin. "We're all here, at the house. Bruno too. He's okay."

I lifted myself onto an elbow and looked over to Sandy's side of the bed. The blanket had been thrown back. She was gone again.

I let my head sink to the pillow again. Terrible. How could this be? What could I do? I had to call someone, talk to Mamma. I saw her in the kitchen standing over the sink, her back to me.

Mamma died in her sleep last night.

Almost seven o'clock. What day was it? Sandy had never gone to work this early before. Today was Monday again. I had to go to work. Did everyone expect me to start missing work?

I closed my eyes. I was too tired today. That goddamned Bea – she had her nerve calling this early in the day.

What do you do when someone dies? You have to go there and stand around. People cry. And it's forbidden to talk too loud, forbidden to smile.

She was looking so weary these past few weeks, so discouraged and down. We should have known something was wrong.

It's not my fault. Everybody has to die. And Waldman had it coming to him.

I suppose it's all up to me now. Funeral arrangements. You expect me to get ahold of Sandy, call Rochelle, get dressed, get right over there, take care of everything.

Goddammit!

Goddammit! Goddammit! Goddammit! I have to stop right in the middle of everything. And Waldman can go to hell!

Your own mother.

It's up to you Sal, to make the funeral arrangements. You're the oldest son.

I always wanted her to teach me how to make her bread.

Mamma, Mamma. I cried and cried.

"Sal, where in the hell have you been? It's almost noon."

I have been away too long, and now it's too late. Looking for Sandy. Where in the hell was she all this time? I had a hard time getting in touch with her.

My father, with Edna across from him half-turned away, sat staring blank-eyed at the bedroom door. Bruno stood next to him, his eyes darting about behind the bandages covering his face, and Guido was in the kitchen leaning on his stick. Kate, her bulge conspicuous beneath a tight print dress, was in a corner, her head in her hands.

"They took her away already, Sal," Bruno whispered in a hoarse voice. "The ambulance came and took her away about an hour ago."

"So what if I wasn't here," I snapped. "It wouldn't have made any difference if I was here." But she would have wanted me to lift the sheet and look one last time at her face. She would have wanted me to see the weariness frozen there, the lines worn on her face by worry and work. And when they wheeled her out on the stretcher she would have made them stop at the door so she could say, I've had enough. I'm leaving and never coming back. No one can convince me to come back – not you, my husband. You who have locked me into your heart and never let me out; not you, daughter, you who fool around in unthinkable ways; not you, Bruno – you have no

285

time for anyone; and not you Sal, the one who first tore through my body with an unimaginable pain and who, when the pain turned dull, became my greatest grief. So I'm leaving and nothing will convince me to stay, not even you Sal. I will put up with all of you no more, no more.

I know the ambulance men had a hard time getting her stretcher through the doorway into the hall. I know the hallway is too narrow, and I know everyone watched and wept as the men twisted and turned to get her out the door.

I put my head in my hands and saw it again. Her bedroom, the wallpaper that always seemed so old. They told me it was the first thing I opened my eyes to when, screaming more loudly than Mamma's pain, I was brought into the world. The wallpaper. Faded, wrinkled here and there. The background not beige, a dirty pink. Small lifeless flowers – yellow and blue – everywhere.

Did she know what was happening to her when, day by day, she missed her cycle the first time? Did she say anything to Papa? I remember when I was fifteen, maybe seventeen, I found a rag under some newspapers in the trashcan in back. The rag was bloody and not quite dry, and I remember leaning down to catch a hint of it with my nose, how strange it smelled, how good.

We washed the walls every spring with warm water and a sponge. Every year we all had to help. One night after we finished with the walls, she tore dishes out of the kitchen cupboard and smashed them one by one on the floor. Papa never said a word. He quietly slipped out and I found him sitting alone in the cellar grinding his teeth.

Then one Sunday she announced she wanted new wallpaper in every room. He didn't say anything, just looked away. Six months later she repapered the kitchen walls.

"What did the doctor say?" I asked Bruno. "Do they know for sure?"

He shrugged. "Heart attack."

"Not cancer? Are they sure?"

No, the doctor couldn't be sure without doing the tests. He said there was an unusual lump in her neck, but he said it was a heart attack.

"And you, Bruno, how are you?"

"My head hurts, but don't worry about me. I'll be okay."

"What did the doctor say?"

"The ringing in my ears. He's a little worried about the ringing in my ears."

When I was a small boy there was a leak in the roof after a big thunderstorm, and in one corner of Mamma's bedroom the wallpaper got wet. She didn't know what to do. She tried wiping the stain off with a cloth, and later she tried the sponge with warm water and soap. She was afraid to rub too hard, and the stain never came out. Yet every spring she tried again and again to get rid of the stain.

"What will happen now to Papa?" Bea asked.

Bruno didn't know.

"Edna has him hooked," I said.

"I can't see it," Bea complained. "I can't see her moving in and taking over Mamma's place. I just wouldn't be able to stand coming here."

"Imagine the two of them sleeping together in Mamma's bed."

"Oh Sal! Shut up! Sometimes all you see is smut!"

Edna saw us talking and put on a smile.

"Dad wouldn't really fall for her, would he?" Bea asked.

"She had Mamma talked into being a Protestant," I replied.

"Papa can't stay here all alone," Bruno said.

"Would you be willing to take care of him?" I asked Bea. "Would you be willing to be his little wife?"

"Oh Sal!"

"Maybe we would get used to Edna after a while," Bruno said.

"Maybe we would." Maybe we could get some new furniture and paint the kitchen and living room. Maybe we could get new wallpaper for the bedroom too.

Finally I escaped, went back home. Nobody was waiting there for me, no cops. Waldman could go to hell. Nothing mattered but Mamma. And where was Sandy? I just wanted to lie next to her, put my head down on her chest, say nothing, think nothing more. Nothing mattered any more.

Mamma would be ready for the funeral home by Tuesday noon. People would come and go and I would have to listen to their words, show all of them a sad face. I would have

Mamma there in the same room with me, not able to turn my back on her. It is wrong to turn your back on your mother when she is dead.

"Sal, the flowers are just beautiful. They're just the way your mother would have wanted them."

"She was such a good woman, Sal. She worked so hard and never complained. But I don't need to tell you."

"Oh Sal, Sal, I can't believe everything happened so fast. And here it's almost Christmas coming on."

"You never know these days."

"Sal, who's that lady sitting next to your dad?"

Yes, rather good-looking, isn't she? Calls herself Saved. "Her name is Edna. She was somebody Mamma knew right before the end."

"Oh that's wonderful."

"How is your father taking it?"

"Hard, very hard."

"What will he do? He can't live alone. He was so sick himself just a few weeks ago, poor man. What will he do?"

"Maybe Guido and Rosina will move in with him. I'm not sure. Rosina is still strong, able to get around. Maybe they'll move in with him. But I'm not sure."

"Oh that would be wonderful. That's the way your mother would want it to be."

"Oh look. There's the DeSantini family – Fred and Sue."

"Everybody's here."

"That's the way your mother would want it, Sal."

Maybe even Maggie would come. She would appear at the door all dressed in black, give me one glance through a black veil, and while everyone turned to stare she would walk solemnly up to Mamma's casket, lift the veil away from her face, whisper some words, and lay one small flower next to her hand. A silent murmur would shudder through everyone's heart. They would know there was some secret, some wrong. And they would know I was the one in the wrong because, because Maggie would pause to stare at me just before she disappeared from the room, and everyone would see the hurt on Mamma's face caused by the words that Maggie whispered to her.

Not until Tuesday night in the funeral home did I dare to look at Mamma's face.

"Oh Sal, she looks so beautiful," my aunt Teresa said. "She looks so beautiful and calm."

"She was a good Catholic – and she looks heavenly," I said loud enough for Edna to hear.

Too much makeup. No sadness around her eyes, and their sympathetic softness gone, closed in. Her jaw seemed set, like a mind locking in a belief to keep it safely off the streets, and her eyelids never moved. Her cheeks and lips were too red, the makeup caked on. If she were awake she would make Bea wash it off.

"Oh God bless him," I heard a woman whisper behind my back while I kneeled before Mamma. "That poor boy, that Sal."

"And her poor husband Paul – he won't even look at her."

Nor can son look at her, for he sees death's woman, one more body used up in the charnel house of life.

She worked so hard and never complained.

Everything is just the way she would have wanted it. Except where is Sandy, Sal's wife? Why isn't she here?

Forgive me Father, for I have sinned. And now she is dead. Forgive me Father, for now maybe I'm free of her.

Kate had a strong grip on my arm. "Sal, Sal, your father wants to talk to you right away."

My father, a red flush on his face, pulled me to one side. "Did you see the goddamned bill?"

"How am I supposed to know about funerals?"

"I should have made the arrangements myself. Jesus Christ," he said. "Your mother was right. You never do anything right."

On Wednesday morning we buried her. A cold day but bright and blue. Only about twenty – those closest to us – followed the hearse to the Parkview Cemetery thirty-seven miles away.

"Where's your goddamned wife?" Papa asked.

Again I didn't know. She had come and gone from the apartment without leaving word, and when I called her at work she was already gone. What could I do but lie?

"Her boss laid it on the line. Either she works or she's fired."

"Those bastards," Bea said.

289

Bruno had called the Bishop to ask for a requiem Mass, but the Bishop did not return his call. Finally Bruno went to the rectory in person, and a priest told him it was too late for a Mass. So we took Mamma from the funeral home to the cemetery without the requiem. Bruno vowed revenge on the church, swore it would have to give Mamma her Mass. A priest from a suburban parish was waiting for us when the motorcade arrived, and within twenty minutes Mamma was lowered into the ground.

We stood around after that, all but Guido who refused to come. Afterwards we met at the house, where Edna had prepared cake and tea. The priest from the suburbs returned with us, and we found Guido, his eyes darting back and forth as if expecting more bad news, waiting for us. The room seemed too warm and the coffee too thin. We stood and then we sat. We felt tired and wandered about. Only Bruno raised his voice, for he kept calling the rectory every ten minutes until the Bishop finally agreed to talk to him. "All right then," Bruno shouted into the phone. "On Friday then. Friday at 6:30. A.M. But I want an organist there, a good one. I want the organ and everything."

"Shouldn't a requiem be held before a burial?" I asked.

"It doesn't have to be that way. This is something we do for her. She was born in the Church, lived near St. Paul's all her life, and was proud that Nonno's father had a hand in building it. It's the least we can do."

"I don't want to go near that creepy place," Bea complained. "I'll probably get accused of stealing another rosary."

"You've got to go. Everyone's got to go."

"I'm not sure Mamma will want to be there," I said. "Edna says she accepted Jesus Christ as her Lord and Savior before she died."

"She did what?"

"Became a Protestant."

"Bullshit," Bruno said. "Once a Catholic, always a Catholic."

"We'll go just this one last time," Bea said, taking hold of Dylan's hand. "But as soon as it's all over I'm becoming a Catholic with a very small 'c'."

"Wait a few years," Kate said to her. "Things all over the world will be so bad you're going to want to break that big old monstrosity church into apartments so people will have a roof over their heads."

"You'd probably want to get rid of the organ too," Bruno said. "That place has a wonderful organ. What would you do with that?"

"Who needs organs?" she replied humorlessly.

When the alarm clock sounded at four on Friday morning I knew the truth about my wife. Again she wasn't there, but Mamma was, in the strange way all things are present when we awaken in the dark. She was in the kitchen calling me to get out of bed. I could hear her at the sink, the water turned on and off, and again she was standing at the door, blocking my way, not letting me go out unless I had something to eat. The apartment was cold, the dismal December day whistling through cracks in the windows. Did bodies in graves freeze during winter months, or would the frost not touch them that far down? Poor Mamma. Nothing had gone all right for you. Never never in your whole life did you find happiness for more than one moment at a time. An hour here and there, but never never one whole day. Yes, yes, I will get out of bed now.

"Sandy, wake up. We've got to go to Mamma's Mass."

I shook myself awake. There was no one next to me in the bed. I shuddered and dressed in the dark.

God lived in a cave that was damp and cold on December Friday mornings at six. Just outside the altar rail stood a catafalque made of wood, on it a framed picture of Mamma taken the summer after she gave birth to Beatrice. Her hair was long, pulled together by a white ribbon in back, a serene smile touched by sadness on her face. No early morning sun yet shone through the stained glass, but the organ, its middle range solemn and deep, sent a soft vibrato through the empty space above. Eight of us sat in the first two rows, but over my shoulder I could see shadows slowly moving along the stones, and out of the corner of my eye I could see Mamma smiling at me from the catafalque. Ten thousand years ago men had huddled near here before, painting on stones the figures of animals and faces of unsmiling gods.

How in the world did the priests heat a place like this? An enormous coal furnace underground, sending its ductwork up like tentacles. And down there tending it must be a man grimy and black, paid to do nothing but shovel coal.

Bea was sullen, almost asleep in the pew. "What's wrong?" I asked.

"Don't you think this is an anti-climax? I mean, she's been buried two days now." She turned away as if it were all my fault.

"Bruno wanted a requiem." The organ. He wanted to hear it played for her. He wanted music to carry Mamma out of the world, just as it carried him away, the organ humming the lullaby vaguely present in his past.

The priest entered from the right, and I saw Bea shrink. Father Francis. Those damned devils had decided that Father Francis should say the Mass. Rubbing the rosary in our wounds.

"Requiem aeternam dona eis."

We stood and we kneeled and we went through all the motions learned by heart.

Then Father Francis ascended the pulpit steps.

"Gloria Maria Ferucci Amato. It is to mark this woman's passage to the other world that we, friends and family, are assembled today. She came naked into the world, she served her Lord and Master, and now she has left this earth. Do we dare ask any more of a woman? Since 1921, when she first took communion in the Parish of St. Paul, Gloria Amato has been faithful to her church, her goodness far outweighing her sins, merely human sins to which we are all from time to time subject, and for which, by God's good grace, we may all earn forgiveness. She brought into the world three children, showed them the way of the Church, and performed her earthly duties as mother to them. In this she was like the mother of Christ herself. What more is there to say about someone as such? That family and friends will miss her presence among them. That her good works will live on. That she shall receive her just reward in heaven – she who provided for those she loved here on earth in the hope that one day the Lord God of heaven, receiving her spirit purified of all sin, would provide for her. May we, like her, all devote ourselves to the work of the spirit, and may we all remember her in this day's prayers by saying a

292

rosary for her. And now let us all prepare to share the bread, the body of our Lord, and consecrate the body of Gloria Amato to God. Amen."

As we approached the communion rail, the organ breathed deeply, and the dome of St. Paul's opened into full view, empty enough to hold all our prayers and regrets. Lifting my head I again saw the carelessness crossing the dome – Raphael's cross, the mistake in magnificence he could not endure. If Raphael had had his way, St. Paul's would have been the most beautiful cathedral in America. It would have taken forever to build, would have required money and labor and sacrifice, but it would have been the most beautiful cathedral in America. And now it was too late. The Magdalene, woman who gave herself, who loved, who was no saint, fell further from grace the day Raphael walked away from his work, St. Paul biding his time to take her place. Looking back one last time, Raphael must have uttered one final curse as he lost sight of his dream, the female form ascending to the clouds as a shrine made of stone.

Now there was too much weight, all of it boorish and blunt, and nothing could lighten the burden or correct the mistakes. We could try moving away, but St. Paul's shadow would lengthen and take us back in. We might never escape what we had made of things not so many years ago. Everything was inside everything else.

Father Francis saw my disdain as he placed the Host on my tongue. He mumbled his words and quickly moved on. The Host dissolved and sent a wave of hunger through me. I wanted eggs and toast, butter, jam, sausage, everything.

Ah Mamma – but she could cook.

She smiled at me from atop the catafalque. Beatrice had just been born, and Mamma was still young, her ageing begun years ago with the pinprick of a weary sadness that left its indelible mark. It grew slowly, imperceptibly, and she kept it all in, the confusion, the pain. Everything. And what was everything? The times I wailed in the night, afraid of the dark – and then Bruno and Beatrice after me, year after year, night after night, hour after hour until every minute of our wailing became every night of her life? Was it the afternoons Papa returned from work with no more than a nod of the head, his own congealing heart dulling the memory of the passion to which she had abandoned herself, perhaps against her will and in spite of the shame requiring silence and humorlessness? Was everything the daily bread she prepared for us so often that her hands knew by rote what to do with the lumps of dough? Was it that she had to hit us with words and guilt so that he, Papa, would not hit her with words and guilt because someone outside the house had hit him with words and humiliating stares? Who was this woman so vital, so much taken for granted, so gone?

"Sal?" Bea nudged me. "Sal, what's the matter Sal?"

And now, Mamma, there you are – in a hole. This a sunken cathedral set on a cavernous earth, whole galaxies swallowing their tails, falling into black holes. Mamma, Mamma. On your final bed, so many loveless nights, now.

"Nothing."

"Then get up. Everyone is staring at you."

Forgive me, Mother, for not loving you the way you deserve, for betraying you because you were no longer young and beautiful.

"Sal...Sal!" Bea took my arm and led me back to my seat. Father Francis, with the altar boys behind, had the last say. *"Requiescant in Pace,"* he pronounced with a sideways glance my way. We all said Amen. Then he descended the altar steps, incensed and aspersed the catafalque, and pronounced the benediction over all of us.

But I could not stop my tears, and could not lift my face from my hands.

31. *"No. I can't stay here. No, thank you, please, no. I have to go home."*

She wasn't there any more. I turned this way and that, waiting for her to call, walk in the door. In my gut I had this sense that there was something terribly wrong. More than anything I wanted to let myself go, just fall back, let her cradle me. Where could I go now? Who was there for me?

"Nonna," I said through the door, "can I come in?"

She was in a white nightgown yellowed by the light behind her chair. Across from her the Virgin was in her usual place, the coffee table centered under the window facing east, presiding with serene eyes over the apartment's worn sofa, frayed area rugs, formica table, and old gas stove. The Queen of Heaven's eyes had that eerie blank look few sculptors can remove from stone, but she wore her crown and royal robe with dignity.

"Ah Salvatore," she began, "your Nonno goes to bed early now, but I stay awake thinking of many things. Listen to that nose of his in bed. You men. How little you know. Your Mamma, she died – why not me instead? You cry all night and can't sleep thinking of her. But I think of the living, not the dead. Your Mamma, you know, has a mother too, Serafina, still alive, your other Nonna who went back to Italy. Imagine her now. The pain she will feel when she gets the word. Do you see the news on TV, all the sons who die in the wars? It is a violation of God and natural law. Mothers should die first. When the sons die first it is a knife in the mother's womb, and nobody can wash from a mother's sheets the blood of all those boys who die in faraway wars. All that blood we shed. Have you ever seen the blood women pass every month, and the

295

blood of birth? You men. Maybe someday you will learn how to give birth. Then it will be right for their children to die first. So do not weep for your Mamma. She died in her good time. Her children, you, still live. Weep for Serafina and the pain she will feel in her womb. If I could have died instead of your Mamma, Serafina would not feel the pain.

"And now Guido tells me your wife has left your house. Where can she go? There is no Old Country for her. Does she have a mother's house waiting empty for her? You men. Why does it surprise you when your women go away, want nothing more to do with you? Where do you go every day? Away from our house. You look at the news. All the boys who go to some war. They leave us behind, the mothers and wives, and why? To learn how to kill and be killed, find some new woman or whore in some faraway place, some girl they can abandon again. What do they care about the pain we feel when we're alone? And when they come back they are never satisfied with us any more. They are no longer boys, and we have grown old. They want somebody new, the girl abandoned in the city they destroyed. Always somebody new to make them forget they are getting old."

"But Guido never went to war."

"All the worse for him. Maybe he would have gone if food was not always on the table waiting for him. No, Guido never went to war. He went to his little store, or to that little throne he made for himself next to the back fence. I let him go, turned the other way so his little witch could whisper to him, give him her remedies for his little aches and pains. How nice the way she too stood there all day, waiting for the tree to bear a few figs. I never liked them myself, the way he split them open with his thumbs, that crooked smile on his face when he did. They were never really sweet enough in America, and even there in that store surrounded with the vegetables and fruit, olives, cheeses, and grains, he never got enough to eat. When he got hungry he always came home, sat by the kitchen table until what he liked appeared under his nose. He fooled me at first, but not any more.

"You know, you also will get old. That's what I want to tell you, Salvatore. If now you can't keep your woman in your house, what will happen when you get old? Think about your Nonno, that old goat. Where can he go now? I'm not like your wife – remember that. We own nothing, never did. But this apartment, these chairs, this table and this gas stove – they are mine. Your wife left and where is she now? What does she have? A house of her own? No, how can she have her own house unless there is one waiting for her in Italy? She is like your Nonno, gone all the time to his store. Now he has no place to go, and where is she, your wife?"

She gazed at the Virgin and crossed herself.

"Forgive me," she said. "I wish no one harm. Your Nonno cannot help himself any more. For us it is too late. When you have been married for seventy years, you too will see that you were children when you stood before the priest and made your vows. Our Lord said it is better to marry than to burn, but he never intended us to live a hundred years. Look at Him, how young He was when He died for us. He was gentle and beautiful, like his Mother the Queen. He fed the hungry and nursed the sick back to health. He did what the women do. That's why the soldiers hunted him down and hung him on the cross. He hid among the women, but they were slaves like me. What choice did we have in those days? Your Nonno came looking for a bride, and it turned out to be Donna Anna or me. He chose me. And now most of all I think about my little Beatrice. I see her getting closer and closer to that boy with long hair. Soon it will be too late for her. He will ask her to marry him, and she, poor girl, will say yes. She will be where I was when I was her age. Married to that boy with hair like a girl. The next thing you know she will be like your wife, the one with the job, all alone with no house of her own.

"So where is she now, this wife of yours?"

"In an apartment, Nonna."

"Listen to me. She will come back to you. Before Christmas. You listen to me. She will not be able to live all alone. I will say the rosary for you, and the Mother of God will send her back. I know her. She will do what you ask. All she wants is you to pay attention to her. All these years and no baby comes. What do you expect? Just listen to my words, and don't forget to say the rosary every morning and night by your bed. You'll see then a baby will come."

She ran the palm of her hand over her brow just as Guido made a strange wheezing sound in his sleep. Then she pulled herself up and opened the refrigerator.

"What can I get for you?" she said. "I have nothing in the house. I have some of yesterday's soup, and there's a nice piece of provelone. But I don't know what else I can offer you – maybe some cookies or a piece of toast?"

"No, please, Nonna. I'm not hungry at all. It's almost midnight. Please no."

She went to the closet and began rummaging about, her back turned to me as she talked.

"I want to do something for you, but I don't know what. You don't know, but your Mamma and I we talk about it all the time, how unhappy you are, what we can do to make you a happy boy."

She turned toward me smiling, a bundle of sheets in her hands.

"I remember when your were born, both your Mamma and me how happy we were. Salvatore. Right then we gave you to God, held you in our arms and said the rosary. Take him, we said to the Queen of Heaven, and make him do your work. Give him, we prayed, a special mission in life."

She sat in her chair again, the bundle still in her hands, an absent faraway stare in her eyes.

"Over there, in the Old Country, the women had no choice. By the time they were thirty years old they had their half-dozen kids. They were worn and old, and their men worked all day and then wanted nothing to do with them. Our mothers knew how to yell at their men, keep them in line when they got lazy and drunk, and many of the women paid the price by suffering the blows that came their way. A few of us managed to escape, thanks to the Queen. We left and never went back. Some were only thirteen when they entered the nunnery, and I should have been one of them."

She got up, went to the sofa, and began unfolding the sheets.

"What are you doing, Nonna?"

"I'm making a little bed for you. I want you to stay here tonight. You don't know how much I worry about you all alone. I'll make a nice little bed for you."

I stood and began backing toward the door. "No. I can't stay here. No, thank you, please, no. I have to go home."

32. *...the pulses increased for the advent of the game, the more than eighty thousand cheering souls.*

Many things happened as if suddenly, but they all were happening many years ago.

Sandy moved out the day after the requiem. She took her clothes, most of the kitchen stuff, the TV, and her favorite record albums. She left me the rest, though when I was away she kept coming back to claim a vase, a painting, old photographs and a few other objects that mattered to her. I stayed away from my father after I broke the news. "Are you finally happy?" I said as I left his place. "At least I've got a regular job." A week later a banker called. Would I be interested in wisely investing the money in my trust account? Trust account? What trust account? Yes, eleven thousand two hundred and thirty-three dollars, money Mamma had spirited away over the years – a dime, nickel, penny at a time. Still too confused to feel the surge of power and satisfaction the money conferred on me, I politely told the banker no thanks, I had other plans. My fingers trembled as I wrote Sandy the letter. She could pay for college with it, and I would hold the job. Would she come back? She called to say no, she still loved me, but she loved him too. It was something she couldn't explain. Could we talk about it some day, maybe after the craziness of Christmas was done? I was too quiet at work and Rochelle kept taking me aside, trying to buck me up. There were cabinets to be made, and I began hating the searing sound of the table saw. At first the fragrance of new-cut wood had its allure, but by the end of the day the workplace had a dry acrid smell. In the bathroom I looked at myself in the mirror: The sawdust drifting down made my hair look grey. And there was always more work to do – always right angles to cut, joints to fit perfectly into other joints, surfaces to plane, sand smooth. I was a worker too now, a member of the rank and file, just one more pair of hands, centuries old, that had tilled the soil, slapped laundry clean on rocks, chipped away bit by bit on stones for somebody's arch of triumph, palace, or cathedral. No, not like this, this lining words up in rows, one after the other one, to make them stand still, behave, make sense for a change – a little like this but not like this at all. Yes, finally here I was a worker too, dragging myself in every morning to my task, this time a drawer or countertop, all for the greater glory of strangers desiring cabinets for the kitchen of their dreams. Ah, Progress and America. Yes, finally I was learning first-hand what books had whispered to me: The Meaning of Work. Work is what people are required to do that they do not want to do. And the obvious stared me in the face and laughed: Those who do the most unpleasant tasks generally work hardest, do the most vital tasks, and are paid least. Nurses, workers on the assembly lines, housewives, ditch-diggers who dig the holes for the telephone poles that carry the messages some boss deems the most important in the world. Rochelle knew – gave me an early Christmas bonus. We got along fine. Working side by side, we shared a lot of unspoken thoughts and dreams, not the least of which was the hope that some lady or gentleman would walk in the door with the sketch of another beautiful bed, this one to be made from the Tree of Life. When no one appeared with such a sketch, we retreated to the back of the shop to fondle his violins. And little by little I learned the properties of wood.

"Should I start thinking of you as a partner?" he asked out of the blue one day.

"I can't," I said. "I can't shake my little dream. I talked to Danko again last week. He said everybody wants old stuff, but used books would just sit there and stare at me. I still want to make room for the books. I've got a line on tons of them, all of them smart, full of ideas. On Monday I'm going to the bank for a loan. I can't get Danko's place out of my mind."

Bruno was long gone from Guido's store.

"I asked him: And now where do you go?"

Bruno didn't seem concerned.

"He's okay in my place for now," Kate said.

"How are you going to get a piano up those steps?"

"We'll just leave it downstairs."

"In the headquarters of your local friendly socialist club – a piano there? Would the Party allow such a thing?"

"We could put it someplace in back," Kate said.

Bruno had other ideas. "I have to be in front. Maybe a little closer to the window. I need to see people passing on the streets."

"We'll see. I'll see what the Central Committee says."

"What are you going to do when the baby comes?"

Bruno gave a shy smile. "Get married."

"And move into Kate's room? Won't your style be cramped?"

"Babies are the future of the world," Kate announced.

Bruno nodded as if he heard. "Do you think there's going to be some way of keeping people from going in and out while I work?"

And Bea had ideas of her own.

"First, Papa asks me to move back home," she complained, "and he makes me do it even though he sees me crying and just knows it'll ruin my entire college life. Then I move in for a week and he tells me I'm a tramp and I have to get the hell out. I'm telling you, I was lucky to get my old apartment back."

"How did you manage that?" I asked.

She said nothing, looked askance.

"Well?"

"Dylan moved in, took over my lease."

"And now the poor boy will have to stay, because there's no way he'll be able to get his old place back."

She sneered at me the way teenagers do when you ask them to explain why their music is always so loud. "Don't be such a smart-ass with me."

"I bet you have an old sofa too. Dylan can sleep on it."

"Quit being a jerk, Sal. We'll screw wherever we feel like screwing – on the bed, floor, sofa, kitchen sink, standing on our heads. It's almost 1976. Declaration of Independence. Remember all that stuff from the Sixties?" She put her hands on her hips and smiled for me, as if waiting for the pictures to appear and reappear, my little sister Bea naked in every one of them. "Dylan and I – we decided we're not going to play the games all the people your age play."

No more games. Nothing but tough talk from now on. So I tried tough talk on her. "Do you think Papa asked you to move out so he could shack up with Edna?"

Her jaw dropped and eyes widened in disbelief. "Go on! He said I had to move because, because it wouldn't look good, Edna living alone with him. You don't think?"

"She's taking care of his leg."

"My God, Sal. You men are something else. Mom just died a month ago. You don't really think they're screwing or anything?"

"No, Bea. Our dad wouldn't do anything like that. But I wouldn't trust Edna. She's got that look in her eyes."

Many things happen – as if suddenly, unexpectedly, maybe because we walk blindly backward into our pasts, our futures no more and no less than the dream-memories we conjure in present moments that keep recurring when we're only half-awake.

A few things never happened. The police never appeared at my door. Waldman's confusion apparently was also too much for them to fathom, and my fear of being caught and desire to confess faded as one. If he had wronged us and I had wronged him, our wronging made nothing right. If he was a haunt, then so was I when he encountered me in his house that night.

The rosary found its way back into Sonia's hands when I shook it out of a sock in my underwear drawer and walked back to the rectory with it. "What in the hell was this all about?" I asked as I handed it to her. "Let's just say," she replied slyly, "that I thought I wasn't getting the little raise I deserved, and the thing just disappeared when your sister was here. They were very upset about it all, but I got my little raise and since then have had my little change of heart about how deeply to punish their little wrong. I'll be sure to tell them your sister brought it back of her own free will."

I just wanted her to keep talking so I could keep looking at her.

And when I went to the bank for a loan to buy Danko's place, the loan officer also knew something I did not. "Sorry, the answer has to be no at this time," he said with a smile I knew would turn into laughing behind my back. That same afternoon, just before closing time, a man with a briefcase asked to see Rochelle. He was not carrying a plan for a remake of Penelope's fabulous bed. After the man left Rochelle sat with his head in his hands. Then he flung a screwdriver across the room, grabbed his coat and slammed the door on his way out. He called me later that night. "We're finished. The building, everything, has to go. The city wants the land." It took more than a week to find out what for. Papa and Kate also received word. The city was paying market value for their properties, plus fifteen percent to cover moving costs and inconveniences. My landlord informed me by mail: I had six weeks to find another place. And Danko was doomed, but he had suspected all along. Only Guido and Rosina survived. The Metropolitan Sports Commission wanted the half-mile square bounded by Franklin, Second, Locust, and Sixth. Demolition was schedule to begin February 16.

It snowed the evening before the bulldozers went to work, another warm snow that covered roofs and sidewalks like a thick layer of down. I walked through the old neighborhood one last time, mesmerized by the silence, the sidewalks and streets empty of people and cars, the windows on all sides with their blank, condemned stares. How many bricks on one city block – each one pulled from some kiln, counted, carted, unloaded, then laid in a row by some workman's hands? And all the properties of wood – the trees felled in some forest, logs dragged to the saws, beams rough cut, boards planed, subtle mouldings shaped, made to fit. Could all that be wrecked in one fell swoop, turned into a heap of colossal waste? I passed by Guido's store one last time, gazed in the window at the remembered stacks of oranges, cabbages, potatoes, apples, pears. In my short lifetime I had seen the Decline; tomorrow the Fall.

Right after midnight a storm came in from the northwest. Blasted by flurries and cold air, the old snow froze hard. Even from my apartment almost a mile away I heard the machinery lumbering up Third – bulldozers, cranes, earthmovers, dumptrucks. I dressed in the dark, then walked to the perimeter of the scene in time to see Kate and three of her socialist friends being led away, kicking and screaming, by police. "Don't lay a hand on them!" I shouted as I slammed my hand on the squad car pulling away. "Can't you see how pregnant she is?" I felt ashamed. I should have been there with her.

Bruno was lucky to have a woman like her. And where was he?

And then the things of steel began to destroy the things of clay, sand, stone, and wood. It was no match, and the faces of the people watching were solemn until the walls staggered, then crumbled into heaps. Little shouts went up as the walls fell, and there were smiles of triumph all around. All day the violence went on, the machines gaining confidence as they went from row to row wrecking everything in sight.

I returned again late at night. The wind had died but the air was cold. The cranes stood lifeless next to their work, their steel limbs flexed, indifferent to the frozen skies, their wrecking balls as still as the pendulums of broken grandfather clocks. I tried to discern any lettering on the steel, some indicator of whether Waldman's boys were doing this work. Numbers, but no names.

I looked again for Guido's old store, but the spot was already bare. Across the field of rubble St. Paul's looked larger than ever before, rising out of the ground like a massive grey rock. I gazed in awe at this thing suddenly looming present again, at once ancient and new, the machines of steel lifeless and limp on all sides, powerless to touch the dark raw beauty of its hard silent face. Where Guido's old store once stood would arise a side entrance to the new sports colosseum approved by the City Fathers. It would be oval, several stories high, its rim almost equal in height to the towers of St. Paul's. There would be sufficient parking for twenty thousand vehicles, and the freeway would move over to accomodate the flow. On Sundays the press of traffic would be impossible, pulses beating wildly for the advent of the game, the more than eighty thousand cheering souls.

33. *The End.*

We all went our own ways, each of us renting apartments on streets facing every which way. Now we all had privacy, and sooner or later we would all own cars. We had those moments too – the quiet, solitary ones – when more than anything we wanted to go back home. But what did we expect? Mamma was gone. Rosina wasn't up to making feasts any more, in fact admitted that years ago she had confessed to the Holy Mother that she hated to cook. She and Guido had to face the parking lot, but what did it matter any more that they had not been forced to move? In their own way they too soon would be on their way out.

And here I was again out of a job. Danko and his wife had fled to Florida, and Rochelle was trying to find a new place, all of us beneficiaries of a little severance allotment that left us feeling tided over rather than drowned. Maggie was a memory that kept walking by, and I kept revisiting the light in the window of Waldman's house. And Sandy kept in touch, still in love with us both. The Other Man, apparently very handsome, athletic, and intelligent, was someone I never had the pleasure to meet. "Sometimes I feel like such a whore," she said, but no, she was not sure she wanted a divorce. Could we keep seeing each other off and on? And was I seeing somebody new?

I was and was not. Every day on a street corner, in the library or a coffee shop, somebody new was still there, always beautiful, intimidating, and strange. Should I smile, walk up to her and introduce myself, follow her down the street? What did I really see in her, in *Them,* I who had spent all my roused years unable to see beyond form to flesh? Woman – what was she? A beautiful creation of mind, like what Raphael dreamed when he went searching for cathedrals in France. Queen of Heaven, yes, but also plain old person exhausted at the end of the day – yes, mother too, and everyone in between. What did I know about Her? Maybe even less than what she knew about Me. But this I felt deeply and therefore knew all along: That she was vital to my work, that she who could bring new life out of passion (call it love) had the power to create and conserve I craved, that in her absence all work went wrong.

Was I seeing someone new? Indeed, and ancient too.

I saw Edna and Papa on June third. He was moving to Brown's Crossing, twenty-six miles away. "What do you expect with my lousy retirement plan?" he explained. "Edna owns a house there now."

Edna was quick to disagree. "The Lord owns everything in our lives."

I pulled him aside. "What'll we do – I mean with Nonna and Nonno?" He knew what I meant. How could we abandon them?

"You ask me that? You who never gave a damn, never came over to say hello to anyone. You expect them to move into Edna's house?"

"But what if Nonno suddenly dies?"

"It's her house. I'm married to her and it's her house, so it's up to her what I do now. This is what I get for all my work."

He grimaced as a pain shot through his leg. "Thank God I'm through," he said. "Thank God I'm almost dead myself."

We planned a picnic for the Fourth of July. It was Bruno's idea. "We'll have a bit of news by then," he said.

"What news?"

He looked at the ground. "Kate and I – we're tying the knot."

"Oh God," I said, "the death of sin."

"I've already been a dad for three months. Can you believe?"

"I remember Thanksgiving. Kate looked like she'd swallowed a watermelon even then. Remember how much food Mamma fixed?" I lowered my voice. "Are you making ends meet?"

"Kate's got the Central Committee lining up places – union halls, places I never played before. Thirty bucks a night. We get by."

"A real wedding – in a church? Not just some sort of secular socialist post-Mayday historical dialectical development event?"

"August ninth. In a church – somewhere. But I don't think we can get St. Paul's."

"You looked into it?"

"Kate handles all the practical stuff."

"A real marriage. Think of that."

"We talked and talked." Then he winked. "She's ready to be tied down."

I pulled him toward me, embraced him the way men do not embrace, and he stiffened at my touch. "She's really sexy, man."

"Mainly," he said, "she has a very good heart."

"So where will the picnic be?"

"At Old River Park – right downtown."

"There? Do you think we'll be able to stand the smell?"

"I think it'll be okay. It's early yet. The river doesn't begin smelling too bad until after the Fourth of July."

So we all gathered at Old River Park. I brought the lasagne and Edna brought jello, potato salad, and paper plates. Papa brought enough wine to last the day, and Rosina, helping Guido take his small steps, brought a salad made of tomatoes, onion, basil, garlic and olive oil. Kate brought a brown bagful of homemade chocolate chip cookies in one hand and tiny Leah in the other, and Bruno a new biography of George Sand. Dylan brought his two guitars, and Beatrice brought him.

We all waited to see what Papa would do when he saw the new baby, but he didn't even give her one long look. At the table I made the announcement and proposed a toast. Papa lifted his glass as high as mine, though Edna didn't dare take a sip.

"Per cento anni," Guido, his eyes already bloodshot from the wine, said to the sky.

"For a hundred years."

On both sides of the river the city hummed on. Brown-bricked warehouses lined the water's edge, the brick faded and worn from a hundred years of wind and rain. This was the same river that carried the stone for St. Paul's, the same river Raphael travelled by steamboat on his way to building the most magnificent shrine in America. Along the banks piles of rubble – old lumber, tires, scrap iron – rose above litter the weeds concealed, and culverts spewed their streams into the flow snaking toward some distant delta in the south. On the railroad tracks following the river's course empty boxcars waited to carry on, while beyond the warehouses lining the banks the city towers looked down at us from the sky. This was Waldman's city, the city of all the Waldmans of the world. A city full of people who had turned their backs to the water that brought their life to them.

It would rain before the afternoon was done. I sat alone under a tree, wondering if Sandy would call again soon. Then a familiar voice broke in on me. Above, high on the bluff, Markels sat on the grass waving at us. "Come down," I yelled. "Come down. We have lots to eat and lots of wine." No, no, he said. Some other time, some other day. He wanted nothing more than to sit and watch.

So the afternoon passed, the river carried downstream by a current stronger than itself. Bruno and Kate wandered with their baby, Kate pointing upstream from time to time toward the city, her words, lost in the wind, always explaining, arguing, pleading, and he, deaf to her, nodding in agreement with the rhythm of her walk. Bent over on a picnic bench, Rosina sat in silence looking at Guido, while Dylan sat on a table strumming tunes for his Beatrice. Papa, his hand surrendered to Edna's, was listening to what I had to say about the properties of wood.

"And what about that book you said you were writing?" he asked. "You got it done?"

"Book?"

"What you said you were doing when you were supposed to be looking for a job."

Ah yes, my Book. Waldman. Is Character Fate? I could never write a book. How could I be historian, poet, and waiter too?

"It's still in pretty rough form."

"Why don't you finish it? You could get a lot of money these days for a book. What's it about?"

"Me."

"You?"

The noise arrived just in time. Two cars – a black Buick and a big red Chevrolet – raced to a stop just short of the railroad tracks on the outskirts of the picnic ground, and nine teenagers, all of them dressed in sharp dresses and suits, clamored out. One, a dark-haired youth with a sharp jaw, began sprinting toward the river bank.

Before I had time to see what he was running from, I saw a football float over his head. He caught it without breaking stride, then turned to bow as the others broke into a cheer. "Here, Louie, here," someone cried, and Louie threw the ball high into a crowd of four boys pushing each other to get at it. The boys taunted each other, jostled, and ran out for passes toward the river bank, their shirts coming out of their pants as they ran, their ties like horses' manes. "Here, here," they yelled, "throw it here."

The leader of the pack was a black-haired girl in a bright blue dress. She emerged from the Buick more slowly than the others and had taken something from the trunk of the car. As she approached, I saw that she was carrying a wreath of flowers, also that she was beautiful and young.

The ball landed at my feet, and two boys ran over to pick it up. "Wedding?" I asked the first boy.

"Nope," he said as he ripped it away and ran off. "My grandpa died and he wanted to be buried at sea. This sure ain't no sea, but what can you do, eh?"

He ducked away from the other boy and ran toward the girl in blue, but she kept walking toward the river bank. Finally, when she arrived at a spot that seemed just right, she yelled until everyone gathered in close. One of the youngest boys, perhaps fifteen, produced a small camera, stepped back from the group and began snapping shots. The girl with the wreath said some words, then she bent down at the water's edge, placed the wreath on a large styrofoam plate, and pushed it away from shore. They all watched a moment, half-expecting the river to sweep it away, but the wreath bobbed and danced at the water's edge, unwilling to leave the shore. Then one of the braver boys waded out in his shoes and gave it a shove. All but the girl in blue cheered as they saw a current catch and begin swirling the wreath away.

One of the boys threw the football at the youngest girl. "Here," all the boys yelled as they took swipes at her.

I bided my time, then abandoned my place under a tree when I saw the girl in blue coming my way. "Hey," I called as our paths crossed, "what's going on? A funeral?"

"My grandpa," she said through a smile that made her dark eyes light up.

"What's your name?"

"Scorpino. You look Italian too."

I nodded yes.

"We're doing this for him. He always wanted to go back."

"Yes, I know. The Old Country."

I took flight to Edna's suburban house, perched myself on a branch of the tallest cottonwood tree in sight, and looked down. It was a squat suburban house, white with green trim, on a quarter-acre of well-mown land, the property line marked by a border of lilac bushes beyond which the land stretched in patches of green and gold. Papa, busy polishing his car, looked as small as Guido but wore a smile that resembled the one I saw curled on my face in my high school yearbook photo. He stood in the driveway waiting for me, then motioned for me to come down.

"Come with me, Sal. Come in back. Come to the garden with me." He lifted his arm for me to help him along, and together we took small steps. The sun was low on the horizon, all the colors of the sunset spreading themselves over the land in a soft fragrant haze. We entered the garden by a white picket gate.

"Look," he said, extending his hand.

The rows were perfect and straight, the tomatoes, tied by ribbons of white cloth to tiers of hickory stakes, lording it over the smaller rows. Not a weed, the ground, hoed fine, showing no footprint anywhere.

"I didn't know you were such a gardener."

"Ah," he said, "there are many things about me you didn't know. Thirty-three years I worked in the factory. But always I wanted a garden like this – here in back, on a little piece of ground."

He led me past the rows to the farthest corner of the plot. "You ever see an apple tree? Someone put it here. Here, for you." He made a gesture to pick a small gnarled one just out of reach on a low-hanging branch.

"No, Papa. Too green. Not ready yet. Let it stay."

"Bah! What good will it do you then? You won't be here when it's ready to eat."

There was a garden hose looped over the main lower limbs of the tree. Papa saw it too and suddenly seemed to remember why he had come to the garden. "I gotta water some of these plants. I gotta turn the water on when I get back to the house."

We left the garden when the sun was halfway down. Behind us the gate closed of itself, and beyond the lilacs the evening mist began to rise over the grass. Papa led me to the side of the house. "Here," he said, "here's the faucet. You turn it on for me. I'm too damned stiff now to bend."

The faucet seemed rusted shut, but with a hard twist it broke itself open. When he saw the water, Papa, a wide grin on his face, turned toward the garden again. Still looped over the lower limbs of the tree, the hose sent a fine spray over the garden rows.

"See," he said. "See what a good system I have. Automatic. I don't have to do nothing no more."

We watched until Edna called. "Come inside now. It's time to come inside for a little tea."

I shuddered and flew back to my perch on the cottonwood tree. From there I could see far away – the grey grime hanging like a shroud over the city miles away, the river turning south, curling past St. Paul's, the highways all leading inexorably away from home, cutting through rows of small square houses planted in fields, all of the houses facing away, all longing for the sunset in the west.

"Jesus Christ!" Papa yelled, "are you coming in or not?"

I left him standing in the doorway alone. As he grew small in the distance, I waved one of the few farewells left to us.

Simple thanks here do not express the depth of gratitude and debt owed to Ray Howe, Joan Prefontaine, Lynn Nankivil, Carole Stoa Senn, and, again, to my wife Monica Drealan DeGrazia, all of whom provided caring and careful critical comments as I chipped away trying to find my way into, and out of, these words.